Case Analyses FOR Intellectual Property Law AND New Media

Steve Jones
General Editor

Vol. 107

The Digital Formations series is part of the Peter Lang Media and Communication list.
Every volume is peer reviewed and meets
the highest quality standards for content and production.

PETER LANG
New York • Bern • Frankfurt • Berlin
Brussels • Vienna • Oxford • Warsaw

Steven L. Baron, Edward Lee Lamoureux, and Claire Stewart

Case Analyses FOR Intellectual Property Law AND New Media

PETER LANG
New York • Bern • Frankfurt • Berlin
Brussels • Vienna • Oxford • Warsaw

Library of Congress Cataloging-in-Publication Data

Baron, Steven L., author.
Case analyses for intellectual property law and new media /
Steven L. Baron, Edward Lee Lamoureux, Claire Stewart.
pages cm. — (Digital formations; vol. 107)
Includes bibliographical references and index.
1. Intellectual property—United States—Cases.
2. Digital media—Law and legislation—United States—Cases.
3. Multimedia systems—Law and legislation—United States—Cases.
I. Lamoureux, Edward Lee, author. II. Stewart, Claire, author. III. Title.
KF2979.B374   346.7304'8—dc23   2015019689
ISBN 978-1-4331-3101-1 (paperback)
ISBN 978-1-4539-1605-6 (e-book)
ISSN 1526-3169

Bibliographic information published by **Die Deutsche Nationalbibliothek**.
Die Deutsche Nationalbibliothek lists this publication in the "Deutsche
Nationalbibliografie"; detailed bibliographic data are available
on the Internet at http://dnb.d-nb.de/.

Cover design concept by Edward Lee Lamoureux

The paper in this book meets the guidelines for permanence and durability
of the Committee on Production Guidelines for Book Longevity
of the Council of Library Resources.

© 2015 Peter Lang Publishing, Inc., New York
29 Broadway, 18th floor, New York, NY 10006
www.peterlang.com

Printed in the United States of America

Table of Contents

Preface to the 2nd Edition

The 2nd edition of *Intellectual Property Law and Interactive Media: Free for a Fee*, improves on the 1st edition in form and content. Although developments in the law tend to move somewhat slowly, the new media environment changes rapidly, such that while the decisions that are made follow time-worn practices (the law), the case specifics present new, innovative, and challenging legal dilemmas. The 2nd edition moves our coverage of case analysis to this separate volume, *Case Analyses for Intellectual Property Law and New Media*, enabling us to focus our attention, and that of our students and readers, on important trial and legal procedures that attend applying extant law to, largely, new circumstances. Moving the case analyses to this separate volume enables students/readers to focus their attention on history and theory while reading the conceptual text, then bring understandings derived there to bear on cases found in this analytic text. The approach offers relief from information overload and arms one with time and space to "shift gears" between concepts and cases. The 2nd edition includes the most important cases presented in the 1st edition, and updates case selections to include the most recent key cases prior to publication.

Each case summary begins with a brief statement highlighting the importance of the litigation's outcome. This element is added to our approach in the 1st edition where we left this interpretation to the reader/student. The new précis provide focus that is especially important given the complexities found in many of the cases. The authors are well aware of, and sensitive to, the fact that few in our target audience have experience with legal terms or protocols. Providing focused interpretations in addition to analysis aids understanding and learning.

Full case citations are given within this text. Having the proper case citation is crucial for accurate searching. When we note cases in the concept text, and when we analyze them in detail, here, in the companion volume, we provide a full case listing using Harvard Law Review Association's *The Bluebook: A Uniform System of Citation*, 19th ed. (2010, sixth printing, 2012) style. Additionally, readers/students may go to our companion website, *freeforafee.com*, and find there a list of URLs that link to case files from the litigation covered in this text.

Marc Cooperman and Robert Resis authored portions of the case analyses in the 1st edition. Many of those passages have been edited/modified and the attributions (that appeared in the 1st edition) are removed in this 2nd edition. Nevertheless, we thank these outstanding intellectual property lawyers for allowing us to build on their work. Additionally, Steve Baron expresses sincere gratitude to attorney Tina Salvato who assisted in compiling case summaries for this 2nd edition.

CHAPTER ONE

Copyright Cases

Traditional Media Copyright Cases with New Media Implications

Baker v. Selden, 101 U.S. 99 (1879).

Baker v. Selden, well prior to the Copyright Act of 1909, deals with the idea versus expression dichotomy in copyright law and the differences between copyrights and patents.

The US Supreme Court (SCOTUS) in *Baker v. Selden* considered what aspects of Selden's book relating to an improved bookkeeping system could be protected by copyright. Selden's book contained mostly bookkeeping forms and descriptions of how to use the new bookkeeping system. The case involved an attempt to keep Baker from selling a book describing a similar system. The Court held that, although copyright law granted Selden the right to prevent others from printing or publishing any material part or his entire book, the system that Selden devised was merely an idea and therefore not subject to copyright protection. The specific layout and presentation of Selden's book was subject to copyright protection, but Baker was not copying the text or presentation from Selden.

The Court went on to distinguish copyright and patent laws. The particular description of the system itself (the expression of ideas) can be protected by copyright, but not the abstract idea of the method or system—inventions, if they qualify, are protected by patent.

Mazer v. Stein, 347 U.S. 201 (1954).

Mazer v. Stein supported the validity of copyright protection for certain kinds of design elements.

Stein designed statuettes of male and female dancing figures intended for use as bases for table lamps. The statuettes, without any of the components used for lamps, were registered with the Copyright Office as works of art. Stein then sold the statuettes for use as the bases on fully equipped lamps. Mazer copied the designs of the lamp bases and sold them as fully equipped lamps as well. Stein sued Mazer for copyright infringement.

The SCOTUS evaluated whether a work of art, intended for use as an element in a useful manufactured article, is copyrightable. The Court affirmed the appellate court and held that such a use of a copyrighted work of art does not affect the ability to protect against copyright infringement of the work of art. The Court held that the statuettes in *Mazer* were an original, tangible expression of the author's ideas and that the reproduction of the statuettes as lamps did not bar or invalidate the statuettes' copyright registration.

The Court found that the statuettes were subject to copyright protection: "the dichotomy of protection for the aesthetic is not beauty and utility but art for the copyright."

Sony Corp. of America v. Universal City Studios, Inc., 464 U.S. 417 (1984).

Sony v. Universal City Studios is a seminal case involving consumer rights to copy and time shift broadcast television and for device manufacturers to provide recording equipment. The case also speaks to issues of private use and fair use.

In *Sony*, various movie studio companies elected to sue Sony for copyright infringement based on its production of home video recorders. The studios argued that notwithstanding some non-infringing uses, the primary purpose of home video recorders was to make unauthorized copies of copyrighted material. Sony argued that: (1) recording copyrighted broadcasts to be watched at a later time for noncommercial use was simply time-shifting, that—even if unauthorized—is a fair use, and (2) there were substantial non-infringing uses, including the copying of non-copyrighted material or copyrighted programming whose owners consent to such copying.

The SCOTUS established a test for determining whether video tape recording devices violate copyright law. In a narrow majority, the Court stated: "the sale of copying equipment, like the sale of other articles of commerce, does not constitute contributory infringement if the product is widely used for legitimate, unobjectionable purposes." The Court examined whether the allegedly infringing device "is capable of commercially significant non-infringing uses" and agreed with Sony that there were substantial non-infringing uses and that recording programming for a noncommercial home use is a fair use of the copyrighted material. The Court emphasized that the public was invited to view the broadcast free of charge; the home video recorder allows them to do that, but at a later time.

Harper & Row v. Nation Enterprises Case Media, 471 U.S. 539 (1985).

Harper & Row v. Nation Enterprises Case Media examined publishing copyright protected material based on the theory of "the public's right to know" as it is related to fair use in news and publishing.

Former President Gerald Ford licensed publication rights to Harper & Row for memoirs relating to his decision to pardon Richard Nixon. Harper & Row had, in turn, contracted with *Time* Magazine to print portions of Ford's memoirs. *The Nation* magazine obtained and published significant excerpts without permission from Ford, Harper & Row, or *Time* Magazine. Once *The Nation* published excerpts, the value of the publication rights for excerpts was reduced, so *Time* withdrew from its contract with Harper & Row, as allowed by a clause in the contract. Harper & Row then sued *The Nation* for copyright infringement.

The Nation claimed that the public interest in learning of Ford's reasons for pardoning Nixon was vital, and that its appropriation and publication should therefore constitute a fair use. The SCOTUS found that there was no exception to copyright protection merely because the memoirs were those of a public figure. The Court applied the traditional fair use tests and found that the factors weighed against fair use because it was a commercial use of the significant portion of the copyrighted material that caused an actual harm (the cancellation of the contract) despite the fact that the nature of the work was informative.

Feist Publications, Inc. v. Rural Telephone Service Co., 499 U.S. 340 (1991).

In *Feist v. Rural Telephone*, the SCOTUS addressed the minimum originality requirement for copyright protection. The Court held that effort and the expenditure of resources are not protected by copyright and rejected the "sweat of the brow" doctrine.

Rural provided telephone service in Kansas and was statutorily required to provide a phone directory to customers free of charge. Feist compiled telephone directories from larger areas than did Rural. When Rural refused to license its local directory to Feist, Feist copied Rural's listings. Rural was able to detect the copying because it had placed some phony numbers in its listings for just that purpose.

Rural sued Feist for copyright infringement, alleging that Rural's "compilation" of phone numbers warranted copyright protection. Prior to *Feist*, investing a significant amount of time and energy into a work helped qualify content owners for copyright protection. *Feist* rejected that aspect.

Feist clarified that the point of copyright protection is to encourage creative expression, thereby "promot[ing] the Progress of Science and useful Arts." Prior to *Feist*, it had long been settled that information itself could not be protected by copyright, but that collections of information could be. The Court in *Feist* indicated that in order to be copyrightable, a work must possess "a minimal degree of creativity" and that the copyright only applies to those creative aspects of the work. The Court held that an author's selection and arrangement of a compilation of facts can warrant copyright protection, although in this case, Rural's arrangement of names and phone numbers in alphabetical order was not remotely creative and did not warrant copyright protection.

New Media Cases and Copyright Law

Cases Involving Thumbnail Image and Hyperlinking to Protected Content

Kelly v. Arriba Soft Corp., 336 F.3d 811 (9th Cir. 2003).

Kelly v. Arriba Soft addresses the copyright status of image thumbnails; in effect, it set precedent for use of modifications of otherwise protected content in online/WWW searches.

In 1999, Leslie A. Kelly, a professional photographer, sued Arriba Soft Corporation for copyright infringement. Arriba operated an Internet search engine that functioned by presenting thumbnails, reduced-size versions of entire images, both as search results and as hyperlinks to larger versions (where licensed versions could be legally acquired). At trial, Kelly requested summary judgment against Arriba's use of thumbnail images, arguing both that Arriba infringed his copyright and, in removing copyright management information, violated the DMCA. The District Court disagreed with Kelly, finding that Arriba's use was fair and that no DMCA violation had occurred.

At the time the suit was filed, most search engines operated by presenting search results in textual form. Arriba's was among the first to operate by displaying a downsized "thumbnail" version of the content itself. The case was an important test of the application of copyright law and traditional infringement defenses on the Internet. Arriba conceded that it had both copied the images and then displayed Mr. Kelly's images, at reduced size, on its site, but denied removing or altering any copyright management information.

The DMCA requires that copyright management information, for example, the title of the work and the identification of the copyright owner, not be falsified, removed, or altered. Judge Taylor found that, since the copyright identification information was in the text surrounding but not included within the images on Mr. Kelly's website, no removal had occurred in the act of copying images to Arriba's database. Although the thumbnails were displayed in the Arriba search engine without the text accompanying them on Kelly's website, "Defendant's users could obtain a full-sized version of a thumbnailed image by clicking on the thumbnail. A user who did this was given the name of the Web site from which Defendant obtained the image, where any associated copyright management information would be available, and an opportunity to link there."

In his analysis of the four fair use factors, the judge found that two of the factors weighed in favor of a fair use finding, and two against. The first factor, the character and purpose of the use, focuses on the way(s) the "new" work uses the protected work. Although Arriba used the images in the context of a commercial enterprise, the judge found the use was a minimally commercial use as it did not offer the work for sale or directly use it to promote other sales. In addition, he found that the use of Kelly's work was transformative, that is, the work was used in a substantially new way in the process of creating a new and useful service. The transformative evaluation, introduced in a 1990 *Harvard Law Review* article by Pierre Leval and famously applied by the SCOTUS in the 2Live Crew/Pretty Woman parody case (*Campbell v. Acuff-Rose Music, Inc.*, 1994) is increasingly seen as an important part of a fair use evaluation.

Evaluation of the second factor, nature of the copyrighted work, weighed against a fair use finding. The protected works were of a highly creative nature, which typically receives more copyright protection than factual works. The third factor determines whether the amount of the work copied was reasonable in light of the intended purpose. Here, the judge evaluated both the thumbnail-sized display and the intermediate linking page that displayed the image full-size alongside a link to the originating site. Although the thumbnail display prevented users from reprinting or otherwise reproducing the image at full size, the judge also felt that the intermediate page created a problem and was not necessary to fulfill the purpose of the search engine: "The Court finds the third factor weighs slightly against fair use."

The final factor evaluates the use against its likely effect on the market for the work. Kelly argued that the Arriba search service made it more likely that users could copy and reuse his work in violation of his copyright, while Arriba argued that the service increased Kelly's market. Since Kelly did not present any evidence of actual harm, the judge found Arriba's argument more compelling and ruled in favor of fair use for the fourth factor.

Although two factors favored fair use and two did not, the use was found to be fair overall, with the first factor playing a key role in tipping the scales: "Defendant's purposes were and are inherently transformative, even if its realization of those purposes was at times imperfect. Where, as here, a new use and new technology are evolving, the broad transformative purpose of the use weighs more heavily than the inevitable flaws in its early stages of development."

Kelly appealed the District Court ruling. The Ninth Circuit Court of Appeals ruled that the creation and use of the thumbnails in the search engine was a fair use. However, the appeals court ruled that the District Court should not have decided whether the display of the larger image was a violation of one aspect of Kelly's copyright protection for the originals (the right to publicly display his works), so that part of the case was remanded for further proceedings. Arriba Soft went out of business before Kelly obtained a large judgment against them, at the District Court, for infringement of the full-sized images.

Perfect 10, Inc. v. Amazon.com, Inc., 508 F.3d 1146 (9th Cir. 2007).

Perfect 10, Inc. v. Amazon.com, Inc. re-examined the use of thumbnail images and extended analysis to linking to protected material. The case continued fair use exemptions for basic functions enacted by search technologies and firms.

The Ninth Circuit revisited thumbnail images a few years later when Perfect 10, a company selling subscription photos of nude models, sued Google and Amazon for infringing its display and distribution rights by using thumbnail images and linking to copyrighted full-sized images.

The court reasoned that infringement depended on whether Google actually stored and displayed copies of the images on its servers or merely linked to the information. Since Google's use of full-sized images merely linked to Perfect 10's content, the court held that Google could not be liable for infringement of the full-sized images. In contrast, Google could be liable for its use of thumbnail images because Google's servers actually stored copies of Perfect 10's copyrighted images. However, the court ultimately concluded that Google's use of thumbnail images constituted fair use under *Kelly v. Arriba Soft*, finding that the search engine put the images "to a use fundamentally different than the use intended by Perfect 10," thereby providing "a significant benefit to the public."

As for whether Google could be liable for infringement committed by search engine users, the court found that Google lacked the ability to stop or limit third-party infringement and thus Perfect 10 could not establish a likelihood of success under a theory of vicarious infringement. But the court did not resolve the issue of contributory infringement, finding that factual disputes remained over whether there were reasonable and feasible means for Google to refrain from providing access to infringing images.

Cases Involving DeCSS and the DMCA (Digital Rights Management)

The DMCA, almost a footnote in the *Kelly v. Arriba Soft* case, took center stage in a series of cases involving the distribution of a computer program designed to circumvent the Contents Scrambling System (CSS) used, to prevent unauthorized access, in many commercial DVDs.

In 1999, Jon Johansen, a teenager living in Norway, reverse engineered the CSS encryption. The version of the Linux operating system that Johansen was using did not have a DVD software player licensed by the DVD Copy Control Association (DVD-CCA), so he wrote a software program to defeat CSS and copy unencrypted movie contents to a computer. This code, released as a Windows program called DeCSS, was later redistributed and linked to from hundreds of sites around the world, including the online "hacker" magazine *2600*. The publishers of *2600* and others who had linked to or posted the code were sued in New York and Connecticut by eight movie studios for violation of the DMCA, and in California, several individuals were sued by the DVD-CCA for violation of trade secrets. Analysis of three related cases follows, below. Chapter Six of Volume Two includes material about DeCSS and trade secrets; Chapter Nine of Volume One includes material about DeCSS and digital rights management.

Universal City Studios, Inc. v. Corley, 273 F.3d 429 (2nd Cir. 2001).

Universal City Studios, Inc. v. Corley tested the degree to which certain kinds of online publication (DeCSS; computer code) should receive blanket First Amendment/ free speech protection, whether publication of code elements should receive a fair use exemption, and challenged the applicability of the anti-circumvention components of the DMCA to the publication of encryption research findings.

In defending themselves against the accusation that they violated section 1201 of the United States Copyright Act (the anti-circumvention portion of the law enacted by the DMCA), Eric Corley (publisher of *2600*), Shawn Reimerdes, and Roman Kazan argued that they had been improperly targeted as parties in the suit, cited the encryption research anti-circumvention exemption, and argued that the DMCA was unconstitutional because it violates both the fair use exemption in the copyright law and the First Amendment right to free speech. The District Court disagreed and enjoined the sites from posting or linking to DeCSS. In late 2001, the Court of Appeals upheld his ruling. The District Court found the fair use argument irrelevant, since the suit had been brought for violation of anti-circumvention provisions, not for infringing the plaintiff's copyrights. In other words, only the circumvention actions were challenged, not the copying of any video content. The free-speech argument consumed most of the Court's attention in both the district and appellate stages, but ultimately the judges felt that while it could plausibly be argued that computer code is speech, the functional aspects of the computer program could not be so protected (Merges, Menell, and Lemley 514).

321 Studios v. Metro Goldwyn Mayer Studios, Inc., 307 F. Supp. 2d 1085 (N.D. Cal. 2004).

321 Studios v. Metro Goldwyn Mayer Studios, Inc. tested the practical commercial implications of rulings against software that enabled circumvention of DRM.

Despite the ruling in *Universal City Studios, Inc. v. Corley*, 321 Studios, a small San Francisco software company, attempted to market software to copy the contents of DVDs, including a package called "DVD X Copy," that allowed DVDs encrypted with CSS to be duplicated to a blank DVD disc. In 2002, 321 Studios, fearing a suit from the film industry, proactively asked a California District Court to find that, because its software had substantial non-infringing uses and allowed consumers to use content as allowed under the fair use clause, its manufacture and distribution were not in violation of the DMCA. The non-infringing uses argument refers to the standard established in the *Sony/Betamax* case, when the SCOTUS found that, because the commercial videocassette recorder could be used for a variety of purposes (including many that did not infringe copyrights), its manufacture could not be prohibited. In ruling on the *321 Studios* case, however, US District Court Judge Susan Illston instead relied heavily on the findings in the *Universal* DeCSS case. She declined to rule specifically on the claim that DVD X Copy supports fair use, focusing instead on the circumvention and trafficking bans and finding 321 Studios in violation of both. Not long thereafter, 321 Studios went out of business.

Realnetworks, Inc. v. DVD Copy Control Ass'n, 641 F. Supp. 2d 913 (N.D. Cal. 2009).

Realnetworks, Inc. v. DVD Copy Control Ass'n revisited the practical commercial implications of rulings against software that enabled circumvention of DRM in light of a potentially changed new media environment. Both the passage of time and the commercial successes (in the digital space) of Realnetworks suggested that perhaps a commercial product with features and constraints would be acceptable to big content. Further, the case tested the "reach and strength" of the DMCA against the fair use principles established (for recording broadcast television programs, for personal use, with VCRs) in *Sony*.

Following the *321 Studios* case, Realnetworks brought a similar action against the DVD-CCA and several major motion picture studios, asking the court to find that it did not violate the anti-circumvention provision of the DMCA by manufacturing and distributing its RealDVD software, that allowed users to copy DVDs onto their hard drives so that they would not need the physical DVD to watch the content. Realnetworks argued that CSS was no longer an effective technological measure because it had already been cracked and published on the Internet. However, the District Court found that the technology was still effective for the average consumer and the product thus violated the copy-control provision of the DMCA.

In addition, Realnetworks argued that the studios and the DVD-CCA did not have a legal right to prevent consumers from making personal or "backup" copies of the DVDs under copyright law, and also that the RealDVD software was capable of substantial non-infringing use under the *Sony/Betamax* standard. The District Court rejected these arguments, noting that the *Sony* case was superseded by the DMCA, and finding that the DMCA permits copying of a work to be fair use under certain circumstances, but that this exemption applies only to individual users. Thus, "while it may well be fair use for an individual consumer to store a backup copy of a personally-owned DVD on that individual's computer, a federal law has nonetheless made it illegal to manufacture or traffic in a device or tool that permits a consumer to make such copies."

Cases Involving Digital Transmission and the Public Performance Right

Cartoon Network LP, LLLP v. CSC Holdings, Inc. (Cablevision), 536 F.3d 121 (2nd Cir. 2008).

Cartoon Network LP, LLLP v. CSC Holdings, Inc. is the first in a line of cases (continuing to the date of publication of this 2nd edition) examining the copyright implications of various digital methods and business models for time and place shifting of content and programs.

In 2006, the cable television provider Cablevision announced its plans to sell a remote storage digital video recorder (DVR) system. Unlike traditional DVRs, which required appliances in the home of the user, the Cablevision DVR stored content on servers in Cablevision's facilities. Under the system, content requested by a particular user was stored independently and made available only for the user who requested it.

In response, a consortium of networks and studios sued for direct copyright infringement, alleging violations of their reproduction and public performance rights. The District Court ruled in favor of the copyright owners. However, on appeal, the Second Circuit reversed, finding that Cablevision's proposed DVR system did not directly infringe on any of the plaintiffs' exclusive rights. In particular, the court held that the system's use of content buffering (the creation of RAM copies) did not qualify as a "copy" because the data was not perceivable "for a period of more than transitory duration." The Circuit Court also held that Cablevision could not be directly liable for creating playback copies because those copies were actually made at the direction of the cable company customers. Lastly, the Circuit Court held that the transmissions of playback copies were not performances "to the public" because Cablevision transmitted only the copy requested and recorded by a particular user to that same user. Though controversial, this decision is often credited with bolstering the legality of cloud-based storage and DVR services.

American Broadcasting Cos., Inc., et al. v. Aereo, Inc., f/k/a Bamboom Labs, Inc., 13 US 461 (2013).

American Broadcasting v. Aereo (re)presents issues that first appeared decades earlier in copyright battles between broadcasters and cable television. "Retransmissions" of copyright protected material challenge interpretations of a variety of those rights. In this instance, however, retransmissions are combined with digital storage and delivery.

The issues in *Cablevision* were again raised with the development of Aereo, an online TV service that allows subscribers to view and record live broadcasts. Aereo uses individual antennas to capture free over-the-air television signals that it then digitizes and stores on its servers for individual customers. After the product launched in 2012, a consortium of major broadcasters and content providers sued Aereo for copyright infringement, seeking to shut down the service. The broadcasters argued that Aereo was a threat to their business model, noting that cable companies have to pay broadcasters for the right to carry their signals; on the other hand, Aereo obtains and retransmits the very same signals without permission or fee/royalty payments.

The Second Circuit held that Aereo's transmissions to subscribers did not constitute copyright infringement because they were not "public performances" under the Copyright Act. Relying on the *Cablevision* case, the court focused on Aereo's transmission to subscribers instead of the underlying public broadcast signal, finding that it was not "capable of being received by the public" and was thus a private transmission. In response to this ruling, several networks and sports leagues have threatened to take their content from free TV to cable or satellite, and the broadcasters appealed the case to the SCOTUS.

Complicating the matter, other courts have come to the opposite conclusion in cases involving FilmOn, another online TV service and Aereo competitor. In contrast to the Second Circuit's findings in *Cablevision* and *Aereo*, district courts in D.C. and California found that the retransmission service infringed on plaintiffs' exclusive right to perform the work publicly, with the D.C. court issuing a nearly nationwide ban on FilmOn's services (see *Fox Television v. FilmonX*, 2013).

The SCOTUS overturned earlier rulings by the trial and appeals courts. The majority declared that Aereo's services do constitute a public performance of copyright protected works and that Aereo does not merely provide consumers with equipment. Therefore, Aereo's services/transmissions infringe. The case was remanded to the Circuit court for further action.

Cases Involving Copyright Term Extension and the Public Domain

Eldred v. Ashcroft, 537 U.S. 186 (2003).

Eldred v. Ashcroft tested the constitutionality of the Copyright Term Extension Act (CTEA) of 1998.

Eric Eldred, a former computer systems administrator, published online editions of public domain texts for several years prior to the Copyright Term Extension Act (CTEA). He looked forward to expanding his project at the point when the copyright terms of various content, set by the Copyright Act, 1976 (CA, 1976) expired. The Copyright Term Extension Act (CTEA) delayed Eldred's project (and similar efforts by others) by increasing the term of copyright protection from life of the author plus fifty years to life of the author plus seventy years. Eldred joined forces with several groups that were also using public domain works, and with the support of noted copyright scholars including Lawrence Lessig and Jonathan Zittrain, filed suit in Washington, D.C. District Court in 1999 challenging the constitutionality of the CTEA.

The plaintiffs argued that Congress exceeded its authority in extending the term, by violating both the constitutional mandate that copyrights be secured for only "a limited time" and the First Amendment right to free speech. The District Court and the appeals court both disagreed with these arguments. The SCOTUS agreed to hear the case. On October 9, 2002, Lawrence Lessig argued the case before the Court; on January 15, 2003, in a 7–2 opinion, the SCOTUS agreed with the lower courts that the CTEA was constitutional and must be allowed to stand.

Key factors in the Eldred case were the true meaning of the phrase "limited times," specifically as it pertains to existing copyrights, and the question of whether the right to free speech in any way applies to the use of copyrighted works. The justices did not agree that repeated extensions of the copyright term were, in effect, creating a perpetual and unlimited right, even when the extensions applied both to new and existing works. Although a life-plus-seventy-years term is considerably longer than the fourteen-year term granted when the copyright law was enacted for the first time, "… a timespan appropriately 'limited' as applied to future copyrights does not automatically cease to be 'limited' when applied to existing copyrights. And as we observe … there is no cause to suspect that a purpose to evade the 'limited Times' prescription prompted Congress to adopt the CTEA" (*Eldred v. Ashcroft*). The Court likewise rejected the First Amendment argument, finding that a limited monopoly on expression is not incompatible with the right to free speech, further noting that the CA, 1976 already contains limitations, such as the 107 fair use exemption, that act as safeguards in cases where the protected speech must involve the use of a copyrighted expression.

Cases Involving Peer-to-Peer File Sharing

In the mid-1990s, a compressed audio file format known as MP3 (officially: MPEG-1, layer 3) became a popular format for sharing recorded music online. The bulletin boards and newsgroups that were once popular for swapping pictures and other media were soon replaced by websites functioning as "peer-to-peer" file sharing systems. Big content, especially the recording and movie industries, responded to challenges presented via the exponentially increasing numbers of files shared among users, through computers and networks, by leveraging copyright law in litigation against peer-to-peer networks and file sharers.

UMG Recordings, Inc. v. MP3.Com, Inc., 92 F. Supp. 2d 349 (S.D.N.Y. 2000).

UMG Recordings, Inc. v. MP3.Com presented the courts with questions that foreshadowed file and content management issues to come, including time and storage shifting and file copying.

The first major challenge to online music sharing was against MP3.com, a company that sought to make digital copies of CDs in order to allow their subscribers to access MP3 versions of their music collections online from anywhere in the world (a practice that is now common to cloud based services such as those provided by Apple). A group of record companies sued MP3.com for copyright infringement based on its digitizing and replaying services. In response, MP3.com argued that its copying service was fair use because it provided a transformative "space shift" by allowing subscribers to enjoy their music from anywhere without having to lug around the CDs themselves. The District Court rejected this argument as "an insufficient basis for any legitimate claim of transformation," calling it "simply another way of saying that the unauthorized copies are being retransmitted in another medium."

MP3.com also argued that it provided a useful service to consumers that, in its absence, would be served by "pirates." But the court held that this claim lacked merit, finding that "defendant's 'consumer protection' argument amounts to nothing more than a bald claim that defendant should be able to misappropriate plaintiffs' property simply because there is a consumer demand for it. This hardly appeals to the conscience of equity."

A&M Records, Inc. v. Napster, Inc., 239 F. 3d 1004 (9ᵗʰ Cir. 2001).

A&M Records, Inc. v. Napster, Inc. presented the first of a virtually unending string of technological innovations that allowed users to share files not only with one another, but across vast numbers of Internet users.

Shawn Fanning, then a freshman at Northeastern University, wrote a simple program (Napster) that allowed users to share lists of the music stored on their computers (by way of Napster) and then to directly connect and swap selected music files (or collections of files). Record companies and the Recording Industry Association of America (RIAA) took notice of Napster and other peer-to-peer, or P2P, services. In 1999, they filed suit against Napster in California District Court, alleging both contributory and vicarious copyright infringement.

Napster attempted to have the case dismissed, arguing that it qualified for protection under the DMCA's safe harbor provision limiting liability for the Internet service providers (ISPs) who merely provide bandwidth and base services for users' network activities. The record companies countered that Napster had both the right and the ability to monitor and prevent illegal activities by its users, and, since it had attracted more than $13 million in venture capital, had a strong financial incentive to support users' infringing behaviors. The District Court agreed with the record companies' argument that Napster failed to qualify for ISP protections and ordered Napster to halt trading copyrighted files. Although an appeals court gave Napster a brief reprieve, the injunction was eventually allowed to stand. Bertelsmann purchased Napster's assets and closed down the P2P service before an appeal could be considered.

Metro-Goldwyn-Mayer Studios Inc. v. Grokster, Ltd., 545 U.S. 913 (2005).

Metro-Goldwyn-Mayer Studios Inc. v. Grokster, Ltd. presented most of the same legal issues as did the *Napster* case. But because Grokster utilized decentralized networking in a way that was quite different from the Napster model, the RIAA and record companies needed litigation to invalidate alternative technological approaches.

Dozens of peer-to-peer services appeared on the Internet, (even) after the *Napster* decision. In late 2001, a coalition of film and recording studios filed suit against another group of P2P services, including Grokster. These services operated on a slightly different basis than had Napster in that they were completely decentralized, without a central catalog of music residing on a specific computer or (set of) server(s). The *Grokster* case was eventually argued before the SCOTUS, and, as with the *321 Studios* case, the defense raised the *Sony* standard, arguing that technology with substantial non-infringing uses cannot be prohibited under US copyright law. In a unanimous but narrow ruling, the justices declined to respond to the non-infringing uses argument, finding instead that Grokster was liable for inducing the infringing behavior of its users. After the ruling, both sides claimed victory—the content industries for successfully making an inducement argument and Grokster for successfully preserving the *Sony* standard. The decision did not definitively resolve the P2P issue one way or the other, but as with *321 Studios* and *Napster*, although the case was remanded to the lower court for further action, Grokster ceased operations shortly after the SCOTUS decision was handed down.

Recording Industry Ass'n of America, Inc., v. Verizon Internet Services, Inc., 359 F.3d 1229 (D.C. Cir. 2003).

Recording Industry Ass'n of America, Inc., v. Verizon Internet Services, Inc. found the content industries attempting to solve the peer-to-peer problem via litigation against users (rather than systems). However, in most cases, users "hid" behind anonymity or various alternative identities (avatars, pseudonyms, nicknames, etc.). Users have to be identified before litigation can take place.

Responding to what they perceived as serious threats to their members' businesses and profitability, the RIAA began, in 2001, to take direct action against users sharing music online through P2P systems. As part of their copyright infringement suits against users (or "pirates," as they called them), the RIAA sought to compel Internet service providers (ISPs) including Verizon, Inc., to disclose the identity of users who were engaging in large-scale music sharing. Several providers did identify their users, but when presented with a subpoena, Verizon refused to do so. The RIAA then took Verizon to court. Verizon made three arguments. First, Verizon argued that limitations on Internet service provider liability in section 512 of the CA (a section of the DMCA) exempted them from responsibility for activities that involve content that travels across Verizon-administrated network connections but is not directly stored on servers or other devices operated by them. Verizon maintained two additional arguments, based on ways of reading the DMCA, that asserted constitutional grounds for protecting them from the demands in the RIAA action.

The D.C. District Court disagreed with all three of Verizon's arguments and had ordered them to identify users, but the Court of Appeals overruled by agreeing with the first argument: "We conclude from both the terms of §512(h) and the overall structure of §512 that, as Verizon contends, a subpoena may be issued only to an ISP engaged in storing on its servers material that is infringing or the subject of infringing activity." However, the Court declined to consider the constitutional arguments that Verizon had raised.

Columbia Pictures Industries, Inc. v. Fung, 710 F.3d 1020 (9th Cir. 2013).

First released in 2001, the BitTorrent protocol is a popular variant of P2P file sharing. Instead of simply transferring a file between two users, BitTorrent breaks large files into smaller pieces, allowing users to quickly download pieces of a file (torrent files) at the same time from different peers. Once a user has downloaded all the pieces, the file is automatically reassembled into its original form. BitTorrent users rely on torrent sites, that track and list basic indicating information about available downloads.

Several studios sued torrent website operator Gary Fung and his company, IsoHunt, claiming that the services and torrent sites maintained by the defendants induced third parties to download infringing copies of the studios' copyrighted works. Fung argued that he could not be liable for infringement because he neither developed nor provided the BitTorrent protocol used for downloading and his sites merely indexed available files. However, under the inducement liability standard in *Grokster*, the Ninth Circuit found overwhelming evidence that the vastly predominant use of Fung's services was to infringe copyrights and that Fung operated his services with the object of promoting infringement. The court also held that Fung was ineligible for any of the DMCA safe harbor provisions. The court reduced terms of the district court's injunction that would have prevented Fung from working in computer network industries. Fung and the studios later agreed on a reported $110 million dollar settlement (and the closing of IsoHunt).

It should be noted that there are numerous legal uses for the BitTorrent protocol, including some that are licensed to and by various "big content" companies (television, film, video games, radio, etc.).

Cases Involving Internet Service Provider Liability under the DMCA

Viacom International, Inc. v. YouTube, Inc., 676 F.3d 19 (2nd Cir. 2012).

Viacom International, Inc. v. YouTube may stand as one of the most important copyright cases in the late 20th and early 21st centuries. Not long after Internet search giant Google acquired YouTube (for roughly $1.65 billion dollars), Viacom sued YouTube/Google for massive copyright infringement. Regardless of the outcome (YouTube/Google win), it's clear that YouTube hosts many infringing files, that YouTube/Google might be able to do more (than they do) to limit infringing materials, but to do so would require radical changes in the ways that YouTube works (and the ways that users participate with media artifacts on the Internet). The case tested the viability of the DMCA in a standoff against the ISP safe harbor and content producers.

In 2007, several film studios, television networks, music publishers, and sports leagues filed a billion-dollar lawsuit against YouTube for copyright infringement of thousands of unauthorized clips that appeared on the video-hosting website from 2005 to 2008. The lawsuit alleged that YouTube knowingly and intentionally allowed the exploitation of Viacom's intellectual property and derived substantial profits from the use of unauthorized copyright content. YouTube sought refuge in the DMCA safe harbor provisions, that allow qualifying service providers to limit their liability for claims of copyright infringement.

The lawsuit considered what level of knowledge of infringing activity would disqualify a service provider from DMCA protection. The District Court held that YouTube was protected by the DMCA despite the company's general knowledge that users had uploaded *some* copyrighted material. The court stated that requiring the website to police every video would contravene the structure and operation of the DMCA (its take-down procedures require specification of individual files) and noted that YouTube had successfully followed the DMCA takedown procedures.

On appeal, the Second Circuit agreed that actual knowledge or awareness of specific infringing activity will disqualify an ISP from DMCA protection, but vacated and remanded the case to determine whether YouTube had such knowledge with respect to specific clips. The court reasoned that, although YouTube was not required to police each video, a service provider cannot turn a blind eye toward infringing activity. On remand, the District Court again ruled in favor of YouTube, finding that the website did not have actual knowledge of any specific instance of infringement and therefore could not have willfully blinded itself. The court also held that YouTube did not have the ability to control infringing activity and did not encourage or induce infringement.

UMG Recordings, Inc. v. Shelter Capital Partners LLC, 718 F.3d 1006 (9th Cir. 2013).

UMG Recordings, Inc. v. Shelter Capital Partners shows that principles articulated in the *Viacom v. YouTube* case apply to similar cases involving a variety of websites that host third-party video content.

The Ninth Circuit addressed a similar infringement case against Veoh.com, another video-sharing website. The court upheld the District Court's ruling that Veoh was entitled to safe harbor protection under the DMCA, finding that knowledge of infringing activity on the site has to be specific in order for an ISP to lose protection. "Merely hosting a category of copyrightable content, such as music videos, with the general knowledge that one's services could be used to share infringing material, is insufficient to meet the actual knowledge requirement." The decision further reiterated that the burden of identifying infringing material must fall on the copyright holder and not the service provider.

After ruling in 2011, the court issued a superseding opinion in 2013 to align its holdings with the Second Circuit's opinion in *Viacom v. YouTube*. The decision clarified that a service provider has "control" over infringing activity sufficient to lose protection under the DMCA safe harbor provisions if it exerts "substantial influence" on the activities of users, meaning "high levels of control over activities by users," or by "purposeful conduct, as in *Grokster*." Merely having the ability to block users from posting content was insufficient to disqualify Veoh from safe harbor protection.

Learning Objectives and Discussion Questions

- Connect significant court cases to the principles established through them. Can you:
  o Discuss the "idea versus expression" dichotomy in copyright law;
  o Identify the status of the "sweat of the brow" doctrine;
  o Discuss users' right to time shift and other non-infringing actions with media content recorders, including the factors considered when deciding if DVRs and cloud storage infringe copyrights;
  o Define and describe the theory of "the public's right to know" as it relates to fair use in news and publishing;
  o Describe copyright protection for manufacturing design elements;
  o Discuss whether displaying thumbnails or linking to images (that users might copy) is infringement;
  o Discuss whether computer code (programming) should qualify for First Amendment and free speech protection;
  o Discuss whether/how the DMCA preempts the publication of encryption research that identifies DRM circumventions;
  o Identify the arguments for/against software that enables circumvention of DRM?

CHAPTER TWO

Three Copyright Issues Cases

Traditional Special Copyright Issues Cases with New Media Implications

Grand Upright Music, Ltd v. Warner Bros. Records Inc., 780 F. Supp. 182 (S.D.N.Y. 1991).

Grand Upright Music, Ltd v. Warner Bros. Records Inc. set a standard against sampling as fair use in the US popular music industry.

Singer-songwriter Gilbert O'Sullivan brought a copyright infringement action against rapper Biz Markie after Markie sampled portions of O'Sullivan's hit song "Alone Again, Naturally". The court ruled that sampling without permission and/or license constituted copyright infringement. However, that decision ruled that the sampling was infringement only if the amount and substantiality failed to gain fair use exemption because the sample "rose to the level of legally cognizable appropriation." That standard stood until *Bridgeport v. Dimension Films* (2005) ruled that even *de minimis* samples infringe and must be licensed.

Computer Associates Int'l v. Altai, 982 F.2d 693 (2d Cir. 1992).

While it is the case that aspects of computer software can be protected by copyright, features that were taken from the public domain cannot be so protected.

Computer Associates Int'l v. Altai helped establish an important and oft-used test that determines whether software can be protected, and a major aspect of that test depends on analysis of the public domain.

Computer Associates (CA) created a job scheduling program (CA-SCHEDULER) for IBM computer systems. Altai established their own scheduling program (ZEKE) for the VSE operating system, but also reverse engineered a version that would run on various operating systems (including standards used in the Computer Associates' program). CA sued for copyright infringement and trade secret misappropriation.

The court had to parse aspects of the code that did or did not infringe. As part of the process, the appellate court engaged in a three-step test (the abstraction, filtration, comparison test) to determine which parts of the code processes could be protected by copyright. An important part of that process is determining which parts of the code are in the public domain and are therefore not protectable. The appellate court's analysis verified the findings of the district court, that Altai had not infringed on significant portions of CA's protectable code. Just as "prior art" is not protectable intellectual property via patent law, information that is in the public domain is not protectable via copyright law.

Monster Communications, Inc. v. Turner Broadcasting Sys. Inc., 935 F. Supp. 490 (S.D. N.Y. 1996).

Monster Communications v. Turner Broadcasting suggests that *de minimis* can be a factor toward a fair use finding, particularly in informational contexts.

Monster Communications produced, and was scheduled to premiere, a film about Muhammad Ali, *When We Were Kings*, focusing on the 1974 championship bout, in Zaire, between Ali and George Foreman (the so-called "Rumble in the Jungle"). Monster learned that Turner Broadcasting had produced, and was about to air, a month before the scheduled film premiere, a documentary special titled *Ali—The Whole Story*, in which a number of clips of the Zaire fight appear (perhaps 41 seconds worth). Monster sought an injunction against Turner and the program, arguing that the footage was protected by a copyright they had acquired, so was an infringement (that threatened the market for their film).

The court ruled against Monster and refused to issue the injunction, largely by finding that it would be very difficult for audience members to detect, and be influenced by, footage from the fight that appeared in both video projects. In effect, even if a technical rights infringement had occurred, the amount was insufficient to cause significant market harm to the rights holder.

Dr. Seuss Enterprises, L.P. v. Penguin Books USA, Inc., 109 F.3d 1394 (9th Cir. 1997).

In a case that adds a dimension to parody considerations in fair use cases, *Dr. Seuss v. Penguin Books* sides with the rights owner when the infringing work is satire rather than parody.

Publication of the book, *The Cat NOT in the Hat! A Parody by Dr. Juice*, was enjoined, at the district court level, by a preliminary injunction based on copyright infringement. Penguin Books appealed, claiming that the work deserved fair use protection as a parody. Authors Alan Katz and Chris Wrinn, respectively, wrote and illustrated *The Cat NOT in the Hat!* satirizing the O.J. Simpson double murder trial. According to an advertisement for the book (quoted in the case file):

> Wickedly clever author "Dr. Juice" gives the O.J. Simpson trial a very fresh new look. From Brentwood to the Los Angeles County Courthouse to Marcia Clark and the Dream Team, The Cat Not in the Hat tells the whole story in rhyming verse and sketches as witty as Theodore [sic] Geisel's best. This is one parody that really packs a punch!

In this case, "Seuss" is a California limited partnership that controls many of the copyrights and trademarks in the late Theodor S. Geisel's (Dr. Seuss) estate. Seuss sued Penguin for copyright and trademark infringement.

In deciding the matter, the court considered the parody definition provided by Justice Souter in the Acuff-Rose "Pretty Woman" case:

> For the purposes of copyright law, the nub of the definitions, and the heart of any parodist's claim to quote from existing material, is the use of some elements of a prior author's composition to create a new one that, at least in part, comments on that author's work. If, on the contrary, the commentary has no critical bearing on the substance or style of the original composition, which the alleged infringer merely uses to get attention or to avoid the drudgery in working up something fresh, the claim to fairness in borrowing from another's work diminishes accordingly (if it does not vanish), and other factors, like the extent of its commerciality, loom larger.

In other words, to qualify as parody, the work must present the copied object as the *object of the parody* rather than merely as a vehicle for getting attention.

The court upheld the preliminary injunction, and the findings of copyright and trademark infringement.

Northland Family Planning Clinic v. Center for Bio-Ethical Reform, No: SACV 11-731 JVS (C.D. Cal. June 15, 2012).

Northland Family Planning Clinic v. Center for Bio-Ethical Reform broadened the usual interpretation of what counts as parody, in a fair use defense, by de-emphasizing comedic and/or entertainment aspects.

Defendants Center for Bio-Ethical Reform, a pro-life/anti-abortion group, created videos by borrowing clips from Northland Family Planning Clinic's pro-choice videos and juxtaposing that material with footage from actual abortion procedures, along with added/new narration that contradicts the sound track of the original. Northland sued for copyright infringement.

The court found that the new videos did not infringe the originals, largely because they were fair use based on parody. In this case, the court noted that parody need not depend on comedy or entertainment. Rather, fair use can be established via content that criticizes/makes negative commentary on the original.

Golan v. Holder, 132 S. Ct. 873 (2012).

In *Golan v. Holder*, The SCOTUS considered whether Congress had the power to restore copyright protection to foreign works that were already in the US public domain.

Plaintiffs brought a Copyright Clause and First Amendment challenge to a statute enacted to comply with US treaty obligations under the Agreement on Trade-Related Aspects of Intellectual Property Rights (TRIPS). The statute extended protection to works that had never been protected in the US, but had not fallen into the public domain in their countries of origin.

The Court upheld the principles established in *Eldred*, finding that Congress did not exceed its authority when it removed works from the public domain. The Court emphasized that compliance with international copyright treaties would expand the foreign markets available to US authors and invigorate protection against piracy of US works abroad. *Golan* also clarified that the "traditional contours" of copyright contain "built-in First Amendment accommodations" found in the idea/expression dichotomy and the fair use defense, and thus there was no need to apply heightened judicial scrutiny.

New Media Special Copyright Issues Cases

Field v. Google Inc., 412 F. Supp. 2d 1106 (D. Nev. 2006).

Is displaying a cached website in search engine results a fair use or an infringement? According to the ruling in *Field v. Google*, it's not infringement when it's the user who decides whether to retrieve the material.

Field, an author, sued Google when the company's cached search results directed end users to copies of copyrighted works. The court found that Google could not be sued for actions that users take. Additionally, Field failed to turn off the cache functions on his website, essentially allowing the copying that he was accusing Google of facilitating.

Warner Bros. Entertainment, Inc. v. RDR Books, 575 F. Supp. 2d 513 (S.D. N.Y. 2008).

It is not uncommon for copyright litigation to "follow the money." *Warner Bros. Entertainment, Inc. v. RDR Books* features an instance when a not-for-profit online Harry Potter fan site moved to for-profit print publication, resulting in Potter rights owners suing for infringement.

Steve Vander Ark operated an online fan site, the Harry Potter Lexicon, for a number of years. Potter rights holders, including author J.K. Rowling herself, took no action against the popular and informative site. However, an independent publisher, RDR Books, convinced Vander Ark to print a version of the site (in a number of works). Rowling and Warner Brothers sued for copyright infringement.

The court ruled in favor of Rowling and Warner Brothers, finding that the Vander Ark/RDR works were not sufficiently transformative to qualify for a fair use defense. However, the trial judge's ruling articulated ways that works such as these are or could be transformative as well as ruling against Rowling's claim that the Vander Ark/RDR works limited or compromised the market for subsequent works she might produce. While denying fair use for Vander Ark/RDR, the verdict strengthened the position of transformative works against attempts at hegemony by the derivative rights owners.

Katz v. Chevaldina (S.D. Fla. June 17, 2014).

Katz v. Chevaldina is a fair use case that illustrates at least two important concepts. First, the case stands against a strategy lately tested/used by high profile targets of negative, online criticism: the targets make claims of copyright infringement against the critic. Second, the case lends further expansion to what counts as transformative use of copyright protected material in a fair use defense.

Defendant Irina Chevaldina has a long-standing riff with Plaintiff Raanan Katz. Katz is a prominent Miami businessman with extensive real estate holdings and a partial ownership interest in the Miami Heat basketball team. Chevaldina posted negative criticisms of Katz and his firms (RK Associates and RK Centers) on blogs specifically targeted at Katz. Her derogatory comments sometimes appeared alongside photographic images of Katz taken from the WWW after a Google images search. Katz acquired the copyright to one of the images, from the originating photographer, then sued Chevaldina, claiming copyright infringement. Chevaldina sought defense via fair use.

The court applied the 4-factor test, with the conclusive factors loading within the determination of the first factor: the nature and character of the use. The court ruled that Chevaldina made non-commercial use of the copyright protected item and that her use was transformative. Here the court issued an interpretation that, if validated by an appellate ruling, would further widen the scope of the transformative standard for fair use.

Citing another district court case as well as an appellate ruling (*Nunez v. Caribbean Int'l News Corp*), Southern District Court judge Chris McAliley reasoned that because the original photograph of Katz was presented along with largely favorable material ("Haaretz used the Photo to identify Plaintiff, in an article about the possibility of Plaintiff acquiring an ownership interest in an Israeli basketball team. Notably, that article cast Plaintiff in a favorable light."), while Chevaldina's uses of the photograph were all presented within highly *unfavorable* contexts, Chevaldina's use of the photograph was transformative and thereby merited fair use protection.

White v. W. Pub. Corp., 12 CIV. 1340 JSR, 2014 WL 3057885 (S.D.N.Y. July 3, 2014).

The transformative standard for fair use was bolstered further by the results of *White v. W. Pub. Corp.*, a class action infringement lawsuit.

The court's analysis indicated that even though the Lexis and Westlaw systems are a commercial interpretation of publicly filed legal briefs (both systems are subscription-only searchable and do not seek the permission of lawyers/authors), the numerous transformations performed on the documents qualifies them for fair use. Further, the market and purposes for the documents are also different (though being "about the law and relevant cases," they may not seem that way). In the first instance, the lawyers produce the documents in the employ of clients so as to execute cases. In the second case, Lexis and Westlaw provide legal research services to the legal community as a whole, thereby placing their efforts outside of commercial infringement.

Fox News v. TVEYES, Inc., 13 Civ. 5315 (S.D. NY Sept. 9, 2014).

In the music industry (and laws that apply therein) sampling recordings requires a license. According to the *Fox News v. TVEYES* ruling, in the television and website news industries, for clipping and indexing, activities that make "snippet" copies not unlike samples, the transformative nature of the work can receive fair use protection.

TVEyes is a media monitoring service using a subscription model. Clients, for example, politicians or celebrities, pay the service to keep track of instances of media coverage. The service monitors information outlets and records instances when those target clients are mentioned/presented. The clients can go to the TVEyes service, call up a list of those instances, and watch the clips.

Fox News sued for copyright infringement, claiming that the copies made by the clipping service created a substitute for watching Fox, harmed the ad revenue of their website (by directing traffic for their programming elsewhere), and competed with Fox's licensing programs (for their clips).

The court rejected Fox's arguments, primarily on fair use grounds based on the transformative nature of the use. Although entire segments (about a given person) were copied and used, the purpose for the copying and use was transformative. Based on the work that TVEyes included in the service, their database is searchable and is used in a way that is different from normal viewing. The service provides the material as part of a research and learning function not available via normal Fox programming and presentational technologies.

Learning Objectives and Discussion Questions

- Connect significant court cases to the principles established through them. Can you:
  o Discuss the relationships among copying, sampling, fair use, licensing, and *de minimis* use;
  o Discuss the relationships between copyright protection and the public domain;
  o Describe and discuss nuances of the transformative standard for fair use protection;
  o Describe and discuss nuances of parody for fair use protection;
  o List and discuss factors of education and information that might cause instances where entire sets of material are copied but are not considered infringement, based on fair use;
  o Discuss the potential costs and benefits (to plaintiffs and defendants) of using copyright law in defamation litigation over comment and review sites? Discuss this question/issue now, then return to it after reading the chapters about the content torts, especially defamation, and the terms of the safe harbor provided by the Communications Decency Act (CDA)?

CHAPTER THREE

Patent Cases

Traditional Media Patent Cases with New Media Implications

Markman v. Westview Instruments Inc., 517 U.S. 370 (1996).

Markman was the most important patent case of its decade. In a unanimous opinion, the SCOTUS affirmed the Federal Circuit and held that determining the meanings of patent claims is a task for the courts to decide as a question of law, not questions for juries to decide as questions of fact.

Before this case, determining the meanings of patent claims (often called "construing the claims") was a task for a jury; a process that often led to unpredictable outcomes even after years of litigating the patent.

Now, common practice is for District Courts to hold *Markman* hearings, where the words of the claims that are disputed by the parties are construed by the Court. Determining whether an accused product infringes a claim of a patent is thus a two-step process. First, the Court construes the claims; second, a jury determines whether the claims fit the accused device or process.

In *Markman*, the patent at issue was directed at managing inventory at a dry cleaner. Claim 1 of Markman's patent stated that the claimed product could "maintain an inventory total" and "detect and localize spurious additions to inventory."

Thus, the term "inventory" was a disputed term. The jury found infringement of Claim 1, but the District Court subsequently granted the defendant's motion for judgment as a matter of law based upon the Court's own construction of the term "inventory." Markman appealed this ruling, but both the Federal Circuit and SCOTUS affirmed, holding that it is within the province of the Court to construe the claims of a patent.

Graham v. John Deere, 383 U.S. 1 (1966).

Graham is the first modern SCOTUS case to address the critical issue in patent law of "obviousness."

As previously discussed, to secure a patent on an invention, the invention must be new, useful, and non-obvious. Before Congress revised the Patent Act in 1952, obviousness was a creature only of the common law. *Graham* was the first case after the 1952 revision when the SCOTUS heard a case involving the obviousness standard.

In *Graham*, the Court set forth the test that is still used by courts today. Under *Graham*, courts look at four factors (often called the "*Graham* factors") to determine if an invention would have been obvious at the time the invention was made to a person of ordinary skill in the art to which the subject matter pertains. These factors are: the scope and content of the prior art; the differences between the prior art and the claims at issue; the level of ordinary skill in the art; and, finally, secondary considerations of non-obviousness, such as commercial success, long-felt but unsolved need, and the failure of others.

The patent at issue in *Graham* covered a device that was "designed to absorb shock from plow shanks as they plow[ed] through rocky soil [which] prevent[ed] damage to the plow." The Court determined that this invention was obvious, because it was not sufficiently different from the prior art. Thus, the Court affirmed the finding of the lower court that the patent was invalid.

KSR Int'l Co. v. Teleflex Inc., 550 U.S. 398, 127 S.Ct. 1727 (2007).

In *KSR*, the SCOTUS rejected the "rigid approach" of the Federal Circuit in favor of an "expansive and flexible approach" on whether a patent claim was obvious in view of prior art.

In *KSR*, the patentee sued the defendant for infringement on a patent claiming an adjustable vehicle control pedal connected to an electronic throttle control. The defendant argued that it was merely obvious, and therefore not patentable, to combine these elements. The defendant's win in the District Court was overturned by the Federal Circuit. The Federal Circuit held that there was no teaching, suggestion, or motivation (TSM) to combine prior art that in combination disclosed the claimed invention. The SCOTUS rejected the Federal Circuit's rigid TSM application.

The SCOTUS stated that "[a] person of ordinary skill is also a person of ordinary creativity, not an automaton." The SCOTUS held that the "obviousness analysis cannot be confined by a formalistic conception of the words teaching, suggestion, and motivation, or by overemphasis on the importance of published articles and the explicit content of issued patents." The SCOTUS stated that "[i]n many fields it may be that there is little discussion of obvious techniques or combinations, and it often may be the case that market demand, rather than scientific literature, will drive design trends." Thus, the SCOTUS noted, "[g]ranting patent protection to advances that would occur in the ordinary course without real innovation retards progress and may, in the case of patents combining previously known elements, deprive prior inventions of their value or utility."

Turning to the facts in *KSR*, the SCOTUS held that the District Court was correct to conclude that, as of the time of the alleged invention, "it was obvious to a person of ordinary skill to combine [a pivot-mounted pedal] with a pivot-mounted pedal position sensor." Indeed, "[t]here then existed a marketplace that created a strong incentive to convert mechanical pedals to electronic pedals, and the prior art taught a number of methods for achieving this advance."

Graver Tank & Mfg. Co. v. Linde Air Products, Co., 339 U.S. 605 (1950).

Graver Tank is the first SCOTUS case to squarely address patent infringement under the "doctrine of equivalents."

It is now commonly recognized that there are two types of patent infringement: literal infringement and infringement under the doctrine of equivalents. To prove literal infringement, a patentee must prove that the words of the claims of the patent "literally" read on the accused device (essentially, copy the original). Alternatively, as set forth by the Court in *Graver Tank*, in order to prevent an infringer from making minor changes that would place the accused device outside of the literal words of the claims, a patentee may prove equivalent infringement by showing that the accused device "performs substantially the same function in substantially the same way to obtain the same result." Here the Court agreed with the trial court: A patent that claimed a welding composition having a combination of an alkaline earth metal silicate (e.g., magnesium) and calcium fluoride was infringed under the doctrine of equivalents by a welding composition having silicates of calcium and manganese (manganese is not an alkaline earth metal). Even though this minor change places the accused recipe for the welding composition outside of the literal words of the patent claim, the accused recipe performs substantially the same function in substantially the same way to obtain the same result, so is infringement under the doctrine of equivalents.

State Street Bank & Trust Co. v. Signature Financial Group, 149 F.3d 1368 (Fed. Cir. 1998).

State Street Bank is an important Federal Circuit decision because it establishes that "business methods" can be patented.

A business method patent (or process) is a patent that covers a way of doing something in a business or transactional setting. The Federal Circuit held that as long as the way of doing something produces a "useful, concrete and tangible result," then the invention is patentable subject matter under section 101. To be patentable, the business method must also meet the other criteria for patentability, namely, it must still be new and non-obvious.

The patent at issue in *State Street Bank* was for a "Data Processing System for Hub and Spoke Financial Services Configuration." The "spokes" were mutual funds that pooled their assets into a central "hub." This method produced a share price that was used for several types of investment decisions. Because this process produced a "useful, concrete, and tangible result," namely, a share price, the Federal Circuit held that the patent was not invalid for failure to claim statutory subject matter as required by Section 101.

Since the *State Street Bank* case, the US Patent Office has issued numerous business method patents, many of which are Internet-related. Later cases, especially *Bilski v. Kappos* (2010), have reaffirmed the validity of business method/process patents. The legal theories that establish the validity of business method/process patents provide much of the superstructure for software patents.

Bilski v. Kappos, 130 S. Ct. 3218 (2010).

In *Bilski*, the SCOTUS, in addition to deciding the particulars of the case at hand, reaffirms the validity of business methods/process patents, deferring speculation that these, and the software patents that depend on business methods/process, might be set aside as non-patentable.

This case involved the question of whether a patent could issue on a procedure for instructing buyers and sellers of commodities how to protect against the risk of price fluctuations in the commodities market. Recognizing that Section 101 of the Patent Act covers "any new and useful process, machine, manufacture, or composition of matter ..." the Court acknowledged that the subject matter of the claimed invention must meet the definition of a process. The court below had strictly applied the so-called "machine-or-transformation test," that defines an invention as a "process" only if: "(1) it is tied to a particular machine or apparatus, or (2) it transforms a particular article into a different state or thing." The SCOTUS found that the Court of Appeals incorrectly concluded that the "machine-or-transformation test was the exclusive test to determine whether a process met the criteria of patentability. Although the SCOTUS was reluctant to limit process patents to the "machine-or-transformation test," the Court nonetheless found the claims not patentable because the claims were attempts to patent abstract ideas.

It will take years for the full impact of *Bilski* to be known, even though business methods and software patents survived *Bilski*. As a result, start-up companies may face increasing risks of defending against other companies' process/methods patents.

Phillips v. AWH, 415 F.3d 1303 (Fed. Cir. 2005) (en banc).

The issue before the Court in *Phillips* was the role that extrinsic evidence should play in construing a patent claim. In *Phillips*, the Federal Circuit set forth that extrinsic evidence is useful, but that it is less significant than intrinsic evidence.

Phillips was a decision that was heard *en banc* (i.e., by all the judges on the Federal Circuit), as opposed to the typical panel of three judges that usually hears an appeal. The issue before the Court in *Phillips* was the role that extrinsic evidence should play in construing a claim. There are two categories of evidence that courts look to in construing a claim. The first is intrinsic evidence, consisting of the claim itself, the specification, and the prosecution history. The second is extrinsic evidence, consisting of dictionaries, encyclopedias, expert testimony, and anything else that is not intrinsic evidence.

In *Phillips*, the Federal Circuit ruled that extrinsic evidence is useful, but that it is less significant than intrinsic evidence. Thus, *Phillips* generally requires a District Court to consult extrinsic evidence only if the intrinsic evidence is insufficient to construe a claim. Nonetheless, the Court explained that extrinsic evidence can play a role in claim construction, depending on the specific facts of a case.

The patent in *Phillips* was for a type of vandal-resistant wall that contained "internal steel baffles." The Federal Circuit looked to the intrinsic evidence, i.e., the claims, the specification, and the prosecution history, and construed the disputed term "baffles." The Court reached a different construction for the term "baffles" than the District Court and accordingly sent the case back to the District Court for further proceedings.

New Media Cases and Patent Law

Alice Corp. Pty. Ltd. v. CLS Bank Int'l, 134 S. Ct. 2347 (2014).

Alice Corp. v. CLS Bank case presents the question of patent eligibility of an invention implemented by computers. It is also the first time in forty years that the SCOTUS has addressed the propriety of patent protection for software.

Since the 1970s, thousands of software patents have been granted, and patent litigation surrounding software patents has also grown exponentially. At issue in the case are Alice Corp.'s patents for "the management of risk relating to specified, yet unknown, future events." In particular, the patents relate to a computerized trading platform used for conducting financial transactions where a third party settles obligations between a first and a second party so as to eliminate "counterparty" or "settlement" risks. Settlement risk refers to the risk to each party in an exchange that only one of the two parties will actually pay its obligation, leaving the paying party without its principal or the benefit of the counterparty's performance. Alice's patents address that risk by relying on a trusted third party to ensure the exchange of either/both party's/parties' obligations. There are several patent claims involving "method," "system," and "computer-readable medium" claims.

In what some claim to be a muddled *en banc* decision, a plurality of the D.C. Circuit Court of Appeals concluded that the asserted claims are not patent eligible and thus invalid. The SCOTUS unanimously affirmed those findings. However, the SCOTUS tailored its findings narrowly, conforming to the specifics of the case instead of addressing the broader issues of software patents in general.

Amazon.com v. Barnesandnoble.com, 239 F.3d 1343 (Fed. Cir. 2001).

Amazon.com v. Barnesandnoble.com provided important insights into the nature of business methods/process patents applied to the Internet, in this instance, the foundational "1-click® ordering method."

In this Internet technology case, Amazon.com (Amazon) brought a patent infringement lawsuit against Barnes & Noble (BN) based on its business method patent for its 1-click® ordering method, that Amazon still uses today. Based on prior use of the Amazon.com website, the website "remembers" a user's information so that shipping address, billing address, and the like do not need to be reentered to order an item. Thus, as the feature's name implies, a user simply clicks the 1-click® button, and the item is scheduled to be shipped.[1]

BN, on its website, installed a similar feature to Amazon's 1-click® button, which it called "Express Lane." This feature allowed a user to click one button to order a product. Amazon brought suit against BN, alleging that the Express Lane feature infringed Amazon's patent.

The trial court agreed with Amazon and granted a preliminary injunction in its favor (effective November 4, 1999—during the winter holiday shopping season), prohibiting BN from using the Express Lane feature. To grant a preliminary injunction in a patent infringement case, a court must determine that it is likely a patentee will prevail on its claim of patent infringement.

The trial court determined that it was likely that the Express Lane feature infringed Amazon's patent, and thus it granted the preliminary injunction (upon Amazon's filing of an undertaking of $10 million to be awarded to BN should it be determined later that the preliminary injunction should not have been granted).

On February 14, 2001, the Federal Circuit, however, reversed. It found that while Amazon was likely to prevail on its claim of infringement, BN presented prior art evidence sufficient to cast doubt on the validity of Amazon's patent, and the Court reversed the preliminary injunction. Ultimately, the parties reached a confidential settlement, and the validity of Amazon's patent was not fully determined. Although an appellate ruling of this nature usually sets precedents for future cases, subsequent litigation and Patent Office actions move precedents away from this ruling in favor of other legal determinations. These details are discussed below.

IPXL Holdings, L.L.C. v. Amazon.com, Inc., 430 F.3d 1377 (Fed. Cir. 2005).

IPXL Holdings, L.L.C. v. Amazon.com, Inc. further established the validity of Amazon's patent holding over 1-click® shopping. However, please see the *Special note* following the analysis of this case as it further clarifies the matter.

In *IPXL Holdings*, Amazon was also a defendant concerning its claims over the 1-click® technology. In this case, IPXL sued Amazon, claiming that Amazon's 1-click® system infringed several claims of IPXL's in a US patent entitled "Electronic Fund Transfer or Transaction System." Amazon prevailed on a motion for summary judgment and also was awarded its attorney's fees. On appeal, the Federal Circuit upheld the summary judgment in Amazon's favor but reversed the award of attorney's fees because Amazon did not timely file its motion for attorney's fees. This ruling further solidified the importance of the 1-click® patent and remains a potent example of the power of business process patents in the Internet economy.

Special Note Concerning the 1-click® Patent

The patentability of 1-click® shopping on the Internet is widely contested. As reported by Ryan Paul in 2010, the USPTO approved Amazon's revision of their original patent application. The revision came in response to a 2007 challenge by

> Peter Calveley, an actor and patent law enthusiast from New Zealand, [who] launched a campaign against the one-click patent in 2006 and filed for a reexamination with funding that he collected from his supporters. A year later, the USPTO issued a decision rejecting 21 of the patent's 26 claims, largely due to the broad availability of well-documented prior art. Amazon decided to amend the patent in order to address some of the specific issues raised by the reexamination.
>
> The amended version has a slightly smaller scope, limiting the patent's coverage to online shopping cart systems rather than all one-click e-commerce. In its statement today, the USPTO declared that the new version of the patent is valid, despite the fact that it has no functional difference from the original version. ("Controversial Amazon")

The 2007 USPTO ruling appeared to "downsize" the Amazon patent from 1-click® shopping to "shopping cart shopping" such that 1-click shopping that didn't use an Internet "shopping cart" would not be a violation of Amazon's patent. However, the revised patent, approved by the USPTO in 2010, does not appear to differ, substantially, from the original filing, thereby apparently "re-instating" the validity of Amazon's claim over 1-click® shopping. In short, critics of the patent cite the incident as evidence of the shortcomings in both the processes for software patent and patent reviews/appeals.

Rambus Inc. v. Infineon Techs. AG, 318 F.3d 1081 (Fed. Cir. 2003).

Rambus is an important case in the field of standard-setting organizations. Standard-setting organizations ensure that certain technical standards are agreed upon so that electronic devices can be designed to communicate and work with other electronic devices in accordance with those technical standards.[2]

For several years in the 1990s, Rambus was a member of the Joint Electron Devices Engineering Council (JEDEC). JEDEC is a standard-setting organization for semiconductor technologies, and it is composed of numerous competitors in the semiconductor industry. Importantly, JEDEC required its members to disclose any of their patents and patent applications if they were related to the standards JEDEC was setting.

In this case, Rambus brought a patent infringement suit against Infineon based on its patents for dynamic random access memory (DRAM) technology. Infineon counterclaimed for fraud, based on allegations that Rambus failed to disclose certain patents and patent applications to JEDEC. In order to prove fraud, Infineon had to prove that Rambus made a false representation or an omission when it had a duty to disclose. Although a jury found that Rambus was liable for fraud, the Federal Circuit reversed the finding of fraud against Rambus, agreeing with Rambus that no reasonable jury could find that Rambus breached a duty to disclose to JEDEC.

Eolas Techs. v. Microsoft Corp., 399 F.3d 1325 (Fed. Cir. 2005).

Eolas Techs. v. Microsoft Corp involved technology relating to Internet browsers. The importance of this case lies in its analysis of one of the lesser-used sections of the patent code that defines infringement in a way that blocks companies from ducking infringement claims by using (infringing) components manufactured outside the US.

The patentee, Eolas, sued Microsoft on its patent described as a "distributing hypermedia method for automatically invoking external applications providing interaction and display of embedded objects within a hypermedia context." As explained by the Federal Circuit, Eolas's claimed invention "allow[ed] a user to use a Web browser in a fully interactive environment." Eolas alleged that certain aspects of Microsoft's Internet Explorer (IE) infringed Eolas's patent.

Under 35 U.S.C. § 271(f), an entity commits patent infringement if it ships from the United States a substantial portion of a patented invention in uncombined parts and actively induces the combination of such components outside of the United States. Eolas claimed damages for domestic sales of Windows with IE, as well as for foreign sales under § 271(f).

One of the ways that Microsoft exported Windows was by exporting a small number of golden master disks containing Windows code. Companies abroad then used the disks to replicate the code and place it onto computers for sale outside of the United States. Thus, the Federal Circuit was faced with determining whether Microsoft's shipping of these golden master disks constituted infringement under § 271(f). After reviewing the precise language used in §271(f), the Court held that software code is a patentable invention under § 271(f) and that the golden master disks are components of the computer program invention. Thus, Microsoft's activities constituted infringement under § 271(f).

NTP, Inc. v. Research in Motion, Ltd., 418 F.3d 1282 (Fed. Cir. 2005).

This case is the famous "BlackBerry" case. The case is noteworthy not only for its legal holdings but for the impact it threatened to have on the nation and the saga that it became. The case also set forth important legal principles regarding the degree to which an accused method or system must be practiced within the United States in order to infringe under 35 U.S.C. § 271.

The case began in 2001 when NTP, a patent-holding company based in Virginia, sued Research in Motion (RIM), a Canadian company. NTP claimed that RIM infringed NTP's method and systems covering wireless email technology.

In 2002, a jury found for NTP. The total damages were calculated at $53,704,323. RIM appealed, and the trial court stayed an injunction pending an appeal. The Federal Circuit reversed in part and affirmed in part, sending the case back to the trial court. In March 2004, NTP and RIM announced a settlement wherein RIM agreed to pay $450 million, but the settlement fell apart.

The case went back up on appeal, and in August 2005 the Federal Circuit issued its second opinion, holding that in order for RIM to infringe the asserted method claims, each of the steps had to be performed within the United States. Because the method claims involved the use of hardware located in Canada, the Federal Circuit held that RIM could not infringe the method claims. As to the system claims, however, the Federal Circuit affirmed the jury's finding of infringement. The Court held that the accused system was used within the United States as long as the United States "is the place at which the system as a whole is put into service, *i.e.*, the place where control of the system is exercised and beneficial use of the system is obtained." The Federal Circuit held that the system was effectively located in the United States, even if some of the hardware was located in Canada.

In 2005 and early 2006, the case gained national attention, as it appeared that the District Court might enter an injunction that would have shut down service to all BlackBerry users (at the time around four million people in the United States). Following this threat, the case ultimately settled in March 2006 for $612,500,000.

eBay, Inc. v. MercExchange, 126 S. Ct. 1837 (2006).

The *eBay* case is significant because in this case the SCOTUS rejected the general rule that, absent exceptional circumstances, a permanent injunction restraining further infringements should issue once patent validity and infringement have been determined. In doing so, the SCOTUS held that a permanent injunction should be granted only "in accordance with the principles of equity" as applied in non-patent cases.

The *eBay* case stemmed from a long-running dispute between eBay and MercExchange involving eBay's popular online auction site. At issue in the case was eBay's "Buy It Now" feature that allows customers to purchase items listed on eBay's website for a fixed, listed price, bypassing the bidding process. In 2000, MercExchange had entered into licensing negotiations with eBay relating to its three business method patents. Those negotiations broke down, and in 2001 MercExchange sued eBay.

After a five-week trial, a jury found eBay and Half.com liable for patent infringement and awarded damages totaling $35 million to MercExchange. Both sides filed post-verdict motions, including a motion by MercExchange for a permanent injunction restraining future infringement by eBay. The District Court denied MercExchange's motion for a permanent injunction, holding that issuance of an injunction following a verdict of infringement is not automatic but instead is governed by traditional equitable principles, which require consideration of a four-factor test: (1) whether the plaintiff will suffer irreparable harm if an injunction does not issue, (2) whether the plaintiff has an adequate remedy at law, (3) whether granting the injunction is in the public interest, and (4) whether the balance of the hardships tips in favor of the plaintiff.

On appeal, the Federal Circuit reversed the District Court's denial of MercExchange's motion for a permanent injunction, applying a "general rule that courts will issue permanent injunctions against patent infringement absent exceptional circumstances."[3]

In a unanimous decision, the SCOTUS held that the Federal Circuit erred in its categorical grant of injunctive relief. Noting that the Patent Act expressly provides that an injunction "may" issue in accordance with the principles of equity, the SCOTUS held that the traditional four-factor test applies to disputes arising under the Patent Act and must be used to determine when injunctive relief is appropriate.

The SCOTUS concluded that although the District Court used the proper four-factor test, it erred in applying that test. More particularly, the SCOTUS held that neither a patentee's willingness to license its patents nor its lack of commercial activity in practicing the patents is sufficient to preclude a finding of irreparable harm. The Court recognized that some patent holders, including universities and "self-made" inventors, might reasonably choose to license their patents rather than practice the invention themselves, and that such actions should not categorically preclude them from satisfying the four-factor test and obtaining an injunction.

Without taking any position on whether a permanent injunction should issue, the Court thus vacated the judgment of the Federal Circuit and remanded the case to the District Court for a determination of whether MercExchange would be entitled to an injunction under a proper application of the four-factor test.

TiVo v. EchoStar, 516 F.3d 1290 (Fed. Cir. 2008).

TiVo v. EchoStar was the first of a number of cases testing the strength of TiVo's patents controlling DVR technologies.

Some EchoStar set-top boxes have DVR capabilities. Both EchoStar and TiVo devices enable "time shifting" when the DVRs record live television for later viewing. TiVo filed suit against EchoStar in 2004, alleging that its use of that technology infringed a TiVo patent. A jury awarded TiVo $73.9 million in damages.

On appeal, the Federal Circuit held that there was a failure of proof of literal infringement and reversed the judgment of infringement of the hardware claims with respect to all of the accused devices and remanded for any further proceedings that may be necessary with respect to those claims. The Federal Circuit affirmed the judgment of infringement of the software claims with respect to all of the accused devices. Because the damages calculation at trial was not predicated on the infringement of particular claims and because the Federal Circuit upheld the jury's verdict that all of the accused devices infringe the software claims, the Federal Circuit affirmed the damages award entered by the district court.

The Federal Circuit noted that the district court's injunction was stayed during the course of the appeal and that the stay would dissolve when this appeal became final. The Federal Circuit stated that when the appeal became final, the district court could make a determination as to the additional damages, if any, that TiVo has sustained while the stay of the permanent injunction has been in effect.

This case illustrates an application of the SCOTUS' decision in *eBay*, and that some courts will still enter a permanent injunction even though a defendant has a significant number of customers who will be impacted by the injunction.

Since the time of the Federal Circuit's decision in 2008, the case returned, twice, to the Federal Circuit. In March 2010, the Federal Circuit affirmed a judgment in favor of TiVo, both on the enforceability of its injunction against Echo-Star and a $90 million sanction against EchoStar for being in contempt of court for failing to abide by the injunction [see *TiVo Inc. v. Echostar Corp.*, 597 F.3d 1247 (Fed. Cir. 2010)]. In April 2011, the Federal Circuit issued an en banc opinion modifying the 2010 decision and vacating the district court's finding of contempt of the infringement provision of the permanent injunction but affirming the district court's finding of contempt of the disablement provision of the permanent injunction and the sanctions related to that finding. EchoStar remained on the hook for $90 million [see *TiVo Inc. v. Echostar Corp.*, 646 F.3d 869 (Fed. Cir. 2011)].

Microsoft Corporation v. i4i Limited Partnership, 131 S. Ct. 2238 (2011).

In *Microsoft Corporation v. i4i Limited Partnership*, the SCOTUS held that one who challenges the validity of a patent must show that the patent is invalid with "clear and convincing" evidence, as opposed to the lower "preponderance of the evidence" standard.

i4i held a patent on an improved method for editing computer documents, and it sued Microsoft for willful infringement claiming that Microsoft's Word products infringed its patent. Microsoft claimed that the on-sale bar (that prohibits a patent from issuing on an invention that has been for sale for over a year) rendered i4i's patent invalid, pointing to i4i's prior sale of a software program known as S4. The parties agreed that, more than one year prior to the filing of the i4i patent application, i4i had sold S4 in the United States. They presented opposing arguments to the jury, however, as to whether that software embodied the invention claimed in i4i's patent. Because the software's source code had been destroyed years before the commencement of this litigation, the factual dispute turned largely on trial testimony by S4's two inventors—also the named inventors on the i4i patent—both of whom testified that S4 did not practice the key invention disclosed in the patent.

While not specific to software patents, the SCOTUS' holding in this case affirms that a challenge to the validity of such patents must be mounted with evidence to meet the highest legal burden.

Eolas Technologies, Inc. v. Adobe Systems Inc., Case No. 6:09-CV-446 (E.D. Texas, Feb. 2012).

Eolas Technologies, Inc. v. Adobe Systems Inc. illustrates the difficulties inherent in patents that have been issued for fundamental aspects of new media functionalities, especially those related to the Internet. Eolas had asked for, and received, three affirmative reexaminations of its patents by the USPTO.

Eolas sued Adobe and 22 other companies, claiming that they infringed patents owned by Eolas that were developed at the University of California. The technologies aimed at fostering interactivity, via browser functionalities, on the Internet. Prior to the trial, 9 of the companies settled with Eolas, influenced by a previous case that found Microsoft losing a trial over the patents and settling for $500 million. In *Eolas Technologies, Inc. v. Adobe Systems Inc.*, however, a jury found, based on prior art, that the two web-browser patents that Eolas had been using to garner licensing fees from technology companies were invalid.

Given the relatively short history of software patents, it is often more difficult to find prior art to mount a successful claim of invalidity. Frequently, defendants choose to settle and, indeed, many companies settled before trial of this case. Those defendants that were able to weather the storm of litigation all the way through trial were rewarded with a verdict in their favor, but companies are sometimes not in a position to defend themselves through such a time-consuming and unpredictable process. (Note: This case was filed in 2009 and went to trial three years later; the original Microsoft case was litigated in 2007.)

On the other hand, one can also view this case as evidence against software patents and as an especially damning indication that the USPTO is out of step with the realities of new media innovations, given that they issued the patents and reasserted their validity through three reviews, only to then find them reversed by the patent court.

Learning Objectives and Discussion Questions

- Connect significant court cases to the principles established through them. Can you:
- Detail the functions and importance of Markman hearings;
- Define and describe the doctrine of equivalents;
- Discuss the significance of the machine-or-transformation test to patents for business methods/processes;
- Describe the differences between intrinsic and extrinsic evidence for construing a patent claim;
- Detail and discuss ways that the Amazon 1-click® ordering method cases illustrate weaknesses in the patent system;
- List some complexities of international aspects in patent claims: where components are manufactured, assembled, sold, used;
- Describe the role(s) of standard-setting organizations, especially during infringement litigation?

CHAPTER FOUR

Open Source Cases

New Media Open Source Cases

Jacobsen v. Katzer, 535 F.3d 1373, 1381 (Fed. Cir. 2008).

Since open source software is not patented, movement participants sometimes depend on copyright law to protect open source code. In order to police and enforce compliance with open source standards, originators of open source software may bring legal action when their software is put to use in proprietary ways that violate open source principles. This strategy only works if the copyright for open source software supports the awarding of damages in software litigation. *Jacobsen v. Katzer* first denied, then validated, those damages and that protective use.

Robert Jacobsen was a model railroad train enthusiast who worked with others in the open source community to develop controllers and interfaces for operating model trains. Much of the work was published on a website. Jacobsen brought a copyright infringement action against Katzer, the owner of a company producing and selling items for model trains.

Both parties filed motions for summary judgment on a number of issues. The District Court ruled that the open source copyright did not support damages for copyright violation. Subsequently, the Circuit Court of Appeals reversed the decision, holding that open source license conditions are enforceable as a copyright condition and that the Artistic License is no different in that respect.

Free Software Fdn., Inc. v. Cisco Sys., Inc., No. 1:08-CV-10764 (S.D.N.Y. Dec. 11, 2008).

Proper use of open source software requires adherence to the terms of GPL and Lesser GPL (LGPL) licenses. Commercial companies are not precluded from using open source code in proprietary products, as long as they follow the required GPL and LGPL terms, specifically in this case, by providing complete and corresponding source code.

The Free Software Foundation ("FSF") claimed that Cisco violated copyright law, during the sale of some of their Linksys wireless routers, by distributing open source programs copyrighted by FSF without satisfying the terms of the GPL and Lesser GPL licenses. The parties settled, in 2009, by agreeing that Cisco would appoint a supervisor to ensure future compliance with open source requirements, as well as pay an undisclosed financial contribution to the Free Software Foundation.

Microsoft v. TomTom, 2:09-cv-00247 (W. Dist. Wash. Apr. 2, 2009).

In *Microsoft v. TomTom* (2009), Microsoft alleged that some of TomTom's navigation products infringed on a handful of Microsoft's patents. This case relates to open source software because two of the patents cited by Microsoft cover legacy compatibility features in Microsoft's FAT32 file system, support for which is implemented in Linux.

TomTom countersued Microsoft for infringing its patents for various automobile navigation systems. On March 2009, TomTom settled the patent dispute by purchasing licenses from Microsoft to use the FAT32 file system. Additionally, TomTom joined the Open Invention Network, an intellectual property sharing organization for innovators using Linux. Subsequently, TomTom was involved in numerous lawsuits related to their use of open source software. Although the settlement between Microsoft and TomTom ended the 2009 case, questions remain about the implications for FAT in the broader Linux ecosystem as it is one of the many UNIX- and LINUX-based elements that Microsoft has, from time to time, claimed ownership over.

Ip Innovation LLC v. Red Hat, Inc., 705 F. Supp. 2d 687 (E.D. Tex. 2010).

IP Innovation LLC, a unit of Acacia Research Corp., is sometimes referred to as a "patent troll," in that IP Innovation operates as a non-practicing entity. IP

Innovation sued Red Hat and Novell (two of the principle providers of LINUX-based, open source software solutions) over three very old patents at the heart of graphical user interfaces. IP Innovations has previously sued numerous computer manufacturers, including Apple, over these graphical interface aspects that IP Innovations gathered via a patent portfolio acquisition. Validation of the patents would threaten the foundation of open source software in modern computers.

In 2007, IP Innovation accused Red Hat and Novell of infringing three patents that cover a computer-based graphical user interface that spans multiple workplaces, enabling remote users to access icons remotely ("multiple virtual workspaces and workspace switching features"). The patents in question had been developed, by Xerox at their PARC lab, as early as 1991, though parts of the patent were developed as early as 1984. A jury in Marshall, Texas, sided with Red Hat and Novell's defense that the patents were invalid.

SCO Group v. Novell, Inc., No. 10-4122 (10th Cir. Aug. 30, 2011).

As far back as 2003, the SCO Group filed lawsuits against multiple companies, claiming that the companies' use of LINUX infringed on UNIX copyrights owned by SCO. A finding against Novell, that established SCO as the owner of copyrights relevant to UNIX and LINUX systems, would expose open source users to SCO's royalty demands.

In the late 1960s, Novell acquired AT&T's UNIX program development and licensing business (for over $300 million). Two years later, after modifying some of the business components, Novell sold the UNIX unit to SCO (then known as "Santa Cruz"). Novell excluded copyrights and trademarks from the deal. SCO later moved to market UNIX to LINUX users after claiming that LINUX incorporated important elements of the UNIX code such that LINUX users needed UNIX licenses from SCO. Eventually SCO sued numerous LINUX users for infringements, including of the copyrights in UNIX. Novell took action that countered SCO's ownership claim over the rights; SCO sued Novell, Novell countersued, each claiming ownership over the rights and accusing the other of various civil issues.

Both the district trial court and the appellate court found that the exclusion of copyright and trademark transfer in the original contracts nullify SCO's claims against Novell. The ruling has the effect of "protecting" users of UNIX and LINUX open source software from having to pay copyright royalties to SCO.

Oracle Am., Inc. v. Google Inc., 2012 U.S. App. LEXIS 25335 (Fed. Cir. Dec. 10, 2012).

Prior to the appellate decision in *Oracle America v. Google*, Java-based Application Programming Interfaces (APIs) were generally considered to be open-source and un-copyrightable. However, the circuit court reversed an earlier district ruling and found that aspects of the Java APIs (owned by Oracle) are copyrightable. Google has appealed to the SCOTUS; that Court has asked the Solicitor General for advice on the case. This holding has serious implications for programmers using Java to implement APIs.

Google wrote its own Java code as it developed and implemented the Android operating system. However, Google relied on Java's API structures in order to enable developers to use open source specifications when tying programs and functions to the Android OS. Oracle purchased Sun, the original developers of Java, in 2010, and after a licensing deal fell through, sued Google for copyright and patent infringement.

The District Court rejected Oracle's copyright claims over the APIs, writing that since "there is only one way to declare a given method functionality ... every-one using that function must write that specific line of code in the same way," APIs cannot be copyright protected.

Oracle appealed and the Circuit Court agreed and overturned the District Court's decision on copyright and the APIs (although they returned the case to the District Court for a decision on Google's claim of fair use). If Google submit-ted to the decision leaving the Java APIs under Oracle's control, "winning" the fair use defense on their case would further confirm Oracle's copyright ownership claim, so instead, Google appealed for a review of ruling by the SCOTUS. The SCOTUS recognized the importance of the underlying issue and has asked the Solicitor General's office for advice on the matter. In May, 2015, the Solicitor General recommended that the SCOTUS deny Google's request. The request awaits SCOTUS disposition at the time of printing.

XimpleWare v. Versata, et al., Case No. 5:13cv5161 (N.D. Cal. Nov. 5, 2013).

XimpleWare v. Versata, et al. is one of a series of lawsuits addressing the use, by client-customers, of XML-code parsing software developed by XimpleWare. XimpleWare licensed the software using the GNU Public License version 2 (GPL2) that specifies a number of open source principals. XimpleWare alleged that some of its customers (the 9 defendants named in the suit) violated the terms of the license (by infringing on the software and/or by distributing the software illegally). Although one might think that a decision for XimpleWare would protect open source software, the contrary is true: If XimpleWare was able to sue custom-ers for using its software (including in services they provided for third parties), the court would be handing control over vital open source software to XimpleWare, an outcome violating the spirit of GNU open source licenses.

Prior to the filing of this case, defendant Versata had sued one of its custom-ers, Ameriprise Financial, for breach of software license. In mounting a defense,

Ameriprise contacted XimpleWare, alerting them "that it had discovered Ximple-Ware's source code throughout Versata's DCM product in violation of XimpleWare's GNU Public License." Rather than offer to help Ameriprise, XimpleWare filed lawsuits against Versata and the 8 other defendant enterprises (including Ameriprise), claiming direct and indirect infringement of XimpleWare's patents. In essence, XimpleWare tried to substantiate a series of patent infringement claims by asserting that the defendants abused the terms of service for the open source (and therefore, non-patented) aspects of their software product.

Via a number of proceedings and decisions, the court dismissed most of XimpleWare's claims, largely over whether the customers had met the tests for violating the GNU license standards. The pleadings and evidence presented in the case indicated that the defendants had used the software, including in work for other (third-party) clients, but did so without either the intention or effect of redistribution of the code ("The act of running the Program is not restricted, and the output from the Program is covered only if its contents constitute a work based on the Program—independent of having been made by running the Program") and therefore did not violate the terms of the license. The court stated that

> Because an express license is a defense to patent infringement, XimpleWare's direct infringement claims against Versata's customers turn on whether the customers' distribution is licensed under the GPL. The reason is that the GPL provides that even if the original licensee—here, one of the Versata entities—breaches its license for whatever reason, third-party customers of that original license retain the right to use XimpleWare's software so long as the customer does not itself breach the license by 'distributing' XimpleWare's software without satisfying attendant conditions.

Although the court, over the course of a year and across a number of rulings, dismissed most of XimpleWare's claims, the November 2014 decision left two of the claims standing. In February 2015, the companies settled those claims, ending the litigation.

Learning Objectives and Discussion Questions

- Although it seems paradoxical, the open source software movement depends on copyright law. Can you:
  o Describe the ways that copyright enables open source;
  o Point to case decisions that undergird these relationships?
- The various open source licenses include specific terms for proper use. Can you:
  o List the most important aspects of the licenses;
  o Identify specific cases that validate the strength of open source license restrictions?

- The open source software movement exists in uneasy tension with software patents. Can you:
  - o Describe and discuss ways that software patents "condition" the open source software environment;
  - o Identify and discuss specific cases that illustrate relationships between open source software and software patents?
- So-called patent trolls present numerous challenges to creative and innovative industries as well as both the patent regime and open source movement. Can you:
  - o Describe and discuss ways that patent trolls complicate the environment for the open source movement;
  - o Provide a case-based example illustrating open source questions in litigation involving a so-called patent troll?

CHAPTER FIVE

Trademark Cases

Traditional Media Trademark Cases with New Media Implications

Polaroid Corp. v. Polarad Electronics, Corp., 287 F.2d 492 (2ⁿᵈ Cir. 1961).

Polaroid Corp. v. Polarad Electronics presented a multi-factor test for establishing the "likelihood of confusion" standard in trademark confusion cases.

Polaroid held various US trademarks related to the term "Polaroid" dating back as far as 1936. Polaroid had become a well-known name for sheet polarizing material, products made from such material, optical desk lamps, and stereoscopic viewers well before Polarad was organized in 1944. Polarad was primarily in the business of microwave generating, receiving, and measuring devices, and television studio equipment. Polaroid brought suit in 1956, alleging that the use of the name Polarad infringed Polaroid's trademark rights and constituted unfair competition. In the case, a well-known judge, Judge Henry J. Friendly, stated a non-exclusive multi-factor test for determining whether there is a "likelihood of confusion" when analyzing trademark infringement: (1) the strength of the mark, (2) the similarity of the two marks, (3) the proximity of the products, (4) actual confusion, (5) the likelihood of plaintiff's bridging the gap, (6) defendant's good faith in adopting its mark, (7) the quality of defendant's products, and (8) the sophistication of the consumer. The Court ultimately found for Polarad, because it concluded that Polaroid had unreasonably delayed filing its suit for approximately ten years.

Big O Tire Dealers, Inc. v. Goodyear Tire & Rubber Co., 561 F.2d 1365 (10th Cir. 1977).

Big O Tire Dealers, Inc. v. Goodyear Tire & Rubber Co. established "reverse confusion" as a category in trademark infringement cases.

Big O Tire Dealers, founded in 1962, was a small tire-merchandising company serving a network of approximately 200 independent tire dealers in 14 states. In February 1974, Big O started interstate marketing of some tires (built for Big O in 1973 by Uniroyal) under the name "Bigfoot." In July 1974, Goodyear decided to use the name "Bigfoot" to promote a new tire. When Goodyear discovered Big O's "Bigfoot" tires in late August, Goodyear contacted Big O. After various meetings, Big O made it clear to Goodyear that it was not interested in selling the rights to use the "Bigfoot" name, and Goodyear made it clear that it was going to use it, notwithstanding Big O's objections. Beginning in September 1974, Goodyear launched a massive advertising campaign promoting its new "Bigfoot Custom Polysteel Radial." Big O sued Goodyear in federal District Court in Colorado on November 27, 1974.

The jury found that the mark "Bigfoot" was not descriptive in nature as applied to tires and that Goodyear's adoption of the mark was likely to cause confusion as to the source of the goods. In addition to dismissing Goodyear's claims that certain jury instructions were inappropriate, the Tenth Circuit also noted that this case was different than most regarding confusion in that it involved "reverse confusion." The Court explained that, generally, a trademark infringement suit results from a plaintiff having "a substantial investment in a well-established trademark" and seeking lost profits/damages based on the second user's attempts to trade on the goodwill of the mark of the first user. In *Big O*, with a case of "reverse confusion," the second—or junior—user (Goodyear) merely causes confusion as to the source of the goods but is not trading on the goodwill developed, by the first user (Big O), in the mark ("Bigfoot").

Zazu Designs v. L'Oreal, 979 F.2d 499 (7th Cir. 1992).

Zazu Designs v. L'Oreal helped establish formative standards for "use in commerce" as a trademark issue.

Zazu Designs brought a trademark infringement suit against L'Oreal for using the name "Zazu" for a hair-coloring product sold by L'Oreal's subsidiary, Cosmair. During product development, L'Oreal became aware of a state service mark registration ("Zazu") by Zazu Designs. After starting its national marketing of the new coloring product, L'Oreal three times sent representatives to visit Zazu Designs. No licensing agreement was reached as L'Oreal determined that Zazu Designs did not sell products under the "Zazu" name.

The Seventh Circuit found that Zazu Designs' minimal shipments of its product were merely an attempt to reserve a mark for intended use and that Zazu Designs' initial shipments were insufficient to establish trademark rights. The Court found that the District Court was incorrect to equate "a use sufficient to support registration with a use sufficient to generate nationwide rights in the absence of registration." The Court therefore held that Zazu Designs' sales of its hair product bearing the "Zazu" mark were insufficient, as a matter of law, to grant Zazu Designs national trademark rights in the mark at the time that L'Oreal began selling its coloring products. The Court held that L'Oreal did not infringe a mark held by Zazu Designs because L'Oreal was the first to market with a product bearing the mark and that Zazu Designs' intent to use the mark was irrelevant. Therefore, the Court vacated all previously awarded damages.

Two Pesos, Inc. v. Taco Cabana, Inc., 505 U.S. 763 (1992).

Two Pesos, Inc. v. Taco Cabana firmly established distinctive trade dress as grounds for trademark infringements.

In this case, Taco Cabana sued Two Pesos for trade dress infringement of the interior design of a Mexican restaurant under the Lanham Act. The jury found that, although Taco Cabana's trade dress had not acquired secondary meaning, it was inherently distinctive, and the Court therefore awarded damages to Taco Cabana. The Court of Appeals upheld the District Court's ruling, finding that the instructions to the jury were adequate and that there was enough evidence to support the jury's findings. The SCOTUS reviewed the provisions of the Lanham Act and found that there was nothing in the language of the act that would lead to a difference in analysis between inherently distinctive verbal or symbolic trademarks and inherently distinctive trade dress. The SCOTUS therefore upheld the lower courts' findings that trade dress could be inherently distinctive and that Taco Cabana should prevail, notwithstanding a finding that its unique trade dress had not acquired secondary meaning.

Wal-Mart Stores, Inc. v. Samara Brothers, Inc., 529 U.S. 205 (2000).

In *Wal-Mart*, the SCOTUS addressed the circumstances when a product's design (as opposed to product packaging) is distinctive for determining whether there can be infringement of an unregistered trade dress under the Lanham Act.

Samara makes children's clothing sold by various stores. Wal-Mart, a large, well-known retailer, sells many things, including children's clothing. Wal-Mart photographed clothes from Samara's line of clothing and hired a company to manufacture similar clothing. Wal-Mart sold the knockoffs of sixteen of Samara's designs and made over $1 million in profits. When Samara's attention was drawn to the fact that Wal-Mart and others were selling similar clothing below the price that Samara's distributors were allowed to charge, Samara sent cease-and-desist letters and eventually brought a lawsuit in the Southern District of New York. The suit alleged many counts, including infringement of unregistered trade dress under the Lanham Act. The District Court found in favor of Samara. After the Second Circuit upheld the decision, the SCOTUS granted certiorari.

The Court discussed the breadth of the language in the Lanham Act as covering not just words and symbols but also the design of a product. The Court also explained that product-design trade dress, like a color, can probably not be inherently distinctive, but that it can still attain distinctiveness through secondary meaning. The Court apparently narrowed its holding from *Two Pesos*, stating that the protection for inherently distinctive trade dress applied only to product-packaging trade dress and that product-design trade dress must acquire secondary meaning to be protected under the Lanham Act.

Qualitex Co. v. Jacobson Products Co., 514 U.S. 159 (1995).

In *Qualitex*, the SCOTUS held that a color could meet the legal requirements for trademark registration under the Lanham Act, provided that it has acquired secondary meaning in the market.

Qualitex used a green-gold color for its dry cleaning press pads. Jacobson, a competitor of Qualitex, started selling its own dry cleaning press pads in a similar green-gold color. Qualitex then sued Jacobson for unfair competition and, after registering the green-gold color of its pads as a trademark, added a trademark infringement claim to its lawsuit. The District Court found for Qualitex, but the Court of Appeals set aside the judgment, stating that color alone could not be registered as a trademark. The SCOTUS, however, unanimously determined that the Lanham Act was broadly worded such that nothing prevented a color from being a descriptive trademark that could acquire secondary meaning over time. The Court found that a color could therefore come to indicate the source of the product, the primary goal of trademarks. The SCOTUS also addressed the functionality doctrine, holding that functional aspects generally cannot serve as a trademark, essentially dismissing the idea that such a doctrine would create a general bar from obtaining trademark protection for a color, while acknowledging that if a defendant could prove that only limited colors could be used for the product, the functionality doctrine would then apply.

The issue of single-color marks was recently revisited in the fashion industry when shoe-designer Christian Louboutin sued Yves Saint Laurent (YSL) claiming trademark infringement of its signature red-soled shoes (*Christian Louboutin S.A. v. Yves Saint Laurent Am. Holdings, Inc.*, 696 F.3d 206 (2d Cir. 2012)). The Second Circuit determined that the secondary meaning of Louboutin's mark extended only to red-soles that contrast with the shoe's upper, and thus YSL's monochromatic red shoes did not infringe.

TrafFix Devices, Inc. v. Marketing Displays, Inc., 532 U.S. 23 (2001).

TrafFix Devices, Inc. v. Marketing Displays confirmed the prohibition against trademark registration/protection for mere functionality.

In this case, Marketing Displays owned a patent on a two-spring traffic sign design created to keep traffic signs standing in strong winds. After expiration of the patent, TrafFix started making signs using the same design, and Marketing Displays sued TrafFix for trade dress infringement, alleging that the design of the traffic signs was recognizable as belonging to Marketing Displays. The SCOTUS held that a functional design could not be trademarked and that a patented design was presumed to be functional. The SCOTUS explained that allowing trademark protection for something that is functional would be detrimental to competition based on something other than reputation and therefore improper.

The Court found that the fact that Marketing Displays obtained a patent on the design created a strong presumption that the patented features were functional and that Marketing Displays, as the patentee, had the burden of showing that the characteristic for which protection is sought is not functional. The Court stated that a design is functional if it makes the product work better or less expensive to produce, regardless of whether an alternative design is possible, and unanimously held that the traffic sign design was clearly functional.

New Media Cases in Trademark Law

Panavision Int'l, L.P. v. Toeppen, 141 F.3d 1316 (9th Cir. 1998).

Panavision Int'l, L.P. v. Toeppen served as an early examination and application of trademark law to Internet-based commerce, laying groundwork for definitional distinctions such as use in commerce and cybersquatting.

In *Panavision*, the Ninth Circuit interpreted the Federal Trademark Dilution Act (FTDA) as applied to the Internet. Dennis Toeppen, a so-called "cybersquatter," acquired domain names containing famous trademarks and attempted to sell them to the mark holders. One domain name that Toeppen acquired was Panavision.com, a website where Toeppen displayed photographs of Pana, Illinois. When Panavision attempted to register Panavision.com, it discovered that it already belonged to Toeppen. Panavision then contacted Toeppen, informed him of its trademark rights and requested that he cease use of the mark and the domain name. In response, Toeppen stated that he had the right to use the domain name but that he would sell it and agree not to acquire other domain names that Panavision alleged to have rights to if Panavision paid him $13,000. Panavision refused Toeppen's offer, and Toeppen then acquired Panaflex.com. Panavision brought suit against Toeppen in California under the FTDA, the California anti-dilution statute, and the California Business and Professions Code, alleging that Toeppen was in the business of stealing marks, registering them as domain names, and attempting to sell them to the rightful owners.

After determining that the District Court properly exercised personal jurisdiction over Toeppen, the Ninth Circuit addressed the District Court's grant of summary judgment that Toeppen violated the FTDA and California state law. In order to prove a violation of the FTDA, Panavision had to "show that the mark is famous, (2) the defendant is making a commercial use of the mark in commerce, (3) the defendant's use began after the mark became famous, and (4) the defendant's use of the mark dilutes the quality of the mark by diminishing the capacity of the mark to identify and distinguish goods and services. 15 USC. S 1125I." Toeppen did not dispute the first and third factors. However, Toeppen alleged that the District Court's findings that his use was commercial and that it diluted the quality of Panavision's mark were incorrect. The 9th Circuit agreed that case law supports Toeppen's claim that mere registration of a mark is not a commercial use as contemplated by the FTDA. However, the Court went on to note that Toeppen's business consisted of the registration and sale of the domain names, which is a commercial use. Next, the Court addressed the issue of dilution and discussed the idea that a domain name is more than an address and actually helps to identify the entity that owns the site. Additionally, the Court stated that Toeppen's registration of Panavision.com dilutes the capacity of the Panavision marks to identify goods and services, that potential customers visiting Panavision.com may be discouraged when finding that it is not Panavision's website, and that Toeppen's use of Panavision.com puts Panavision's name and reputation at the mercy of Toeppen. Therefore, the 9th Circuit upheld the District Court's finding of violation of the FTDA.

Bally Total Fitness Holding Corp. v. Faber, 29 F. Supp. 2d 1161 (C.D. Cal. 1998).

Bally Total Fitness Holding Corp. v. Faber examined one of the "grey areas" that emerged as commerce moved to the Internet: using URLs, domain names, and web pages for social commentary.

Bally sued Faber for trademark infringement, unfair competition, and dilution for his use of the phrase "Bally sucks" on a web page. First, with respect to trademark infringement, the District Court pointed out that the "likelihood of confusion test" applies to related goods, and that Bally is involved in the health club industry while Faber is involved in the design of web pages. Further, the fact that Bally uses a website to communicate to its current and potential customers, while Faber used a website to communicate his criticisms of Bally to Bally's current and potential customers, relates to the medium used and "does not make the goods related." The Court then addressed the many factors considered in the likelihood of confusion test (strength of the mark, similarity of the marks, proximity of the goods, evidence of actual confusion, marketing channels used, degree of care likely to be exercised when purchasing the items, the defendant's intent in selecting the mark, and likelihood of expansion of the product line). The Court weighed the factors and found the primary purpose of the accused mark was criticism and not promotion of goods or services related to Bally. Therefore, the Court found that restricting the defendant from the use of the terms would limit the ability to publish critical commentary about Bally. Additionally, the Court found that there is little likelihood that Bally would expand its business to compete with Faber's anti-Bally commentary. Ruling that the factors weighed in favor of Faber, the Court found that there was no likelihood of confusion of the marks and that Faber was therefore not infringing on Bally's rights.

Next, the Court addressed Bally's trademark dilution claim. The Court found that Faber's use of Bally's marks in the context of a consumer product review of Bally's services was not a "use in commerce." Furthermore, the Court held that even if Faber's use had been commercial, it would not harm Bally's marks, since the marks are not tarnished or otherwise diluted, and Faber's use of the Bally marks in his criticism is protected by the First Amendment. Bally's unfair competition claim was based on dilution and trademark infringement. Therefore, the Court granted Faber's summary judgment motion with respect to all claims.

Playboy Enters., Inc. v. Welles, 279 F.3d 796 (9th Cir. 2002).

Playboy Enters., Inc. v. Welles provides an instance when a famous mark may be used by an entity other than the rights holder. Such uses are more common in new media than had been the case when only professionals and large organizations could publish content for wide distribution. In the early days of the Internet, website developers often used metatags in order to attract the attention of search engines (and thereby users). As a result, the content in a page's metatags became the subject of trademark litigation. The algorithms employed by Google eventually lessened the impact of metatags, thereby substantially reducing the number of trademark cases focused on metatags. This case also bolstered analysis of whether the use of marks (especially on websites) was "nominative": Nominative fair use is use of a mark that is solely for the purpose of describing the goods or services (e.g., "We sell Ford automobiles") and doesn't imply ownership so, generally, doesn't infringe trademark rights.

Former *Playboy* Playmate of the Year Terri Welles ran a website that used trademarked terms owned by *Playboy*. In particular, Ms. Welles's website included trademarked terms such as *Playboy* and *Playmate* in the metatags that were used to identify Ms. Welles as a former Playmate of the Year. Additionally, each of the pages of the website used "PMOY '81" as a repeating watermark in the background. *Playboy* sued Ms. Welles, alleging that her use of the trademarked terms infringed and diluted its trademarks.

The court evaluated Ms. Welles's use of the trademarked terms and determined that the use of trademarked terms in metatags should be considered under the same test for nominative use, namely: (1) the product or service cannot be readily identified without using the trademark (i.e., trademark is descriptive of a person, place, or attribute), (2) only so much of the mark is used as is necessary for the identification (i.e., the words but not the specific font or logo), and (3) the user does nothing to suggest sponsorship or endorsement by the trademark holder—which applies even if the nominative use is commercial. Based on this test, the Court held that Ms. Welles's use of the terms in the metatags was nominative (the marks used were descriptive, only the terms were used, and nothing was done to suggest sponsorship) and therefore, by definition, could not dilute the trademark.

March Madness Athletic Ass'n v. Netfire, Inc., 2005 U.S. App. LEXIS 1475 (5th Cir. Jan. 24, 2005).

March Madness Athletic Ass'n v. Netfire, Inc. further illustrates the early developments that extend (traditional) trademark law to uses on the Internet. In this instance, a registered mark (the term "March Madness") had taken on such wide cultural usage that web developers created online products and services without license from the original mark holder.

The Illinois High School Association (IHSA) first used the term "March Madness" to refer to its state championship basketball tournament, in the 1940s.

It is thought that CBS broadcaster Brent Musberger first used the term "March Madness" in reference to the NCAA basketball tournament in 1982, after which the NCAA began licensing "March Madness," from the IHSA, in 1988. The IHSA claimed exclusive rights to the mark and also licensed it to various entities, including other state high school associations, Wilson, Pepsi, and *The Chicago Tribune*. After a lawsuit between the IHSA and one of the NCAA's licensees was adjudicated in 1996, the IHSA and NCAA eventually decided to jointly protect their rights in the mark. In 2000, following the filing of *March Madness Athletic Ass'n v. Netfire, Inc.*, the IHSA and NCAA formed the March Madness Athletic Association (MMAA), transferring each of their rights in the mark to the MMAA.

The defendants acquired the domain name marchmadness.com when one of the defendants falsely stated that Netfire was associated with the NCAA and was the rightful owner of the mark. The defendants then began developing content relating to the NCAA tournament for their site. After receiving a cease-and-desist letter from the NCAA in 1996 stating that the defendants were violating the NCAA's common law rights in the mark, the defendants decided not to operate their site for the 1996 tournament. Subsequently, in 1996, the IHSA sent a separate cease-and-desist letter, stating that the IHSA was the owner of all rights in the mark. Notwithstanding the two letters, the defendants operated their site from 1997 to 1999, when the domain registrar, NSI, took the domain name out of circulation at the IHSA's request. When NSI informed the IHSA that the hold on the domain name would cease absent court papers, the IHSA filed *March Madness Athletic Ass'n v. Netfire, Inc.*

The Fifth Circuit upheld the District Court's rulings, holding that "March Madness" was a descriptive mark that had acquired secondary meaning and that marchmadness.com created a likelihood of confusion with the mark. The Court also upheld the District Court's rulings that the defendants' registration and use of marchmadness.com violated the Anti-Cybersquatting Consumer Protection Act (ACPA), notwithstanding the defendants' lack of profit and that the plaintiffs were not entitled to damages because the defendants' registration and use of the website was prior to the enactment of the ACPA.

Tiffany (NJ) Inc. v. eBay Inc., 600 F.3d 93 (2nd Cir. 2010).

Tiffany (NJ) Inc. v. eBay was the first major decision to address third-party liability for trademark infringement on the Internet, finding that entities that "enable" trademark infringement can be liable, but that eBay did not transgress.

Unlike copyright law, that provides a statutory safe harbor for Internet service providers (ISPs), trademark law relies on the common law principles developed in prior cases to address third-party liability for infringement. In *Tiffany v. eBay*, Tiffany and Co. sued eBay for direct and contributory trademark infringement, trademark dilution, and false advertising, alleging that eBay knew of widespread counterfeiting of Tiffany jewelry on its online auction site and did not adequately prevent such infringement. The Second Circuit held that eBay's generalized knowledge that counterfeit goods were being sold on its site was not sufficient to impose liability for contributory trademark infringement. Rather, such liability requires specific knowledge of infringement.

In reaching this conclusion, the Court first determined that an Internet service provider can be liable for contributory trademark infringement under the standard set forth in *Inwood Labs., Inc. v. Ives Labs* (1982). In *Inwood Labs*, the Court held that:

> [e]ven if a manufacturer [of prescription drugs] does not directly control others in the chain of distribution, it can be held responsible for their infringing activities under certain circumstances. Thus, if a manufacturer or distributor intentionally induces another to infringe a trademark, or if it continues to supply its product to one whom it knows or has reason to know is engaging in trademark infringement, the manufacturer or distributor is contributorially responsible for any harm done as a result of the deceit.

In *Tiffany v. eBay*, the Court reasoned that liability can arise if a service provider (1) intentionally induces another to infringe a trademark, or (2) continues to supply its service to one who it knows or has reason to know is engaging in trademark infringement. Because Tiffany did not argue that eBay induced the sale of counterfeit Tiffany goods, the only issue was whether eBay had sufficient knowledge of infringement to be held liable. Ultimately, the Court determined that "a service provider must have more than a general knowledge or reason to know that its service is being used to sell counterfeit goods. Some contemporary knowledge of which particular listings are infringing or will infringe in the future is necessary" to trigger liability.

However, a service provider is not permitted "willful blindness"—it may not ignore evidence of specific infringement in order to avoid liability. The Court considered eBay's extensive efforts to prevent counterfeiting, including its notice and takedown system and warnings to consumers, and determined that eBay's actions did not amount to "willful blindness."

Keyword/Search Term/AdWord Trademark Claims

As the Internet has evolved, corporations with search engines, especially Google, were quick to understand and leverage the economic power of search terms that users type into search engines. So-called "keywords" (or "AdWords" in Google's parlance) are a large part of the currency of the modern-day search engine, because the companies providing the search engine sell search terms to the highest bidder, usually via a special type of auction. The payoff for the winning bidder is that its sponsored advertisements appear prominently in the sponsored results section of the results returned from a search. Better placement can mean more eyeballs find the bidder's website, thereby leading to more site traffic; more traffic can equate to higher sales volume. It all makes commercial sense. But, what happens if trademark law protects the word or phrase that a search engine puts on the auction block as a keyword? Can Google auction off the word "McDonald's" to the highest bidder? What if that bidder is a competitor, like Burger King? There has been significant litigation in this area over the last decade. Several issues emerge, including (1) whether the use of a word or phrase as a keyword is a "use in commerce," which is a prerequisite to bringing a claim for infringement under the Lanham Act; (2) whether the use of a keyword is likely to cause confusion in the marketplace; and (3) whether search engines like Google are liable for infringement or other claims arising out of the sale of keywords that consist of trademarks. Cases that have grappled with these, and related, issues follow.

U-Haul Int'l, Inc. v. WhenU.com, Inc., 279 F. Supp. 2d 723 (E.D. Va. 2003).

U-Haul Int'l, Inc. v. WhenU.com, Inc. was one of the first cases to consider whether the use of keyword advertising on the Internet violates the Lanham Act. The decision in this "early" Internet case indicated that keyword advertising does not constitute use in commerce so does not infringe trademark rights. The precedents from this (and similar cases) will later be applied to contested keyword searches.

The case involved plaintiff U-Haul's claim that defendant WhenU's pop-up advertising infringed on U-Haul's trademark, constituted copyright infringement, and amounted to unfair competition. U-Haul alleged that WhenU's pop-up advertisements, which crowded the computer user's screen, blocked out U-Haul's website display, infringed on UHaul's registered trademark, and altered U-Haul's copyrighted advertisements.

WhenU, an Internet marketing company, used a software program that was generally co-distributed with other software, such as screensavers. After a program that included WhenU's software was installed on a user's computer, the WhenU pop-up appeared whenever the program determined that the user's computer and Internet activity displayed content from WhenU's targeted companies. The pop-ups required users to navigate away from the WhenU advertisements in order to see the program or site they had been viewing. As a result, computer users impacted by the WhenU software had to endure pop-up advertising along with her ugly brother, unsolicited bulk email (spam), as a burden of using the Internet, even though they had not installed the software purposefully.

The District Court considered whether WhenU's computer software was a form of trademark infringement, copyright infringement, or unfair competition. To prove trademark infringement, a mark holder must show that the defendant made commercial use of a valid mark in a manner that would be likely to cause confusion to consumers. Hence, a fundamental element of trademark infringement is that the defendant is using the plaintiff's mark in commerce. The Court found that WhenU was not copying U-Haul's trademarked material and that U-Haul could not establish how WhenU's advertisements "used" UHaul's marks, because WhenU's advertisements were distinct from U-Haul's site, WhenU didn't promote or advertise U-Haul's marks, and WhenU's software didn't impede Internet users from accessing U-Haul's website by using U-Haul's marks. Therefore, the Court granted WhenU's summary judgment motion of non-infringement.

On the issue of trademark dilution, the plaintiff must prove that the defendant is making commercial use of the plaintiff's mark in commerce after the mark became famous in a way that dilutes the distinctive quality of the mark. Thus, once again, "commercial use" of the mark was a key component for showing that WhenU was diluting U-Haul's mark. On this claim, for the same reasons as with trademark infringement, U-Haul could not support the claim that WhenU used U-Haul's marks. As a result, the Court also granted WhenU's summary judgment motion with respect to U-Haul's trademark dilution claim.

1-800 Contacts, Inc. v. WhenU.Com, Inc., 414 F.3d 400 (2nd Cir. 2005).

In *1-800 Contacts, Inc. v. WhenU.Com, Inc.* the Second Circuit expanded on the *U-Haul* holding to again find that the use of keywords in advertising does not constitute a "use in commerce."

In this case, 1-800 Contacts sued WhenU for causing pop-up ads of 1-800's competitors to appear when users accessed 1-800's website. The trial court entered an order preventing WhenU from using 1-800's trademarks in connection with its advertising. However, on appeal, the Second Circuit reversed, finding that WhenU did not "use" 1-800's trademarks within the meaning of the Lanham Act when it used 1-800's website to trigger pop-up ads.

Citing *U-Haul*, the Court reasoned that the use was an internal, "pure machine-linking function." WhenU's pop-up ads did not display the 1-800 trademark and also did not appear on or affect the 1-800 website. The Court likened WhenU's tactics to the product placement tactics of a drugstore that places its generic brand next to trademarked brands, finding that such acts do not amount to an improper use of a trademark. Because 1-800 could not establish "use" under the Lanham Act, its trademark infringement claims failed.

Rescuecom Corp. v. Google Inc., 562 F.3d 123 (2nd Cir. 2009).

Without overruling *1-800*, in *Rescuecom Corp. v. Google Inc.*, another Second Circuit panel came to the opposite conclusion on the "use in commerce" issue for Google's AdWords program. *Rescuecom* marks the move of Internet-based trademark infringement litigation from pop-up ads and metatags into the more ubiquitous practices found in keyword search and advertising. Courts, since *Rescuecom*, continue to grapple with the business model underlying search terms and results as they relate to trademarks and use in commerce.

In this case, Rescuecom sued Google for trademark infringement, false designation of origin, and trademark dilution based on Google's practice of allowing advertisers to purchase keywords, including trademarks, that Internet users entered as search terms. Rescuecom complained that when users searched for its mark, Google displayed sponsored links of competing brands that had purchased the Rescuecom mark.

The Court emphasized that, unlike the defendant in the *1-800* case, Google was recommending and selling trademarks to advertisers and was in fact displaying, offering, and selling trademarks in the process of selling its advertising services. The Court found that these were not internal uses, and that Google had thus made a use in commerce of Rescuecom's mark. The case was sent back to the trial court without determining whether Google's AdWords program caused a likelihood of confusion.

Network Automation, Inc. v. Advanced Sys. Concepts, Inc., 638 F.3d 1137 (9th Cir. 2011).

Network Automation, Inc. v. Advanced Sys. Concepts, Inc. expanded the examinations of potential trademark infringement within the standard web search model (essentially, Google's business model) to include questions surrounding the likelihood of confusion.

This case addressed the likelihood of confusion issue in a dispute between two software companies with directly competing products. The trial court granted an injunction stopping Network from using System's marks to advertise its products through Google's AdWords program, but the Ninth Circuit vacated the order, finding that the likelihood of confusion test requires a more "flexible approach" in the Internet context. Given the nature of the case, the Court determined the most relevant factors were: (1) the strength of the mark, (2) the evidence of actual confusion, (3) the type of goods and degree of care likely to be exercised by the purchaser, and (4) the labeling and appearance of the advertisements and the surrounding context on the screen displaying the results page. Notably, the Court also acknowledged that Internet users are becoming more sophisticated, stating that "the default degree of consumer care is becoming more heightened as the novelty of the Internet evaporates and online commerce becomes commonplace." Because the trial court had incorrectly applied the likelihood of confusion test, the Court reversed and remanded for further proceedings consistent with its opinion.

Rosetta Stone, Ltd. v. Google, Incorporated, 676 F.3d 144 (4th Cir. 2012).

Rosetta Stone, Ltd. v. Google is another example of a trademark owner taking direct aim at the practices of search engines in selling keywords that are trademarks of the owner. The ruling in *Rosetta Stone* may open the door to additional claims that Google's search business model infringes on trademarks.

In this case, Rosetta Stone, the foreign language learning company, sued Google for direct, contributory, and vicarious trademark infringement; unjust enrichment, and trademark dilution. In 2009, Google modified business policies to permit the limited use of trademarks in advertising text in four situations: (1) the sponsor is a reseller of a genuine trademarked product, (2) the sponsor makes or sells component parts for a trademarked product, (3) the sponsor offers compatible parts or goods for use with the trademarked product, or (4) the sponsor provides information about or reviews a trademarked product. Google's policy shift came after it developed the technology to automatically check the linked websites to determine if the sponsor's use of the trademark in the ad text was legitimate. Rosetta Stone contended that Google's policies concerning the use of trademarks as keywords and in ad text created not only a likelihood of confusion but also actual confusion as well, misleading Internet users into purchasing counterfeit Rosetta Stone software. Moreover, Rosetta Stone alleged that it has been plagued with counterfeiters since Google announced its policy shift in 2009. According to Rosetta Stone, between September 3, 2009, and March 1, 2010, it was forced to report 190 instances to Google when one of Google's sponsored links was marketing counterfeit Rosetta Stone products.

The district court granted summary judgment in favor of Google, but on appeal, the Fourth Circuit reversed, in part, the district court's ruling and reinstated Rosetta Stone's direct infringement, contributory infringement, and dilutions claims and remanded the case back to the district court. The parties agreed to a confidential settlement after the case returned to the district court, so we will never know how a jury might have come down on issues involving trademark confusion. It is safe to say that while Google continues to face legal exposure for selling trademark terms, few trademark owners have the wherewithal to take on a colossus like Google and fight over the intensely factual issues surrounding likelihood of confusion.

Learning Objectives and Discussion Questions

- Detail the primary questions/issues for determining trademark infringement. Can you:
  - o Define "use in commerce" for trademark purposes;
  - o Identify when "likelihood of confusion" entered to compliment "actual confusion" and describe the significance of this nuance;
  - o Discuss relationships among using registered trademarks and free speech in public commentary;
  - o Discuss how anti-cybersquatting statutes differentiate between legal and illegal commerce in website domain names;
  - o List and examine the nuances of "contributory" infringement, especially for website operators and ISPs?

CHAPTER SIX

Trade Secrets Cases

Traditional Media Trade Secret Cases with New Media Implications

Kewanee Oil Co. v. Bicron Corp., 416 U.S. 470; 94 S. Ct. 1879 (1974).

In *Kewanee Oil Co.*, the SCOTUS held that state trade secret law is not preempted by federal patent law.

In *Kewanee Oil*, the plaintiff was a leading manufacturer of a type of synthetic crystal useful in the detection of ionizing radiation. By 1966, this manufacturer had developed a novel, seventeen-inch crystal, using techniques and processes Kewanee Oil considered trade secrets. The individual defendants were former employees of Kewanee Oil who formed or later joined Bicron Corp. As a condition of their former employment with Kewanee Oil, they each executed at least one agreement requiring the signer not to disclose confidential information or trade secrets obtained as employees of Kewanee Oil. The Bicron Corp., formed in August 1969, competed with Kewanee Oil in the production of the crystals and by April 1970 had grown a seventeen-inch crystal. The plaintiff thereupon instituted an action in the US District Court for the Northern District of Ohio seeking injunctive relief and damages for the misappropriation of trade secrets.

The District Court, applying Ohio trade secrets law, granted a permanent injunction against the disclosure or use by the defendants of twenty of the forty claimed trade secrets. Although holding that the District Court's findings of fact were not clearly erroneous, the Court of Appeals for the Sixth Circuit reversed the District Court on the ground that Ohio's trade secret laws were in conflict with the patent laws of the United States (478 F.2d 1074).

The SCOTUS reversed and remanded the case to the Court of Appeals with directions to reinstate the judgment of the District Court. The majority opinion, by Chief Justice Burger, held that state trade secret protection was not preempted by federal patent laws.

PepsiCo Inc. v. Redmond, 54 F.3d 1262 (7th Cir. 1995).

PepsiCo Inc. v. Redmond is an important trade secret case that affirms what is sometimes called the "inevitable disclosure" doctrine. Inevitable disclosure recognizes that even when an employee does not physically remove confidential or trade secret information, the employee may inevitably disclose confidential information that the employee acquired during the course of the prior employment.

This case involved fierce beverage-industry competition in the 1990s between Quaker and PepsiCo, especially in "sports drinks" (also called "isotonics") and "new age drinks" (such as non-carbonated drinks like tea and fruit drinks). In 1994, PepsiCo developed extensive plans to increase its market presence, while Quaker was trying to solidify its lead by integrating Gatorade and Snapple distribution.

William Redmond, Jr. worked for PepsiCo in its PepsiCola North America division (PCNA) from 1984 to 1994. Redmond's relatively high-level position at PCNA gave him access to inside information and trade secrets. Redmond, like other PepsiCo management employees, had signed a confidentiality agreement with PepsiCo. That agreement stated that he would not disclose "at any time, to anyone other than officers or employees of [PepsiCo], or make use of, confidential information relating to the business of [PepsiCo] … obtained while in the employ of [PepsiCo], which shall not be generally known or available to the public or recognized as standard practices."

Shortly after Redmond told PepsiCo that he was joining Quaker in November 1994, PepsiCo filed suit against him, seeking an injunction to prevent Redmond from assuming his duties at Quaker and to prevent him from disclosing trade secrets or confidential information to his new employer. At a preliminary injunction hearing, PepsiCo offered evidence of a number of trade secrets and confidential information, to which Redmond was privy, that PepsiCo considered protected, including PCNA's *Strategic Plan*, an annually revised document that contained PCNA's plans to compete, its financial goals, and its strategies for manufacturing, production, marketing, packaging, and distribution for the coming three years. This strategic plan was developed with input from PCNA's general managers, including Redmond. Another alleged trade secret was PCNA's Annual Operating Plan (AOP), a national plan for a given year that guided PCNA's financial goals, marketing plans, promotional event calendars, growth expectations, and operational changes. Another alleged trade secret was PCNA's innovations in its selling and delivery systems.

The district agreed with PepsiCo and entered a preliminary injunction. The Court of Appeals for the Seventh Circuit affirmed. The Seventh Circuit recognized that PepsiCo had not brought a traditional trade secret case, featuring a former employee with knowledge of a special manufacturing process or customer list that gives a competitor an unfair advantage by transferring the technology or customers to that competitor. The Court, however, found no abuse of discretion in the District Court's holding that Redmond could not help but rely on PCNA trade secrets as he worked to plot Gatorade and Snapple's new course for Quaker, and that these secrets would enable Quaker to respond strategically and achieve a substantial advantage by knowing exactly how PCNA would price, distribute, and market its sports and new age drinks.

The Seventh Circuit concluded that the District Court correctly decided that PepsiCo demonstrated a likelihood of success on its statutory claim of trade secret misappropriation based on the combination of (1) the demonstrated inevitability that Redmond would rely on PCNA trade secrets in his new job at Quaker, and (2) the District Court's reluctance to believe that Redmond would refrain from disclosing these secrets in his new position (or that Quaker would ensure that Redmond did not disclose them). Thus, the District Court's order enjoining Redmond from assuming his responsibilities at Quaker through May 1995 and preventing him forever from disclosing PCNA trade secrets and confidential information was affirmed.

In an industry side note, in March 1997 Quaker sold its Snapple business for $300 million, incurring a $1.4 billion loss from its purchase price of Snapple in 1994 for $1.7 billion. In August 2001, Quaker was acquired and merged with PepsiCo.

New Media Cases in Trade Secret Law

DVD Copy Control Assn., Inc. v. Bunner, 116 Cal. App. 4th 241, 10 Cal. Rptr. 3d 185, 69 U.S.P.Q.2d 1907 (Cal. Ct. App. 2004).

DVD Copy Control Assn., Inc. v. Bunner illustrates three "trade secret facts of life" in the age of new media: First, US law does little to control the actions of entities operating outside the US; second, once a secret has been published on the Internet, it's virtually impossible to quash; and third, it's unreasonable (and generally not possible) to hold subsequent publishers (entities republishing the information) responsible for trade secret violations.

While the *Universal City Studios, Inc. v. Corley* (2001) copyright case was unfolding in New York, the DVD Copyright Control Association (DVD-CCA) pursued a trade secrets case against a number of individuals, including Andrew Bunner, in California State Court. In this case, the DVD Copy Control Association, Inc. (DVD-CCA) sued defendant Andrew Bunner and others under California's Uniform Trade Secrets Act (CUTSA) (Civ. Code, §3426 et seq.), seeking an injunction to prevent defendants from using or publishing "DeCSS," a computer program allegedly containing DVD-CCA's trade secrets.

Recognizing the risk of widespread piracy, the motion picture industry insisted that a viable protection system be made available to prevent users from making copies of motion pictures in digital form. Without such protection, it would not have agreed to release movies on DVDs. To provide this protection, two companies—Toshiba and Matsushita Electric Industrial Co., Ltd.—developed the Content Scrambling System (CSS).

> CSS is an encryption scheme that employs an algorithm configured by a set of "keys" to encrypt a DVD's contents. The algorithm is a type of mathematical formula for transforming the contents of the movie file into gibberish; the "keys" are in actuality strings of 0's and 1's that serve as values for the mathematical formula. Decryption in the case of CSS requires a set of "[master] keys" contained in compliant DVD players, as well as an understanding of the CSS encryption algorithm. Without the [master] keys and the algorithm, a DVD player cannot access the contents of a DVD. With the [master] keys and the algorithm, a DVD player can display the movie on a television or a computer screen, but does not give a viewer the ability to use the copy function of the computer to copy the movie or to manipulate the digital content of the DVD. (see *Universal City Studios v. Corley*)

The motion picture, computer, and consumer electronics industries decided to use the CSS technology to encrypt copyrighted content on DVDs and agreed that this content should not be subject to unauthorized copying or transmission, including making the content available over the Internet. To this end, they began licensing CSS technology in October 1996. Under the terms of the licensing agreement, licensees had to maintain the confidentiality of proprietary information embodied in the CSS technology, including the "master keys" and algorithms. The agreement also contained other terms and conditions designed to ensure the confidentiality of this proprietary information. These industries later established the DVD Copy Control Association, Inc. (DVD-CCA) as the entity charged with granting and administering the licenses to the CSS technology.

Despite these efforts to safeguard the CSS technology, Jon Johansen, a Norwegian resident, acquired the proprietary information embodied in the technology—including the master keys and algorithms—by reverse engineering software created by a licensee, Xing Technology Corporation (Xing). Xing's software is licensed to users under an agreement that specifically prohibits reverse engineering. Using the proprietary information culled from this software, Johansen wrote a program called DeCSS that decrypts movies stored on DVDs and enables users to copy and distribute those movies. According to DVD-CCA, DeCSS "embodies, uses, and/or is a substantial derivation of confidential proprietary information" found in the CSS technology. Johansen posted the source code of DeCSS on an Internet website in October 1999.

Soon thereafter, DeCSS appeared on other websites, including a website maintained by Andrew Bunner. Bunner posted DeCSS on his website allegedly because it would enable Linux users to use and enjoy commercial DVDs, thereby enhancing Linux's usability and popularity. Bunner also claimed that he wanted to be sure that programmers had access to information for improving the DeCSS program. Bunner and others were sued by DVD-CCA after refusing to remove DeCSS from their websites.

The trial court granted DVD-CCA's request for a preliminary injunction and entered an order prohibiting defendants from posting, disclosing, or distributing DeCSS or related proprietary material. Bunner appealed. His primary argument on appeal was that the injunction infringed his free speech rights under the state and federal constitutions. The California Appellate Court concluded that the injunction was an unconstitutional prior restraint and reversed.

The California Supreme Court granted review and held that the preliminary injunction did not violate the free speech clauses of the US and California Constitutions, "*assuming* the trial court properly issued the injunction under California's trade secret law." The California Supreme Court remanded the matter to the California appellate court to determine whether the evidence in the record supported the factual findings necessary to establish that the preliminary injunction was warranted under CUTSA. On remand, the California appellate court found that there was not adequate evidence to grant DVD-CCA's request for a preliminary injunction; essentially, the secret was out prior to Bunner's posting.

McRoberts Software Inc. v. Media 100 Inc., 329 F.3d 557 (7th Cir. 2003).

McRoberts Software Inc. v. Media 100 Inc. involved copyright infringement and misappropriation of trade secrets and is important because it establishes that courts can award damages for trade secret infringement based on more than one issue or "theory of the case." This interpretation and ruling strengthens negative sanctions available against infringers.

In 1992, MSI developed a computer software program for character generation called Comet/CG. Character generation is the process of placing text over video and audio, as when words appear over images in a television ad or credits scroll at the end of a movie. Prior to MSI's inventing its software, character generation required specialized hardware that cost up to $100,000, but MSI's Comet/CG software provided similar character generation capability for users of Apple's Macintosh personal computers at around $1,300. Media 100 (formerly Data Translation, Inc.) manufactured video editing equipment, including the very expensive character generation hardware used by advertising agencies and television production studios. When Media 100 decided to enter the personal computing market, it turned to MSI to supply its Comet/CG software for use with its new "Media 100" line of personal video editing board hardware. MSI and Media 100 negotiated three separate licensing agreements, in 1993, 1995, and 1998.

Initially, Media 100's personal video editing boards functioned only on Macintosh computers through a video card component called a NuBus. Windows computers, in contrast, are compatible only with a video component called a PCI bus. Therefore, until Macintosh retooled its computers in 1995 to accept PCI bus hardware, video editing systems could only function on Macintosh or Windows machines but not both. The programming language for Macintosh and Windows machines was similarly incompatible, so MSI's Comet/CG source code could only be executed with Macintosh-compatible video editing boards. Early in the partnership between Media 100 and MSI, the Windows-versus-Macintosh debate remained on the distant horizon, at least in the video and graphic arts world. But it soon became clear that the personal computing market was going the way of Windows. By the time MSI and Media 100 negotiated their 1995 licensing agreement, both companies sensed that a profitable future had something to do with producing Windows-compatible products.

During negotiations for the 1995 agreement, MSI knew that Media 100 had developed a new video editing board based on the PCI bus architecture. While Media 100's new bus hardware made its products potentially compatible with Windows machines, the bundled video editing software (including Comet/CG) that Media 100 agreed to license from MSI still operated only on Macintosh machines. In 1998 Media 100 decided that it could no longer afford to ignore the Windows OS market, so it entered into an agreement with software development firm Vanteon (formerly Millennium Computer Corp.) to translate the Comet/CG source code from Macintosh to Windows (akin to translating English to Chinese, in the words of MSI owner McRoberts). Without MSI's consent or knowledge, Media 100 gave Vanteon a copy of MSI's confidential Comet/CG source code and paid Vanteon nearly $3.2 million to translate the code as quickly as possible. When Vanteon completed the task, Media 100 took the new code, put it into a Windows-compatible video editing system, and began selling it immediately. This new product line was named "Finish" and was essentially the same as the old "Media 100," except that Finish worked on Windows machines and Media 100 worked on Macintosh machines.

Soon after the Finish boards containing the translated Comet/CG code hit the market, MSI complained to Media 100 that it was not licensed to incorporate the Comet/CG software into its Windows-compatible product line, nor was it licensed to use any new version of Comet/CG that operated on PCI bus architecture rather than NuBus. Moreover, MSI demanded that Media 100 give it a copy of the translated Comet/CG code created by Vanteon as required by the licensing agreement. Media 100 refused to give MSI the translated code, but it removed all Finish products containing the translated MSI software from the market, licensed another company's Windows-compatible CG software, and reissued the Finish video boards with the new software. MSI sued Media 100 in Federal District Court, claiming, among other things (1) copyright infringement under the Federal Copyright Act based on Media 100's unauthorized creation and distribution of the translated Windows-compatible Comet/CG software, and (2) trade secret misappropriation under Indiana's Trade Secret Act based on Media 100's unauthorized disclosure of the confidential Comet/CG source code to Vanteon.

The jury awarded MSI $1.2 million for actual damages for copyright infringement, $900,000 in lost profits for copyright infringement, and $300,000 for trade secret misappropriation. In its cross-appeal, MSI claimed that the District Court erred by vacating the jury's award of $300,000 in damages for trade secret misappropriation. In granting Media 100's post-trial motion for judgment as a matter of law on this issue, the District Court ruled that MSI had failed to distinguish between its damages for copyright infringement and its damages for trade secret misappropriation, calling the trade secret damages duplicative and against the weight of evidence. The only explanation offered by the District Court for its decision was its belief that a successful claim for trade secret damages would have required MSI to argue and prove that it had suffered actual damages and lost unique ideas as a result of Media 100's breach of confidentiality.

Unlike the District Court, the Seventh Circuit found that MSI presented ample evidence to support the jury's award of damages for trade secret misappropriation. The jury was clearly instructed by the Court as to how it should properly calculate damages for both trade secret misappropriation and copyright infringement. Because the Comet/CG source code represented both a trade secret and a consortium's copyright, much of the evidence presented at trial could have been used to substantiate damages for either one or both claims. Still, it was undisputed that the jury was instructed to consider different measures of damages in determining each award.

In calculating trade secret damages, for example, the District Court told the jury to consider either "the cost Media 100 would have incurred in acquiring the same information or trade secret through its own experimentation or through other lawful means," or "the actual value of what has been appropriated or the reasonable royalty at the time of the misappropriation." The jury was also reminded that MSI had the burden of proving its damages "for actual loss [proximately] caused by the misappropriation" by a preponderance of the evidence. In comparison, the instruction for computing copyright damages told the jury to determine "the amount of money adequate to compensate [MSI] for the reduction of the market value of the copyrighted work caused by the infringement," as measured by "the amount a willing buyer would have been reasonably required to pay a willing seller … for the use made by Media 100 of [MSI]'s Comet/CG source code." Although both instructions informed the jury that the value of the Comet/CG source code is relevant to determining damages, the value of the code is supposed to be measured differently in each instance. According to the Seventh Circuit, it was neither surprising nor impermissibly duplicative for MSI to have presented numerous theories to the jury for calculating its losses.

The Seventh Circuit noted that as a matter of law, it is possible to recover damages based on more than one legal theory in the same suit, provided the plaintiff provides sufficient evidence of his injuries. The evidence in this record suggested that had Media 100 lawfully gone about acquiring the rights to the Comet/CG source code for the purpose of translating it into Windows, it either would have had to pay MSI to translate it or pay MSI for the right to hire someone like Vanteon to translate it. While Media 100 disputed this evidence, the jury was entitled to draw this inference from what it heard at trial. In particular, the jury learned that Media 100's customers wanted any new Windows hardware to be compatible with their Macintosh hardware running Comet/CG, which meant that Media 100 had a strong incentive to translate the Comet/CG code rather than incorporate Windows-based character generation software from a different company. Moreover, the jury heard evidence from MSI to suggest that the value to Media 100 of acquiring MSI's trade secret in the Comet/CG source code would have ranged from $383,000 to $1.3 million. MSI based these figures on (1) past software development contracts between Media 100 and MSI (as compared with software licensing contracts which the parties also entered into), (2) the profits realized by Vanteon in translating MSI's Comet/CG source code, and (3) MSI's investment costs in the Comet/CG source code. Thus, the Seventh Circuit held that the evidence showed that MSI suffered a measurable loss when Media 100 took its trade secrets in the Comet/CG source code and gave them to Vanteon, a competing software development company. The evidence also showed that this loss was different from the loss that MSI suffered when Media 100 incorporated the translated source code into Windows-compatible products and profited from its unauthorized distribution. For these reasons, the Seventh Circuit held that it was an error for the District Court to vacate the jury's award of $300,000 to MSI for trade secret damages as duplicative of the copyright infringement damages.

IDX Systems Corp. v. Epic Systems, Corp., 285 F.3d 581 (7th Cir. 2002).

IDX Systems Corp. highlights the importance of being able to specifically identify the trade secret(s) in the misappropriation claim.

Both IDX Systems and Epic Systems make software for use in managing the financial side of a medical practice: billing, insurance reimbursement, collections, and the like. During the 1980s, IDX sold this software package to two medical groups that later merged into the University of Wisconsin Medical Foundation, a group that now comprises more than one thousand physicians. The foundation continued to use IDX software until December 2000, when it switched to software developed by Epic. IDX believes that Mitchell Quade and Michael Rosencrance, former employees of Epic who came to manage data processing at the foundation, not only instigated this change but also used their new positions to transfer valuable information to Epic. According to IDX's complaint, over the course of a year Quade and Rosencrance personally, and with the aid of other foundation employees, furnished Epic with details about how IDX's software works, enabling Epic to enhance its own package and ultimately take the foundation's business—and to match up better against IDX in the competition for additional customers.

IDX's complaint under the diversity jurisdiction of 28 U.S.C. §1332 charged the foundation, Quade, and Rosencrance with stealing IDX's trade secrets and breaking contractual promises of confidentiality. The Court granted summary judgment to the defendants on the trade secret claim, after concluding that IDX had failed to identify with specificity the trade secrets that it accuses the defendants of misappropriating (165 F. Supp. 2d 812; W.D. Wis. 2001).

To show that particular information was a trade secret, the Seventh Circuit held that IDX had to demonstrate that it is valuable, not known to others who might profit by its use, and has been handled by means reasonably designed to maintain secrecy. The Seventh Circuit agreed with the district judge that IDX failed to do this. The Court held that IDX had been both too vague and too inclusive, effectively asserting that all information on or about its software is a trade secret and did not match up to the statutory definition.

The Seventh Circuit held that a plaintiff must do more than simply identify a kind of technology and then invite the Court to hunt through the details in search of items meeting the statutory definition. The Seventh Circuit stated that details such as the algorithms that the software uses to do real-time error checking (a vaunted feature of IDX's software), may be genuine trade secrets, but IDX did not try to separate them from non-trade secret elements such as its input and output formats. Nor did IDX contend that the defendants decompiled the object code or otherwise obtained access to the algorithms that power the program; instead, it alleged only that the foundation transferred to Epic those details that ordinary users of the software could observe without reverse engineering.

The Seventh Circuit affirmed the judgment of the District Court to the extent that it granted judgment to the defendants on IDX's trade secret claims.

United States v. M.J. Trujillo-Cohen, CR-H-97–251 (S.D. Tex. 1997).

United States v. M.J. Trujillo-Cohen highlights the importance of legal procedures that control intellectual property in the global setting. Actions that, previous to 1996, would have been prosecuted in civil court, became federal criminal espionage cases after passage of the Economic Espionage Act. Under the EEA, trade secret infraction judgments become convictions that can lead to jail time and/or fines (rather than mere injunctions and fines).

The US Attorney's Office in Houston, Texas, brought a two-count indictment under the Economic Espionage Act of 1996 against Mayra Trujillo-Cohen for allegedly stealing proprietary software (specifically, the "4FRONT for SAP" and "FASTRACK 4SAP" programs) developed by Deloitte-Touche. According to the grand jury charges, Trujillo-Cohen, a former Deloitte-Touche employee, converted portions of the software programs, which she knew to be proprietary to Deloitte-Touche, by selling them to others for her personal benefit. In a plea agreement, Trujillo-Cohen pled guilty to one count under the EEA and one count of mail fraud. She was sentenced to concurrent terms of forty-eight months in prison on each of the EEA and mail fraud counts, followed by three years of supervised release. In addition, she was ordered to pay restitution in the amount of approximately $337,000, payable in full immediately.

EF Cultural Travel BV v. Explorica, Inc., 274 F.3d 577 (1st Cir. 2001).

EF Cultural Travel BV involved application of the Computer Fraud and Abuse Act (CFAA) as well as misappropriation of trade secrets.

EF and its partners and subsidiaries make up the world's largest private student travel organization and had been in business for more than thirty-five years. Explorica was formed in 2000 to compete in the field of global tours for high school students. Several of Explorica's employees were formerly employed by EF.

Shortly after the individual defendants left EF in the beginning of 2000, Explorica began competing in the teenage tour market. The company's vice president (and former vice president of information strategy at EF), Philip Gormley, envisioned that Explorica could gain a substantial advantage over all other student tour companies—especially EF—by undercutting EF's already competitive prices on student tours.

Gormley considered several ways to obtain and utilize EF's prices: by manually keying in the information from EF's brochures and other printed materials; by using a scanner to record that same information; or by manually searching for each tour offered through EF's website. Ultimately, however, Gormley engaged Zefer, Explorica's Internet consultant, to design a computer program called a "scraper" to glean information from EF's website. Zefer designed the program in three days.

The scraper has been likened to a "bot," a tool used to gather information for countless purposes, ranging from compiling results for search engines to filtering for inappropriate content. Like a bot, the scraper sought information through the Internet. Unlike other bots, however, this scraper focused solely on EF's website by using information that other bots would not have. Specifically, Zefer utilized "tour codes"; those codes (and their significance) were not meaningful to the general public. With the tour codes, the scraper accessed EF's website repeatedly and easily obtained pricing information for those specific tours. The scraper sent more than thirty thousand inquiries to EF's site and recorded the pricing information onto a spreadsheet.

Zefer ran the scraper program twice, first to retrieve the 2000 tour prices and then the 2001 prices. All told, the scraper downloaded sixty thousand lines of data, the equivalent of eight telephone directories. Once Zefer "scraped" all of the prices, he sent a spreadsheet containing EF's pricing information to Gormley, who then systematically undercut EF's prices. Explorica thereafter printed its own brochures and began competing in EF's tour market.

The District Court granted a preliminary injunction against Explorica based on the CFAA, that criminally and civilly prohibits certain types of access to computers/networks (18 U.S.C. § 1030(a)(4)). The Court found that EF would likely prove that Explorica violated the CFAA when it used EF's website in a manner outside the "reasonable expectations" of both EF and its ordinary users. The Court also concluded that EF could show that it suffered a loss, as required by the statute, consisting of reduced business, harm to its goodwill, and the cost of diagnostic measures it incurred to evaluate possible harm to EF's systems, although it could not show that Explorica's actions physically damaged its computers. In a supplemental opinion, the District Court further articulated its "reasonable expectations" standard and explained that copyright, contractual, and technical restraints sufficiently notified Explorica that its use of a scraper would be unauthorized and thus would violate the CFAA.

EF alleged that the defendants knowingly and with intent to defraud accessed the server hosting EF's website more than thirty thousand times to obtain proprietary pricing and tour information, as well as confidential information about EF's technical abilities. At the heart of the parties' dispute is whether appellants' actions either were "without authorization" or "exceeded authorized access" as defined by the CFAA. The First Circuit concluded that because of the broad confidentiality agreement, appellants' actions "exceeded authorized access," and it did not need to reach the more general arguments made about statutory meaning, including whether use of a scraper alone renders access unauthorized.

There was ample evidence that Gormley provided Explorica with proprietary information about the structure of the website and the tour codes. Manually gathering the various codes through repeated searching and deciphering of the URLs may theoretically be possible. Practically speaking, however, Explorica's wholesale use of EF's travel codes to facilitate gathering EF's prices from its website, if proven, indicates use—and indeed abuse—of proprietary information that goes beyond normal and/or authorized access to information on EF's website.

Gormley voluntarily entered into a broad confidentiality agreement prohibiting his disclosure of any information "which might reasonably be construed to be contrary to the interests of EF." Appellants would face an uphill battle trying to argue that it was not against EF's interests for appellants to use the tour codes to mine EF's pricing data. Thus, the First Circuit stated that if EF's allegations are proven, it will likely prove that whatever authorization Explorica had to navigate around EF's site (even in a competitive vein), it exceeded that authorization by providing proprietary information and know-how to Zefer to create the scraper. The First Circuit held that the District Court's finding that Explorica likely violated the CFAA was not clearly erroneous.

PhoneDog v. Kravitz, 2011 U.S. Dist. LEXIS 129229, 2011 WL 5415612 (N.D. Cal. Nov. 8, 2011).

In *PhoneDog v. Kravitz*, a company that provides reviews and rating of mobile products and services was able to pursue a claim for misappropriation of trade secrets against a former employee who failed to relinquish use of the Twitter account provided to him by the company. Numerous instances of disagreements, between companies and employees, over the ownership of social media accounts (and the material contained there) make this an emergent trend in new media-based trade secret litigation.

PhoneDog is an "interactive mobile news and reviews web resource," that reviews mobile products and services and provides users with resources needed to research, compare prices, and shop from mobile carriers. Kravitz was employed as a reviewer of products for PhoneDog for several years. He submitted video and written content to PhoneDog and maintained a Twitter account, "@Phone-Dog_Noah." PhoneDog considered all Twitter accounts and related passwords as proprietary and confidential information. When Kravitz left the company, he changed his Twitter handle to "@noahkravitz" but continued to use the PhoneDog account. PhoneDog sued under California law for, among other things, misappropriation of trade secrets.

Kravitz filed a motion to dismiss PhoneDog's claims. The court, however, found that PhoneDog sufficiently described the subject matter of the trade secret with sufficient particularity and has alleged that, despite its demand that Kravitz relinquish use of the password and account, he has refused to do so. At the early stage of the case, the court found these allegations sufficient to state a claim.

The parties settled the case in December 2012. Financial terms were not announced; however "Kravitz announced that he and PhoneDog have reached an agreement under which Kravitz will get to keep his Twitter account—and his followers" (Terdiman).

Christou et al. v. Beatport, LLC, 849 F. Supp. 2d 1055 (D. Colo. 2012).

In traditional trade secret law, client lists are protected trade secrets. *Christou et al. v. Beatport* indicates that social media friends lists (and/or the business relationships they represent) may be the subject of trade secret protection (even when some of the information is relatively public).

Christou, the owner of several nightclubs, sued his former employee (Bradley Roulier) for alleged trade secret misappropriation. During his employment, the former employee had created an online marketplace for electronic dance music, called Beatport, with financial support from his employer. When he left the employer, the employee founded his own competing club and threatened DJs that they would not be featured on Beatport if they performed at Christou's clubs. In rejecting the employee's motion to dismiss, the court found that whether Christou's Myspace friends list was a trade secret was a question of fact and that Christou had alleged sufficient facts to maintain a trade secret claim—at least at the early stage of the suit.

In July 2013, a federal jury found in favor of Beatport founder Roulier and against the trade secret misappropriation claim (Flaherty).

Art of Living Found. v. Doe, 2012 U.S. Dist. LEXIS 61582, 2012 WL 1565281 (N.D. Cal. May 1, 2012).

In *Art of Living Found. v. Doe*, we learn that anonymous bloggers who were former adherents to teachings of an international humanitarian organization were able to defeat trade secret claims arising out of the bloggers' publishing of training manuals and teaching notes from the organization, but only to the extent that such materials were made publicly available previously by the humanitarian organization itself.

Art of Living Foundation ("AOLF") sued the two bloggers when it discovered they had created a blog titled "Leaving the Art of Living." The bloggers were highly critical of the teachings and methodologies of AOLF. In addition, the bloggers posted certain training guides, manuals, and teaching notes of AOLF on the blog. AOLF asserted claims for copyright infringement (not the subject of discussion here) and misappropriation of trade secrets. The bloggers filed a motion to strike the trade secret claims under California's anti-SLAPP law. The court found that because members of the public could readily obtain audio versions of certain teaching materials, including a download from the AOLF-Europe website, and as a CD sold on the AOLF website, to the extent the manuals and teaching notes contained materials from these publicly available media, those portions were publicly known and therefore not protectable under the trade secret statute. As to materials that were not made publicly available and were the subject of non-disclosure agreements, the court found that such materials were capable of being protected as trade secrets and, therefore, denied the motion to strike as to those materials.

Corporate Techs., Inc. v. Harnett, 731 F.3d 6 (1st Cir. 2013).

Corporate Techs., Inc. v. Harnett indicates that an employee who sends an email blast to announce his new job may violate a non-solicitation clause in a contract with his former employer.

Harnett worked for nearly a decade as an account executive/salesman at CTI, a provider of customized information technology solutions to sophisticated customers. Because CTI regarded many of the details of its business operations as proprietary, it insisted that Harnett sign an agreement that contained non-solicitation and non-disclosure provisions when he came on board. Harnett agreed. When Harnett left CTI, he sent an email blast announcing his new job. Although Harnett insisted that he had not solicited CTI's former customers (because they had contacted him), neither the trial court nor the court of appeals was convinced, holding that non-solicitation rights "cannot be thwarted by easy evasions, such as piquing customers' curiosity and inciting them to make the initial contact with the employee's new firm." The trial court entered and the appellate court upheld a preliminary injunction against Harnett.

Learning Objectives and Discussion Questions

- Detail the legal procedures that aid in the adjudication of trade secret cases. Can you:
  - o Define and describe the inevitable disclosure doctrine in trade secret litigation;
  - o Suggest ways that infringement claims can involve more than one theory of the case;
  - o Discuss ways that web scrapers and bots can be implicated/involved in trade secret misappropriation?
- Detail complexities that new media bring to trade secrets. Can you:
  - o List complexities to trade secret law and litigation brought about by social media?

CHAPTER SEVEN

Tort Laws for Intellectual Property of the Persona Cases

Traditional Media Right of Publicity Cases with New Media Implications

Haelan Laboratories, Inc. v. Topps Chewing Gum, Inc., 202 F.2d 866 (2nd Cir. 1953).

In *Haelan Laboratories, Inc. v. Topps Chewing Gum*, the term "right of publicity" is coined in the context of a dispute between competing makers of baseball cards.

A baseball player endorsed Haelan's brand of chewing gum. The player granted the plaintiff exclusive rights to use the player's photograph in connection with the sales of the plaintiff's gum. Later, Topps, Haelan Laboratories' competitor, induced the player to enter into a contract granting Topps the right to use the player's photograph for sales of Topps's gum during the term of Haelan's contract with the player.

Topps's principal argument was that a statutory right of privacy is personal and not assignable. If this argument had been accepted, it would have meant that the player could, at most, grant a release of liability for use of the player's photograph for a commercial purpose. Therefore, the defendant argued that defendant's conduct could not have invaded any right of the plaintiff.

The Court rejected the defendant's argument, concluding that "the ballplayer also promised not to give similar releases to others," and that inducing the player to breach that agreement constitutes tortuous conduct. Essentially, the Court held that in addition to a right of privacy, an individual has the legal right to grant exclusive use of one's image, likeness, or name. The Court found that whether or not such a right was a "property" right was immaterial and coined the term "right of publicity" to describe such a legal right. The Court found that such a right existed and remanded the case to the District Court to determine whether the defendant induced the player to breach a contract granting the right of publicity from the player to the plaintiff.

Zacchini v. Scripps-Howard Broadcasting Co., 433 U.S. 562 (1977).

Zacchini v. Scripps-Howard Broadcasting is a SCOTUS decision holding that the media do not have an unfettered right, under federal law, to appropriate a person's name or likeness and then claim protection under the First or Fourteenth Amendments of the Constitution. To this date, it is the only case the SCOTUS has considered that is specific to the right of publicity.

Zacchini was a performer in a human cannonball act that included being shot out of a cannon into a net sitting hundreds of feet away. Zacchini sued Scripps-Howard, a television broadcasting company, because Scripps-Howard videotaped Zacchini's entire performance at an Ohio county fair and played the videotape on the 11 o'clock news. The Ohio Supreme Court rendered judgment for Scripps-Howard on the grounds that the performance was a matter of public interest and therefore Scripps-Howard was constitutionally privileged to include the performance in its newscasts. The Court went on to state that because there was no intent to injure Zacchini, the right of publicity did not prevent Scripps-Howard from broadcasting Zacchini's performance.

The SCOTUS granted certiorari and explained that prior federal case law involving the First and Fourteenth Amendment privilege exceptions, cited by Scripps-Howard, applied to cases when the press was reporting news events and generally involved defamation cases. The Court distinguished this case, stating that the Constitutional privilege should not be applied where the press is attempting to "broadcast or publish an entire act for which the performer ordinarily gets paid."

The SCOTUS then held that although Ohio could grant such a privilege as a matter of its own state law, there is no Constitutional requirement to allow the press to broadcast such a performance and that the right of publicity protects the proprietary interest of an individual to "reap the reward of his endeavors." To the extent that the Ohio Supreme Court based its finding for Scripps-Howard on the First and Fourteenth Amendments, the Court therefore reversed the Ohio Supreme Court's findings.

Henley v. Dillard Department Stores, 46 F. Supp. 2d 587 (N.D. Tex. 1999).

Playing on the name of a rock star, without permission or license, is enough to trigger a successful right of publicity claim under Texas law, regardless of whether the use produces and/or increases profit.

Don Henley, a prominent rock musician (as a member of the Eagles, and as a solo act), brought suit against Dillard, a department store, for violating his right of publicity. Dillard ran a newspaper advertisement for a shirt styled as a "Henley." To catch consumer attention, the ad presented a model wearing the shirt and ostensibly named "Don," with advertising copy reading "this is Don's Henley." The Court reviewed the case law regarding the "three elements a plaintiff must prove to recover for the tort of misappropriation of name and likeness in Texas: (1) the defendant appropriated the plaintiff's name or likeness for the value associated with it, and not in an incidental manner or for a newsworthy purpose; (2) the plaintiff can be identified from the publication; and (3) there was some advantage or benefit to the defendant."

The Court found that Dillard intended to use the term "Don's Henley" for commercial advantage, believing that the expression would catch consumers' attention due to its similarity to Don Henley's name. The Court also found that the use of the term "Don's Henley" in the advertising was enough to identify Henley. Finally, the Court held that Dillard obtained a benefit from the advertising. Here, the Court found that proving a profit is not necessary and that it is only necessary to show that the defendant received a commercial benefit from use of the plaintiff's name or likeness that the defendant would not otherwise have received. Because of the decision by the advertising designer to run the advertisement, the Court found that the benefit of Henley's endorsement was obtained without Henley's consent, regardless of whether sales from the advertisement were profitable. Therefore, the Court found that Henley's right of publicity was violated and granted his motion for summary judgment.

Abdul-Jabbar v. Gen. Motors, 85 F.3d 407, 415–16 (9th Cir. 1996).

Abdul-Jabbar v. Gen. Motors indicates that a celebrity changing names does not free up the former name for use, without permission, in commercial promotion.

Former basketball player and actor Kareem Abdul-Jabbar sued General Motors (GM) for trademark infringement and violation of his right of publicity under California's state law. In a television advertisement for an Oldsmobile car, GM used, without consent, Abdul-Jabbar's former name (Lew Alcindor) as the answer to a trivia question in a mock game show. The District Court, based on the fact that Mr. Abdul-Jabbar had abandoned his former name and that GM's use of his former name could not be construed as a personal endorsement of GM's product, granted summary judgment in favor of GM.

In addition to discussing aspects of Abdul-Jabbar's trademark claims, the Court addressed GM's primary argument that Abdul-Jabbar had abandoned the name Lew Alcindor with respect to the right of publicity claim. GM argued that, because Abdul-Jabbar had not used the Alcindor name in over ten years and because the name was not in "common, present use," GM could not infringe Abdul-Jabbar's right of publicity by using the Alcindor name. Abdul-Jabbar countered, and the Court agreed, that a name cannot be abandoned and that in addition to a person's right to use his name or identity for commercial purposes, that person also has the right to block use of the identity (to not use it) for commercial purposes. The Court therefore found that Abdul-Jabbar had alleged sufficient facts to state a claim and survive summary judgment, reversing the District Court's grant of GM's motion for summary judgment.

Cardtoons, L.C. v. Major League Baseball Players' Ass'n, 95 F.3d 959 (10th Cir. 1996).

Cardtoons, L.C. v. Major League Baseball Players' Ass'n indicates that parody is an appropriate defense to a claim of misappropriation of the right of publicity.

Cardtoons filed a declaratory judgment action asserting that their parody baseball trading cards did not infringe the baseball players' rights of publicity. An example was a card of a player dubbed "Treasury Bonds," a parody of San Francisco Giants' outfielder Barry Bonds. The card had a recognizable caricature of Bonds, "complete with earring, tipping a bat boy for a 24 carat gold 'Fort Knoxville Slugger.'" The card also contained a team logo for the "Gents" and other humorous text on the back. The District Court held that the First Amendment allowed for a parody exception to Oklahoma's statutory right of publicity, granting Cardtoons's declaratory judgment that the cards do not infringe Bonds's rights of publicity.

The Tenth Circuit evaluated a potential right of publicity claim under Oklahoma law and found that the cards produced by Cardtoons did meet the three required elements—defendant's knowing use of plaintiffs' names or likenesses; on products, merchandise or goods; and without plaintiffs' prior consent—and therefore infringed Bonds's right of publicity. The Court next addressed the "news" exception and a First Amendment–like "incidental use" exception of the Oklahoma statute. The "news" exception allows for use of a person's identity for news reporting, public affairs, political campaigning, or sports broadcasting. The "incidental use" exception exempts uses in commercial media that are not "directly connected with commercial sponsorship or paid advertising."

The Court found that neither exemption provided protection for Cardtoons, because Cardtoons's use of Bonds's likenesses is directly connected with a proposed commercial endeavor. Although the Court held that the defendant's use of Bonds's likenesses in parody trading cards violated the right of publicity, the Court found that the First Amendment protects Cardtoons's right to publish its parody trading cards. The Court discussed the idea that parody is a humorous form of social commentary and that humorous as well as serious commentary on "an important social institution constitutes protected expression." Finally, the Court weighed the effects of limiting the right of publicity versus the effects of limiting free expression and held that the effect of limiting the right of publicity in this case was negligible, while limiting free expression would eliminate "an important form of entertainment and social commentary that deserve First Amendment protection." The Court therefore affirmed the grant of Cardtoons's declaratory judgment that its parody trading cards do not infringe Bonds's right of publicity.

Toney v. L'Oreal USA, 406 F.3d 905 (7th Cir. 2005).

Toney v. L'Oreal USA shows that the right of publicity is distinct from, and not preempted by, federal copyright law.

June Toney, a model, authorized Johnson Products Company to use photographs of her in connection with its hair-relaxing product, "Ultra Sheen Supreme," in national magazine advertisements for a limited time. When L'Oreal, a successor company to Johnson, later used the photographs after the expiration of the initial contract, Toney sued L'Oreal for violation of her right of publicity. The District Court dismissed Toney's claim, asserting that federal copyright law preempted her right of publicity claim.

The Seventh Circuit reversed the District Court's holding, finding that Toney's right of publicity was infringed by the use of Toney's likeness in connection with the packaging and promotion of L'Oreal's hair care product. The Court analyzed the Illinois Right of Publicity Act (IRPA) and the claims in the suit to determine whether copyright law preempted Toney's claims. The Court determined that Toney's identity was not fixed in a tangible medium of expression and that there was no work of authorship at issue because a person's likeness or persona is neither authored nor fixed. Furthermore, the Court found that the rights protected by the IRPA, which allow a person to control the commercial value of her/his identity, are not equivalent to any of the rights protected by federal copyright law.

Newcombe v. Adolph Coors Co., 157 F.3d 686 (9th Cir. 1998).

Newcombe v. Adolph Coors Co. indicates that a violation of the right of publicity may occur even without identifying the claimant by name but merely using, without permission, a photograph that resembles the claimant.

Don Newcombe is a former all-star baseball pitcher who played the majority of his career for the Brooklyn Dodgers and the Cincinnati Reds in the 1950s, with time taken out to serve in the Korean War. Newcombe, a well-known recovering alcoholic who has been sober since 1967, has helped numerous people in their battles against substance abuse and has served as spokesperson for the National Institute on Drug and Alcohol Abuse. Killian's Irish Red Beer, owned by Coors, ran an advertisement in the *Sports Illustrated* swimsuit edition that featured a beer and some text on the right side and a drawing of an old-time baseball game on the right. Although the drawing did not depict a specific team or stadium, the drawing featured a pitcher in the windup position, a single infielder, and an old-fashioned outfield fence. Newcombe, his friends, family, and former teammates immediately recognized the pitcher as being Newcombe in his playing days. The drawing of the pitcher in the advertisement was based on a 1947 photograph of Newcombe on the mound. The District Court dismissed the suit, finding that the intent of the advertisers was to have a generic baseball scene and not to exploit Newcombe's image.

The Ninth Circuit reversed the District Court's finding, holding that there was a "triable issue of fact" as to whether the plaintiff was "readily identifiable as the pitcher in [the] advertisement" and "whether the advertisement made use of Newcombe's likeness." The Court found that the stance of the pitcher in the advertisement was similar to that of Newcombe in the photograph and that none of the other pictures of record depicting pitchers in the windup position included a similar stance. The Ninth Circuit therefore reversed the District Court, holding that the jury may find that Adolph Coors used an image of Newcombe without his permission.

Carson v. Here's Johnny Portable Toilets, Inc., 698 F.2d 831, 835 (6th Cir. 1983).

Carson v. Here's Johnny Portable Toilets, Inc. indicates that unauthorized use of a slogan associated with a celebrity may give rise to a claim for misappropriation of the right of publicity.

Johnny Carson, the long-time host of *The Tonight Show*, sued Here's Johnny, a company involved in the sale and rental of portable toilets, for trademark infringement and violation of the right of publicity. On *The Tonight Show*, each night, Mr. Carson was introduced (usually by announcer/sidekick Ed McMahon) with the familiar phrase, "Here's Johnny." The District Court dismissed Carson's complaint. The Sixth Circuit affirmed the District Court's finding that there was no likelihood of confusion, and thus the trademark infringement claim failed. However, the Court reversed the District Court's finding with respect to the right of publicity and found for Carson, holding that "if the celebrity's identity is commercially exploited, there has been an invasion of his right whether or not his 'name or likeness' is used. Carson's identity may be exploited even if his name, John W. Carson, or his picture is not used."

The Court summarized prior right of publicity cases, clarifying that use of a person's name or picture is not necessary to find that the person's right of publicity has been violated. The Court included references to cases finding infringement of people's rights of publicity when the infringer used the person's nickname, likeness, and, in at least one case, a car that was associated with the person who was a professional race car driver.

Jordan v. Jewel, 743 F.3d 509 (7ᵗʰ Cir. 2014).

In *Jordan v. Jewel*, a former basketball superstar was able to pursue a claim that his right of publicity was misappropriated by a grocery store chain that congratulated him (but did not otherwise promote any specific product) in a full-page tribute in a commemorative issue of *Sports Illustrated* that celebrated his induction into the Basketball Hall of Fame.

Around the time that Michael Jordan was inducted into the Basketball Hall of Fame in 2009, Time, Inc., publisher of *Sports Illustrated*, published a special edition (September, 2009) to celebrate Jordan's career. The special edition was not distributed to regular subscribers but rather sold separately in stores. Time, Inc. approached Jewel Food Stores, Inc. to offer free promotional space in the issue in exchange for Jewel carrying the issue in its stores. Jewel agreed to the deal and had its marketing department design a full-page color ad. The ad combines textual, photographic, and graphic elements, and prominently includes the Jewel-Osco logo and the supermarket chain's marketing slogan, "Good things are just around the corner." The logo and slogan—both registered trademarks—are positioned in the middle of the page, above a photo of a pair of basketball shoes, each bearing Jordan's number "23."

The text of the ad reads as follows:

A Shoe In!

After six NBA championships, scores of rewritten record books and numerous buzzer beaters, Michael Jordan's elevation in the Basketball Hall of Fame was never in doubt! Jewel-Osco salutes #23 on his many accomplishments as we honor a fellow Chicagoan who was "just around the corner" for so many years.

Jordan filed suit, alleging violations of the Illinois Right of Publicity Act (765 Ill. Comp. Stat. 1075/1 et seq.), the Illinois Consumer Fraud and Deceptive Business Practices Act (815 Ill. Comp. Stat. 505/2 et seq.), the Illinois common law of unfair competition, and the federal Lanham Act (15 U.S.C. § 1125). He sought $5 million in damages, plus punitive damages on the state law claims and treble damages (triple the amount) on the Lanham Act claim. Jewel removed the case to federal court. The district court ruled in favor of Jewel on summary judgment, finding that Jewel's ad was noncommercial speech and entitled to complete protection under the First Amendment.

On appeal, the Seventh Circuit relied upon the guideposts in *Bolger v. Youngs Drug Prods. Corp.* 463 U.S. 60 (1983) for classifying speech that contains both commercial and noncommercial elements; relevant considerations include "whether: (1) the speech is an advertisement; (2) the speech refers to a specific product; and (3) the speaker has an economic motivation for the speech." The Seventh Circuit significantly restricted the scope of fully protected noncommercial speech under the First Amendment. The Court held that commercial speech is not limited to speech that directly or indirectly proposes a commercial transaction, noting that "[a]n advertisement is no less 'commercial' because it promotes brand awareness or loyalty rather than explicitly proposing a transaction in a specific product or service." The court stated,

> [i]mage advertising is ubiquitous in all media. Jewel's ad is an example of a neighborly form of general brand promotion by a large urban supermarket chain. What does it invite readers to buy? Whatever they need from a grocery store—a loaf of bread, a gallon of milk, perhaps the next edition of *Sports Illustrated*—from Jewel-Osco, where "good things are just around the corner." The ad implicitly encourages readers to patronize their local Jewel-Osco store. That it doesn't mention a specific product means only that this is a different genre of advertising. It promotes brand loyalty rather than a specific product, but that doesn't mean it's "noncommercial."

New Media Cases in Right of Publicity Law

CBC Distribution and Marketing, Inc. v. Major League Baseball Adv. Media, L.P., F.3d (8th Cir. 2007).

CBC Distribution and Marketing, Inc. v. Major League Baseball Adv. Media, L.P. shows that baseball players' names and statistics as used in fantasy baseball are not protected under the right of publicity. The outcome of this ruling can be extended across a variety of fantasy league activities.

The plaintiff, CBC, brought this action seeking a declaratory judgment against the defendant, Major League Baseball Advanced Media (MLBAM), to establish CBC's right to use the names of MLB players without any license. By selling subscriptions, the plaintiff provided a sports website that included a fantasy baseball league. The fantasy league used the names and performance statistics of actual MLB players. Up until 2005, CBC had licensed the use of the names and statistics from the Major League Baseball Players Association. At the end of its agreement with CBC, the Players Association decided to exclusively license MLB players' names and statistics to MLBAM. CBC thereafter initiated this action to prevent the MLBAM from suing to enjoin CBC's continued use of the players' names and statistics. The District Court granted summary judgment to the plaintiff, holding that the plaintiff was not infringing any state law rights of publicity that belonged to the players, and that even if it were, the First Amendment preempted those rights. On appeal, although the Court of Appeals for the Eight Circuit disagreed with the District Court that the plaintiff was not infringing the players' rights of publicity, it nonetheless affirmed that the First Amendment preempted the claims.

The Court began its discussion by reviewing the District Court's findings regarding the right of publicity claims. The Court noted that the District Court was correct in determining that the plaintiff's use of the names and statistics was without consent. However, the Court disagreed with the District Court's finding that the plaintiff was not using the players' names as a symbol of identity. The Court explained: "The District Court did not understand that when a name alone is sufficient to establish identity, the defendant's use of that name satisfies the plaintiff's burden to show that a name was used as a symbol of identity." The Court also disagreed with the lower court's finding that the plaintiff's use of the players' names was not for a commercial advantage. The Court noted that although the plaintiff's use of the names for fantasy sports did not fall squarely within the recognized categories of commercial advantage, it was clear that the plaintiff used them for purposes of profit. Therefore, the Court found that MLBAM did have a cause of action for violation of the players' rights of publicity.

The inquiry, however, did not end there. The Court determined that the right of publicity claims were preempted by the First Amendment. In so doing, the Court recognized that the CBC's use of the names in an "interactive form" was entitled to First Amendment protection. The Court then noted that the names and statistics are of public interest and value and that the states' interest in protecting an individual's right to privacy was not implicated because the players are handsomely rewarded for their participation in the actual games. Accordingly, the Court held that MLBAM's claim for violation of the right of publicity was preempted. On June 2, 2008, the SCOTUS refused to hear MLB's appeal, thereby maintaining the public domain status of statistics and players' names in the fantasy league context.

KNB Enters. v. Matthews, 78 Cal. App. 4th 362 (Cal. Ct. App. 2000).

KNB Enters. v. Matthews reminds us that the right of publicity belongs to everyone, not just famous people, and is not preempted by federal copyright law.

The plaintiff, KNB, was the owner of a website that displayed erotic photographs. The plaintiff owned—by contractual assignment—the copyrights to several hundred photographs and occasionally posted some of these photographs to various Usenet newsgroups in order to promote its website. The defendant, Matthews, characterized Usenet as "a public forum on the Internet where individuals can participate in the open exchange of information." Essentially, KNB attempted to entice users on Usenet to subscribe to the KNB website by uploading sample images to Usenet. Matthews used a software program that consolidated and copied erotic photographs posted on Usenet. Matthews, without KNB's consent, displayed hundreds of copyrighted photographs on Matthew's website, Justpics—a website where customers pay a monthly membership fee to view erotic photographs taken from Usenet.

KNB brought suit, however, not under federal copyright law, but rather under California state law covering commercial appropriation. Essentially, the plaintiff alleged that the models'—the women who posed in the pictures—right to publicity was violated. The linchpin issue for the Court, then, was to decide whether federal copyright law preempted the misappropriation claims.

The Court began its discussion on California's right of publicity law. The Court noted that although the models were not recognized celebrities, the plaintiff nevertheless was able to allege that the defendant profited by making sales, selling memberships, and saving time and money by "substituting a few moments of copying for what could have been days or weeks of work." After briefly reciting relevant copyright law, the Court acknowledged that the photographs themselves were copyrightable and that unauthorized display of the photographs was copyright infringement, but that the issue was not the photographs but rather the models' likenesses.

The Court continued, citing cases wherein copyright law and preemption of misappropriation claims were at issue. The Court distinguished cases when copyright preemption was found based on the fact that in those cases, the models or actors were suing the entities that lawfully owned the copyrights to the models' or actors' photographs. Unlike those cases, the Court noted, the defendant was not lawfully entitled to distribute or use the photographs, and thus the plaintiff was not using the right of publicity to make up for its lack of copyright rights.

Moreover, the Court cited *Nimmer on Copyright* (Melville B. Nimmer and David Nimmer) for the proposition that "right of publicity claims generally are not preempted by the *Copyright Act* [emphasis added]." Subsequently, the Court stated that while it would find a misappropriation claim preempted "where an actor or model with no copyright interest in the work seeks to prevent the exclusive copyright holder from displaying the copyrighted work," it would not do so "where ... the defendant has no legal right to publish the copyrighted work."

Finally, the Court concluded that the two-part test for preemption—that (1) the subject of the claim must be a work fixed in a tangible medium of expression and be within the subject matter of copyright protection, and (2) the right asserted under the state law must be equivalent to the exclusive rights granted under copyright law—was not met because the subjects of the claims were the actual likenesses of the models, and accordingly were not copyrightable, and the right of publicity does not come within the subject matter of copyright. Therefore, the Court reversed the trial court's finding of summary judgment for the defendant and remanded the case.

Carafano v. Metrosplash.com, Inc., 339 F.3d 1119 (9th Cir. 2003).

Carafano v. Metrosplash.com Inc. shows that a dating website was not liable for misappropriating the identity of an actress who was the victim of a third party's false profile on the site.

The plaintiff, Christianne Carafano, was an actress who went by the stage name of "Chase Masterson." The plaintiff filed her lawsuit against the defendants, operators of the website Matchmaker.com, alleging, among other things, misappropriation of the right of publicity.

Matchmaker.com provided an online service that allowed members to search a database containing profiles posted by other members. All a person had to do to join this online community was to fill out an application and a questionnaire. Eventually, after the running of a trial period, a user was required to pay a monthly fee to continue membership. In 1999, an unknown person created a trial account on Matchmaker.com under the name "Chase 529." The profile created by this anonymous user included four photographs of the plaintiff and the plaintiff's home address and an email address. The user also filled out the online questionnaire using various lewd and licentious answers. As a result, the plaintiff received obscene phone calls, letters, and faxes. After learning of the profile, the plaintiff filed suit against the defendant. In turn, the defendant moved for summary judgment.

As an initial matter, the Court determined that Carafano's various causes of action were not barred by the Communications Decency Act of 1996 (CDA)—an act designed to protect "interactive computer services" from liability for third-party postings. While the Court agreed with the defendants that Matchmaker.com was an "interactive computer service" for purposes of the CDA, the Court nevertheless determined that immunity under the CDA was inapplicable because Matchmaker.com was an "information *content* provider [emphasis added]"—an entity unable to find refuge under the CDA. The Court noted that Matchmaker.com was not simply a conduit of the information that was provided on its website. Rather, by requiring the users to fill out a questionnaire, it was an active player in developing the information that was ultimately posted. Therefore, the Court found that, as a matter of law, immunity from suit under the CDA did not extend to the defendants.[1]

The Court continued its discussion, addressing each of the plaintiff's causes of action. In one of her causes of action, the plaintiff alleged that the use of her photographs in the Matchmaker.com profile constituted an appropriation of her likeness. The defendants argued that summary judgment was appropriate because the plaintiff—a public figure—could not demonstrate that the defendants acted with the requisite constitutional malice. In response, the plaintiff argued that the actual malice standard did not apply because the Matchmaker.com profile constituted commercial speech—which, if classified as such, would allow the plaintiff to avoid having to prove actual malice. The plaintiff's contention rested, in part, on the basis that Matchmaker.com's business depended on getting free trial members to become paying customers by allowing them to access profiles such as the one at issue.

The Court rejected the plaintiff's argument, stating that "[t]he fact that Matchmaker makes a profit from selling memberships does not transform the speech at issue into commercial speech." The Court distinguished a case out of the Court of Appeals for the Ninth Circuit (in which a company, without authority, used a photo of a surfer to promote its clothing) from the case before it, where the defendant allowed members to post information, about themselves, in an online profile. The Court ultimately concluded that the profiles on Matchmaker.com did not constitute commercial speech. Therefore, the Court granted the defendant's motion for summary judgment with respect to the issue of misappropriation of the right of publicity.

Perfect 10, Inc. v. CCBill LLC, 481 F.3d 751 (9th Cir. 2007).

In *Perfect 10, Inc. v. CCBill LLC*, Section 230 of the Communications Decency Act (CDA, 230) offers immunity to interactive computer service providers for claims of misappropriation of the right of publicity arising from content posted by users.

The plaintiff, Perfect 10, the publisher of an adult entertainment magazine and the owner of the website Perfect10.com, filed suit against two defendants, CWIE and CCBill, alleging, among other claims, violation of the right of publicity. The plaintiff's website is a subscription-based site where members pay a fee so that they can gain access to thousands of images of models displayed on the website. Many of the models featured on the website signed releases of their rights of publicity to the plaintiff. The first defendant, CWIE, is a provider of Internet hosting to the owners of various websites. CWIE ensures that its clients' service or website is connected to the Internet. The second defendant, CCBill, facilitated the ability of customers to use credit cards or checks to pay for subscriptions. The plaintiff began sending letters to the defendants alleging that the defendants' clients were infringing not only copyrights but also the state law right of publicity. Notably, the District Court found that the defendants were not immune from right of publicity claims under the Communications Decency Act of 1996. The Court of Appeals for the Ninth Circuit, however, reversed this particular finding of the District Court.

In reversing the District Court finding regarding the right of publicity, the Court noted that the immunity created by the CDA was limited by another section of that act that requires courts to "construe [the act] in a manner that would neither 'limit or [sic] expand any law pertaining to intellectual property.'" The Court, accordingly, explained that the CDA did not shield service providers from laws dealing with intellectual property. The question remained, however, whether intellectual property encompassed federal intellectual property or state intellectual property or both. The Court noted that the scope of federal intellectual property laws, unlike that of the state intellectual property laws, was well established and uniform. The Court further explained that state intellectual property laws varied significantly from state to state. Because Internet websites have material that reaches many different states at any one time, the Court reasoned that to allow "any particular state's definition of intellectual property to dictate the contours of this federal immunity would be contrary to Congress's expressed goal of insulating the development of the Internet from the various state-law regimes." Therefore, the Court construed intellectual property as used in the CDA to mean "federal intellectual property." In a footnote, the Court explained that a number of state law claims, including right to publicity, could be classified as state intellectual property claims such that "an entity otherwise entitled to Section 230 immunity would thus be forced to bear the costs of litigation under a wide variety of state statutes that could arguably be classified as 'intellectual property.'" Consequently, the Court held that the defendants were eligible for immunity under the CDA for all of the state law claims—including the right to privacy—raised by the plaintiff.

Pesina v. Midway Mfg. Co., 948 F. Supp. 40 (N.D. Ill. 1996).

In *Pesina v. Midway Mfg. Co.*, a little known model, who served as inspiration for a video game character, could not prevail on claim for misappropriation of his right of publicity.

The plaintiff, a martial artist, brought suit against the defendant, Midway, alleging, among other things, that the defendant used his persona, name, and likeness without consent, and accordingly infringed his common law right of publicity. The defendant was in the video game business and created the popular martial arts games *Mortal Kombat* and *Mortal Kombat II*. In order to create characters and images for the game, the defendant hired models to perform movements to be captured, edited, and transferred into the game. The plaintiff was one such model and he claimed that Midway improperly used his image in the home version of the two games. The defendant moved for summary judgment.

The Court granted the defendant's motion for summary judgment with respect to the plaintiff's right of publicity claim, because there was no evidence that the plaintiff's persona, name, or likeness had any commercial value and—even if it had any such value—the likeness was unrecognizable in the video game. The Court noted that the video images of the plaintiff "were extensively altered prior to being incorporated into the games," and thus, "after comparing Mr. Pesina and the game character, Johnny Cage, who allegedly resembles the plaintiff, only 6% of 306 *Mortal Kombat* Users identified Mr. Pesina as the model." The Court also dismissed any argument that the use of the plaintiff's name for only eight seconds in one of the games was actionable. The Court intimated that the plaintiff may have been able to argue that he had become associated with the game character, Johnny Cage, such that the character invoked the plaintiff's identity, but that the Court would have nevertheless rejected this argument. The Court found that the evidence showed that the plaintiff was not a well-known martial artist and that the public did not "even recognize him as a model for Johnny Cage." Consequently, the Court granted the defendant's motion for summary judgment.

Michaels v. Internet Entm't Group, Inc., 5 F. Supp. 2d 823 (C.D. Cal. 1998).

Michaels v. Internet Entm't Group, Inc. shows that celebrities can invoke rights of publicity to enjoin the unwanted distribution of personal sex tapes.

The plaintiffs, Bret Michaels and Pamela Anderson Lee, filed for a preliminary injunction against the defendant, Internet Entertainment Group, Inc., to prevent the dissemination of a videotape showing the plaintiffs engaged in sex acts together. The plaintiffs alleged, among other things, violation of the California statutory right of publicity. At the time of the suit, Bret Michaels was best known as a member of the rock band Poison, and Pamela Anderson Lee was primarily known as a television and film actor. The defendant was a corporation in the business of distributing adult entertainment through the Internet and had obtained a copy of the video through a private investigator who maintained he had received the tape from a client claiming to be an associate of the plaintiffs. The Court, prior to issuing the injunction, determined that the plaintiffs would likely succeed on the merits in their claims of copyright infringement, violation of the right of publicity, and violation of the right to privacy.

In regard to the right of publicity claim, the Court, as an initial matter, rejected the defendant's argument that the plaintiffs' state claim was preempted by federal copyright law. The Court found that the plaintiffs had alleged that their names, likenesses, and identities had been used on the radio, television, and Internet to advertise the distribution of the videotape. Therefore, according to the Court, the defendant's conduct was "unrelated to the elements of copyright infringement, which are concerned only with distribution of the Tape itself."

The Court then recited the elements of both the common law right of publicity claim and the statutory right of publicity claim. The Court found that the first element—defendant's use of the plaintiffs' identities—was met, since the plaintiffs' names and identities were used to promote the videotape. Moreover, the Court found that the second element, requiring that the use be to the advantage of the defendant, was likewise met because the defendant used the identities and names to sell subscriptions to its website. Further, the Court determined that the plaintiffs never consented to the use of the tape. Additionally, the Court found that the defendant knowingly used the names for purposes of promotion and that there was a direct connection between that use and the promotion. Finally, the Court found that there was evidence to indicate that the plaintiffs would be injured by the defendant's exploitation of their names and identities based, in part, on the fact that the plaintiffs' images and careers would be damaged by being associated with the pornography trade. Therefore, the Court found that the plaintiffs had shown a likelihood of success on the merits.

Almeida v. Amazon.com, Inc., 456 F.3d 1316 (11th Cir. 2006).

Almeida v. Amazon.com, Inc. shows that an online retailer of books is not liable for misappropriating the right of publicity of a claimant whose picture was featured on the cover of a book for sale online. This is a case from the early days of the Internet when rules for online commerce had not been fully worked out. People, like the plaintiff Almeida, who had given permission for the use of their image in print, were not clear as to their rights when those images were reproduced and used online.

The plaintiff, Almeida, brought suit against the defendant, Amazon.com—a recognized leading Internet retailer with a focus on online book sales—alleging, among other things, violation of her right of publicity under both Florida common and statutory law. The plaintiff had consented to being photographed for a photo exhibit and photo-based book. A resulting image was displayed at the exhibit and in the first edition of the book. Subsequently, the publishers of the book in which the plaintiff's image was displayed decided to publish a second edition. The second edition, although similar in many respects to the first edition, now displayed the plaintiff's picture on the book's cover. Further, the second edition was then offered for sale on Amazon.com's website. Frequently, when Amazon.com offers books for sale, it provides the user with a photo of the book cover. The plaintiff contended that this practice led to a violation of the plaintiff's right of publicity.

The Court began its discussion by explaining that the District Court determined that the plaintiff's right to publicity claim was preempted by the Communications Decency Act of 1996. The Court discussed the parties' various arguments concerning the scope of the CDA but ultimately found that it need not address whether the District Court erred, because the plaintiff's right to publicity claim would not survive a motion to dismiss in any event. The Court concluded that it was unnecessary for the District Court to recognize the preemption issue.

The Court then analyzed the plaintiff's right to publicity claim and determined that Amazon.com did not violate any publicity right because it did not use, as contemplated by the statute, the plaintiff's image for trade, commercial, or advertising purposes. The Court cited relevant case law for the proposition that use of an image in a publication is not commercial simply because that publication is offered for sale. The Court distinguished cases when defendants affirmatively aimed at using their images and emphasizing their role for marketing purposes, stating, "[I]n contrast, Amazon does not make editorial choices as to the book cover images it displays on its website." The Court concluded that Amazon.com's practice of putting up pictures of the covers of books it is selling was not an "endorsement or promotion of any product or service, but is merely incidental to, and customary for, the business of [I]nternet book sales." Essentially, the Court analogized Amazon.com's practice to that of a traditional bookstore having books on the shelf with the book covers facing out toward customers. Accordingly, the Court found no cause of action for right to publicity and, consequently, it affirmed the District Court's grant of summary judgment, albeit on separate grounds.

Bosley v. Wildwett.com, 310 F. Supp. 2d 914 (N.D. Ohio 2004).

Bosley v. Wildwett.com features a television news reporter who was entitled to an injunction to protect her right of publicity to prevent release of a DVD that showed her participation in a wet t-shirt contest.

The plaintiff, Catherine Bosley, a television news reporter who had achieved regional celebrity, filed for a preliminary injunction against the defendants—multiple companies—for violation of the plaintiff's right to publicity. The plaintiff participated in a "wet t-shirt" contest that was filmed by one of the defendants,

Dream Girls, to be part of a DVD called *Spring Break 2003*. Shortly after the plaintiff was filmed, Dream Girls released a video from the contest. Subsequently, Dream Girls released a second version of the video, this time emphasizing the fact that the plaintiff appeared naked on the tape. Thereafter, Dream Girls licensed the video of the plaintiff's performance to a second company, Marvad Corporation. Marvad owned the website, *SexBrat.com*, that distributed adult entertainment over the Internet through a subscription service. Members of *SexBrat.com* who paid a subscription fee were, among other things, allowed to see portions of the plaintiff's performance. The website and video drew substantial publicity and the plaintiff eventually had to resign from her news anchor position. The plaintiff filed for a preliminary injunction to prevent the distribution of her image via the defendants' businesses.

The Court began its discussion with an explanation of the relevant Ohio and Florida statutory and common law claims for right of publicity. The Court then rejected the defendants' argument that the use of the plaintiff's image was not for a commercial purpose. The Court noted that the defendants used the images of the plaintiff to directly promote the sale of videos and website memberships. The Court further explained that the "prominent display" of the plaintiff's name and image on the cover of the video and on the website constituted an advertisement for the Dream Girls video and that the use of the plaintiff's image constituted direct promotion of the defendants' products and services.

The defendants further argued that their use of the plaintiff's image fell under the "public affairs exception." The Court cited case law for the proposition that the test of whether or not the public affairs exception applies turns not on the type of media in which the image appears but rather on whether the use of the image is a matter of legitimate public concern. The Court then noted of the Internet, "In modern times, one could extend this analysis to conclude that information relating to a legitimate public interest on an internet web page is protected communication." The Court explained that images that are otherwise newsworthy are not always protected in the context of advertising. The defendants' use was, according to the Court, clearly advertisement.

The Court also rejected the defendants' argument that the First Amendment barred the plaintiff's right to publicity claim because, as the defendants contended, their use of the plaintiff's image was protected speech. The Court noted that because the defendants were using the plaintiff's image "solely for the use of the purpose of commercially exploiting her fame" and because the use of the images lacked artistic expression and significant editorial comment, the case was distinguishable from cases in which First Amendment protections applied. The Court further found the defendants' prior restraint arguments unpersuasive, noting that the right to publicity bears close similarity to the goals of patent and copyright law and that the First Amendment "is not a license to trample on legally recognized rights in intellectual property." Finally, the Court rejected the defendants' allegations that the plaintiff had consented to the taping. The Court noted that, at the very least, explicit oral consent was required and that all the defendants could allege was tacit consent. Ultimately, the Court issued the preliminary injunction.

Stern v. Delphi Internet Servs. Corp., 626 N.Y.S. 2d 694 (1995).

In *Stern v. Delphi Internet Servs. Corp.*, a prominent radio talk show host could not claim misappropriation of his right of publicity over a full-page ad challenging his candidacy for governor. Being a famous celebrity and running for public office (even if the run is a parody) raises the bar for what might count as misappropriation of the celebrity's image.

The plaintiff, talk show "shock-jock"/host Howard Stern, brought suit against Delphi Internet Services Corporation, alleging commercial misappropriation of his name and picture. Delphi sponsored an electronic bulletin board debating Stern's candidacy for office of governor of New York and included his name and picture as part of the bulletin board. The Court described Delphi as "an online computer network" that had "set up on its on-line electronic bulletin board, a subscriber participation debate on the merits of Stern's candidacy." It was undisputed that Delphi used Stern's name and picture without his permission in a full-page advertisement in *New York Magazine* and the *New York Post*. The ad read as follows:

> Should this man be the next governor of New York? You've heard him. You've seen him. You've been exposed to his Private Parts. Now he's stumping to be governor. Maybe it's time to tell the world exactly what you think. The Internet's the one frontier even the King of (Almost) All Media hasn't conquered. And Delphi's where you get aboard. The online service that "leads the way in Internet access." With Delphi, navigating the Net is as easy as falling down. Assistance is available at every turn. From help files, guides and books, to hundreds of online experts, including Wald Howe, Delphi's resident Internet guru and all around smart guy. So whether you think Howard-the-Aspiring-Governor should be crowned King of the Empire State, or just greased up and sent face-first down a water slide, don't put a cork in it. Sit down, jack in, and be heard.

Delphi's principal contention, however, was that its use of Stern's name and photograph fell within the bounds of the "incidental use exception." Delphi argued that because its advertisements were for a service related to news dissemination—the online forum to discuss Stern's candidacy—it is entitled to protection under the incidental use exception even though Delphi, as a company, was neither solely nor predominately engaged in the dissemination of news.

The Court agreed with Delphi. In so doing, it analyzed various cases dealing with the issue of the "incidental use exception." The Court noted that "New York courts have consistently held that the incidental advertising exception applies to all 'news disseminators,' not just newspapers and magazines." Further, the Court analogized Delphi's online forum—that is only a small percentage of its entire business—to the traditional media, television networks. The Court noted that television networks engaged in both news dissemination and entertainment, but television was given the same privileges as other media where the statutory right to privacy is at issue. The Court concluded, "[b]ecause Stern's name was used by Delphi to elicit public debate on Stern's candidacy, logically the subsequent use of Stern's name and likeness in the advertisement is afforded the same protection as would be afforded a more traditional news disseminator engaged in the advertisement of a newsworthy product." The Court ultimately held that the use of Stern's name to advertise the subject—a debate of Stern's candidacy—on an electronic bulletin board fell within the incidental use exception.

Brown v. ACMI Pop, 873 N.E.2d 954 (Ill. App. 1st. Dist. 2007).

In *Brown v. ACMI Pop*, a stock photo service may be liable for misappropriating the right of publicity of the subjects of the photos it licenses and by displaying thumbnails of the photos on its website. Note the way that this case changes the outcome one comes to expect from cases about copyright (*Kelly v. Arriba Soft*) where use of thumbnails or degraded/watermarked images for search is not infringement. The right of publicity can change the infringement equation.

The estate for the plaintiff, the late recording artist James Brown, brought suit against the defendant (stock image company Corbis—ACMI pop), alleging—among other things—that the defendant infringed the plaintiff's right of publicity through the defendant's unauthorized commercial use of Brown's image on the Internet. The defendant was in the business of licensing copyrighted photographs, doing so by displaying a catalogue of over two million photos on its website to facilitate the ability of customers to identify images they wished to license. The photos displayed on the defendant's website were obscured with a visible watermark or used a very low resolution to preclude unauthorized use of the pictures prior to licensing. The plaintiff alleged that this use of his photo violated his right of publicity. The Circuit Court initially granted the defendant's motion to dismiss the claims, finding that the defendant's use was noncommercial, thus precluding a claim for right of publicity, and that in any event the federal Copyright Act preempted the claim. The Circuit Court, however, upon the plaintiff's motion for reconsideration, reversed all of its initial holdings and thereafter certified two questions regarding its right to publicity findings on appeal to the Illinois appellate court.

The Court of Appeals first analyzed whether the defendant's use of the plaintiff's images on the website could be considered commercial. The defendant argued that unlike the facts in cases cited by the plaintiff, the defendant's use of the images dealt with intangible property—the transferring of a legal right created by the Copyright Act—rather than tangible property, such as, for example, an image affixed to a t-shirt for sale. Essentially, the defendant argued that it was not selling a product but instead offering a license on the copyrights it owns. The Court found that because there was valid disagreement as to whether the use was commercial, the Circuit Court had not erred in denying the defendant's motion to dismiss.

As for the copyright preemption claim, the Court rejected the defendant's argument that the defendant was exercising its rights to reproduce and publish the plaintiff's images under the federal Copyright Act such that any right of publicity claim was preempted by the Act. The defendant's contention centered on its belief that the use of the plaintiff's likeness on the Internet did not extend beyond the use of the copyrighted photos. Further, as the defendant argued, the copyrighted work was not used to endorse a product but rather was used to distribute a license. The plaintiff responded by arguing that the images advertised for sale on the defendant's website constituted a fixed work on the Internet because the "license" resulted in tangible property in the form of a photograph to the end user. The plaintiff further argued that he had never consented to any sale of his photos and never had any control over the copyright interest to release. The Court held that the Circuit Court had not erred in denying the defendant's motion to dismiss.

Fraley v. Facebook, Inc., 830 F. Supp. 2d 785 (N.D. Cal. 2011).

In *Fraley v. Facebook, Inc.*, a group of consumers was able to pursue claims under California law that their rights of publicity had been misappropriated by Facebook's "Sponsored Stories" program.

In this class action, plaintiffs alleged, among other things, that Facebook's "Sponsored Stories" program violated California's Right of Publicity Statute (Civil Code § 3344). Plaintiffs challenge one of Facebook's advertising services in particular, known as "Sponsored Stories," that Facebook launched in January 2011, and that was enabled for all members by default. A "Sponsored Story" is a form of paid advertisement that appears on a member's Facebook page and that generally consists of another Friend's name, profile picture, and an assertion that the person "likes" the advertiser. A "Sponsored Story" may be generated whenever a member utilizes the "Post," "Like," or "Check-in" features, or uses an application or plays a game that integrates with the Facebook website, and the content relates to an advertiser in some way determined by Facebook. For example, plaintiff Angel

Fraley, who registered as a member with the name Angel Frolicker, alleges that she visited Rosetta Stone's Facebook profile page and clicked the "Like" button in order to access a free software demonstration. Subsequently, her Facebook user name and profile picture, bearing her likeness, appeared on her Friends' Facebook pages in a "Sponsored Story" advertisement consisting of the Rosetta Stone logo and the sentence, "Angel Frolicker likes Rosetta Stone."

Plaintiffs alleged that Facebook unlawfully misappropriated plaintiffs' names, photographs, likenesses, and identities for use in paid advertisements without obtaining plaintiffs' consent. Facebook filed a motion to dismiss. Among other things, Facebook argued that it was immune from liability under CDA, 230. As to the right of publicity claims, the court denied Facebook's motion to dismiss and allowed the claims to proceed. The Court stated that in the context of the claims at issue, Facebook was playing the role of an information content provider, not an interactive computer service and thus was not immune under CDA, 230. After the court ruled that the claims could proceed, the parties settled the class action case. Under the terms of the settlement, Facebook was to pay $20 million into a settlement fund for distribution to members of the class of plaintiffs. Facebook also agreed to modify its terms of service to make them more clear and transparent, allow for easier opt-out of "Sponsored Stories," and afford greater protection for minors.

Perkins v. LinkedIn Corp., 2014 U.S. Dist. LEXIS 81042 (N.D. Cal. June 12, 2014).

In *Perkins v. LinkedIn Corp.*, participants in online social media claim that companies use personal data to invade privacy; those claims are often dismissed out of hand. The ToS and EULA for social media rule out privacy claims. Further, users provide personal information to the websites/services. However, there may be limitations to the uses to which social media services can put that data and users' right of publicity provides constraints.

LinkedIn is a social networking website geared toward professional networking with more than 200 million users. Users, who maintain resume-like profiles, utilize LinkedIn to view each other's profiles and to exchange messages. This case centered around one portion of the process that a user must complete to sign up for a LinkedIn account. Specifically, the plaintiffs, nine LinkedIn users who sought to represent a nationwide class of LinkedIn users, alleged that during the sign-up process, LinkedIn harvested the email addresses of the plaintiffs' contacts. Plaintiffs alleged that LinkedIn's harvesting of email addresses and sending of endorsement emails was contrary to several of LinkedIn's own policies.

Plaintiffs filed a class action lawsuit against LinkedIn Corporation. Plaintiffs asserted that LinkedIn, the operator of a popular social networking website, violated common law rights of publicity and other state and federal laws by harvesting email addresses from the contact lists of email accounts associated with plaintiffs' LinkedIn accounts and by sending repeated invitations to join LinkedIn to the harvested email addresses.

LinkedIn moved to dismiss the plaintiffs' claims on both procedural grounds (i.e., that they lacked standing because they could not assert any harm) and on the merits. As to the standing issue, the court found that individuals' names have economic value where those names were used to endorse or advertise a product to the individuals' friends and contacts. This was so because an advertisement bearing the imprimatur of a trusted or familiar source, such as a friend or acquaintance, has concrete value in the marketplace. Here, Plaintiffs alleged that their names were misappropriated by LinkedIn to create personalized endorsements.

On the merits, although the court noted that LinkedIn's sign-up process could and should be clearer, the court concluded that Plaintiffs' allegations that they did not consent to the first endorsement email are insufficient because LinkedIn's sign-up process discloses that LinkedIn will send such an endorsement email. Accordingly, the court grants Defendant's Motion as it relates to Plaintiffs' common law right of publicity action for the first endorsement email. However, the court found that Plaintiffs adequately pleaded lack of consent to the sending of the second and third endorsement emails and that it was plausible that these subsequent emails created independent harm. Accordingly, the court denied LinkedIn's motion as it relates to the common law right of publicity cause of action with regard to the second and third endorsement emails.

Joude v. WordPress Found., 2014 U.S. Dist. LEXIS 91345, 2014 WL 3107441 (N.D. Cal. July 3, 2014).

In *Joude v. WordPress Found.*, two individual citizens of France sued WordPress and its owner, Automattic, Inc., to compel them to take down an anonymously written blog post about them and their family. The court found that the defendants were immune from suit for misappropriation of their rights of publicity under CDA, 230.

Plaintiffs learned of anonymously published blog about Plaintiffs and other members of the Joude family. While some of the entries appeared to state plain facts about plaintiffs' family history, others contained remarks Plaintiffs claimed to be negative. For example, one entry titled "God's Fundraisers" stated that "We [the Joudes] obtain funds through deceit and fraud ..." and "have defrauded victims out of at least 30 million Euros ..." to support the "Legionnaires of Christ." Plaintiff Alexandre sent an email to Automattic via WordPress requesting that they take down the blog because "the author of this blog has usurped my identity to publish defamatory information about family members with photos that I do not know how he was able to obtain." Later the same day, Automattic responded that they "were in no position to arbitrate content disputes" but would remove any content "found to be defamatory or illegal by a U.S. court of law" in a formal order from a United States court.

Plaintiffs sued for, among other things, misappropriation of their rights of publicity. Defendants removed the case to federal court (a tactic that is appropriate if the federal court has proper jurisdiction over the case) and then moved to dismiss. As to the right of publicity claim, the defendants asserted that they were immune from liability under CDA, 230. The court agreed. The court distinguished the decision in *Fraley* from this case because plaintiffs did not allege that Automattic had a role in "creating or developing" the blog, commercially or otherwise. Moreover, Plaintiffs did not claim that Automattic was the blog's anonymous writer. Indeed, by its own allegations, Automattic's role here was limited to "host[ing], maintain[ing], and administer[ing]" the blog-making apparatus. Thus, as a publisher, Automattic has CDA, 230 immunity from Plaintiffs' misappropriation of likeness claim relating to content created by the anonymous blogger.

The *Fraley* and *Joude* cases demonstrate the critical distinction under the law between being labeled a content provider (who may be liable for the content on line) versus a mere conduit (who is not liable for the content of third parties). The *Fraley* and *Perkins* cases demonstrate the perils of operating social media sites and using aspects of someone's identity to endorse a product, whether it is the social media site itself (e.g., LinkedIn) or a third-party product (e.g., Facebook's "Sponsored Stories").

Traditional Media Privacy of the Persona Cases with New Media Implications

Katz v. United States, 389 U.S. 347 (1967).

The Court, in *Katz*, set the requirement that the government must obtain a properly authorized warrant before wiretapping.

At the time of *Katz*, wiretapping had not yet been included in privacy expectations. Katz was convicted of illegal gambling based on wiretaps obtained by the FBI on conversations he had from a public telephone booth. Trial and appeal courts convicted and upheld based on excluding Fourth Amendment claims of protection from illegal search and seizure, finding that there was no physical entrance into Katz's private property. The SCOTUS overturned the conviction, finding that while the Fourth Amendment doesn't protect places (like a public phone booth), it does protect people and matters that they intend to keep to themselves.

Berger v. New York, 388 U.S. 41 (1967).

As with *Katz*, *Berger v. New York* dealt with authorizations for wiretaps; in this instance, noting that authorizations to collect data (should) have reasonable end points.

Berger was indicted and convicted of conspiracy to bribe the chairman of the New York State Liquor Authority based upon evidence obtained via a wiretap. The surveillance was carried out under a New York state law allowing the authorized placement of a wiretap for up to sixty days (with renewal for sixty more, with cause). The SCOTUS found the law violated the Fourth Amendment in that the "authorization to eavesdrop for a two-month period is equivalent to a series of searches and seizures pursuant to single showing of probable cause."

Whalen v. Roe, 429 U.S. 589 (1977).

Some of our most sensitive information are medical data, so not surprisingly, numerous important privacy cases, including *Whalen v. Roe*, involve privacy expectations in health care.

Although not about media as such, *Whalen v. Roe* dealt with important database issues. In 1972, the State of New York passed anti-drug regulations requiring that prescriptions for a class of "dangerous drugs" be written on an official form, in triplicate, with one copy going to the state for database entry. The information included the names of doctors, patients, and medications. Sets of doctors and patients challenged the statute on the ground that it violated Fourth Amendment privacy protections. The SCOTUS found in favor of the State of New York and ruled that the statute was not unconstitutional.

Nixon v. Administrator of General Services, 433 U.S. 425 (1977).

Government officials are also private citizens, but ownership and control of materials that, for purely private citizens, would be proprietary intellectual property may become public documents when generated by elected officials. *Nixon v. Administrator of General Services* examines that dynamic, finding in favor of the public interest.

After former President Richard Nixon resigned from office, he executed an agreement with the administrator of the General Services Administration (GSA) to ship his private papers from Washington to California, where he was to retire and where he expected a presidential library to be built. As part of the agreement, Nixon mandated a process and time frame that would allow him to eventually destroy materials from the collection, particularly audio recordings. Of course, the Watergate crisis had found audio recordings to be particularly damaging to the Nixon presidency.

When Congress learned of the agreement, it acted by passing the Presidential Recordings and Materials Preservation Act (PRMPA), legislation that put into practice procedures for handling the materials and protecting their integrity. The PRMPA obviated the previous agreement between Nixon and the GSA by mandating certain procedures for that agency. Nixon filed suit against the GSA and thereby challenged the PRMPA, claiming that the PRMPA violated a number of principles concerning the separation of powers, various presidential rights and powers, as well as the former president's First, Fourth, and Fifth Amendment rights. In this, Nixon:

> concedes that, when he entered public life, he voluntarily surrendered the privacy secured by law for those who elect not to place themselves in the public spotlight ... He argues, however, that he was not thereby stripped of all legal protection of his privacy, and contends that the *Act* violates fundamental rights of expression and privacy guaranteed to him.

The Court found against Nixon for a number of reasons. While noting that Nixon did retain some expectation of privacy for his personal and/or family matters, the bulk of the materials in question were public documents, and the procedures that had been set up to screen the documents before any of them would be made public were sufficient to protect the former president's privacy.

United States v. Smith, 978 F.2d 171 (5ᵗʰ Cir. 1992).

United States v. Smith points in the direction of new media by illustrating some of the complexities that accompany the development and deployment of new media technologies. In this case, the status of intercepting and recording telephone conversations that are conducted using wireless (rather than hardwired) equipment modified both the federal protection of phone calls and the assumption that wireless calls cannot be private.

A neighbor of Smith's girlfriend suspects that Smith is involved in neighborhood break-ins. The neighbor uses technology to intercept Smith's phone calls, learns that Smith is dealing drugs, and alerts police. The police help the neighbor record phone conversations and then arrest Smith for drug activities. Smith argued that his phone conversations were intended to be private and that the use of intercepted phone messages was a violation of the Omnibus Crime Control and Safe Streets Act of 1968 and the Wire Tap Act of 1968. The trial court threw out the claim and used the information toward conviction. The Court of Appeals upheld the conviction. However, in doing so, the Court's opinion opened the door for the application of privacy issues to cellular and wireless phone conversations.

In general, the reason that cellular and wireless phone conversations are not protected against unauthorized interception is that the technology is so easy to intercept. Because the signals are broadcast over open frequencies, the expectation of privacy is waived. The fine print in cellular phone contracts spells that out but, of course, most people don't read it. However, in *Smith*, the Circuit Court noted that there are ways that citizens can strengthen their privacy expectations when using wireless devices. If the user acquired equipment that specially protects the data transmission, say by encryption or by operating in a frequency not accessed by normal radios or scanners, the citizen could be marking the intention that the conversation is (especially) private. Further, if the interceptor has to go to extraordinary means to intercept the talk, once again, the circumstances might mark a violation of privacy expectations. This area of the law is murky, and *Smith* complicated rather than clarified the landscape and undermined previously held interpretations both of privacy protections in the home and of the exclusion of cellular and wireless phone transmissions from legal protections.

McIntyre v. Ohio Elections Commission, 514 U.S. 334 (1995).

One of the hallmarks of online communication is that often, contributions cannot be tracked to particular individuals. *McIntyre v. Ohio Elections Commission* is the case that validated the right to anonymous speech standard.

In *McIntyre v. Ohio Elections Commission*, the SCOTUS set aside an Ohio state law that prohibited the distribution of campaign literature that did not contain the name and address of the person or campaign official issuing the literature. McIntyre (deceased by the time the case reached the SCOTUS) had been cited and fined for distributing leaflets in opposition of a school levy. Some of the self-produced leaflets did not identify her as the author. The Court's decision upheld the First Amendment right to publish anonymously.

Bartnicki v. Vopper, 532 U.S. 514 (2001).

Bartnicki v. Vopper indicated that a radio host and radio station could not be held liable for violating federal and state wiretap laws simply by playing, on air, the tape of a phone conversation that was illegally procured by a third party.

During collective-bargaining negotiations between a union representing teachers at a Pennsylvania high school and the local school board, a cellular phone conversation took place between the union's chief negotiator and a teacher who was president of the local union. In the course of the conversation, the teacher remarked that because of the board's intransigence, "we're gonna have to go to their, their homes ... [t]o blow off their front porches... ." A person (unidentified) intercepted and recorded the conversation and left the tape in the mailbox of the president of a local citizens' organization that opposed the union's proposals. The organization president, in turn, gave a copy of the tape to a local radio station's commentator, who played the tape on his public affairs talk show. Another radio station also broadcast the tape and some local newspapers published the tape's contents.

The union negotiator and the teacher brought a damages suit in the District Court against the radio commentator, the radio stations, and the organization president. Among the allegations in the suit were that (1) the interception violated federal wiretap laws, that generally made it illegal to intentionally intercept any wire, oral, or electronic communication; and (2) the publication violated other federal wiretap laws, that made it illegal for a person intentionally to disclose the contents of any such communication, where the person knew or had reason to know that the disclosed information was obtained through the illegal interception of the communication. The District Court, in denying the parties' cross-motions for summary judgment, concluded that (1) an individual who disclosed an illegally intercepted electronic communication could be in violation of the law even if the individual was not involved in the interception; and (2) imposing liability on the defendants would not violate the First Amendment.

On appeal, the Third Circuit reversed the District Court's order and remanded with directions to grant such judgment—on the grounds that the federal and the Pennsylvania statutes were invalid under the First Amendment as deterring significantly more speech than necessary to protect the privacy interests at stake.

The SCOTUS granted certiorari and agreed with the Third Circuit and held that under the circumstances presented, (1) the First Amendment protected the disclosure of the conversation's contents, and (2) the application of the federal and Pennsylvania statutes violated the First Amendment, because such application could not be justified by (a) a government interest in removing an incentive for parties to intercept private conversations, as there was no basis for assuming that imposing sanctions upon those who made the disclosure would deter the unidentified interceptor from continuing to engage in surreptitious interceptions, or (b) an interest in minimizing the harm to persons whose conversations have been illegally intercepted, as (i) the negotiations in question were a matter of public concern, and (ii) in the case at hand, privacy concerns gave way when balanced against the interest in publishing matters of public importance.

Riley v. California, 134 S.Ct. 2473 (2014).

Contestations over laws relating to search and seizure and self-incrimination have long struggled with materials and objects gathered during encounters between citizens and law enforcers. New media technologies can up the ante during these confrontations. Digital devices contain vast collections of records about their owner/holder. *Riley v. California* examined the status of such data and provides a level of privacy protection.

The contents of the defendants' cell phones were searched after the defendants were arrested, and evidence obtained from the cell phones was used to charge the defendants with additional offenses. The SCOTUS unanimously held that police officers generally could not, without a warrant, search digital information on the cell phones seized from the defendants as incident to the defendants' arrests. While the officers could examine the phones' physical aspects to ensure that the phones would not be used as weapons, digital data stored on the phones could not itself be used as a weapon to harm the arresting officers or to effectuate the defendants' escape. Further, the potential for destruction of evidence by remote wiping or data encryption was not shown to be prevalent and could be countered by disabling the phones. Moreover, the immense storage capacity of modern cell phones implicated privacy concerns with regard to the extent of information that can be accessed on the phones.

New Media Privacy of the Persona Cases

Steve Jackson Games v. U.S. Secret Service, 816 F.Supp. 432 (W.D. Tex. 1993).

A particular aspect in the PPA of 1980 applies to the protection of intellectual property associated with the privacy of the persona. Material being collected and prepared, toward a publishing effort, is protected prior to publication. Since many new media producers, like Mr. Jackson in *Steve Jackson Games v. U.S. Secret Service*, use computers to prepare and store materials, some protection of intellectual property related to privacy of the persona is leveraged prior to publication.

Steve Jackson Games v. U.S. Secret Service tested the PPA of 1980 against seizure of work output prior to publication when a computer running an online bulletin board and books prior to their publication was seized. Steve Jackson Games published books and board games and operated an online bulletin board for conversations about various computer gaming activities. Due to a number of factors, including the activities of a business associate well known in the hacker community, the Secret Service suspected the company of involvement in hacking. A Secret Service–led raid on the company included the confiscation of computers and data files, thereby closing the bulletin board and taking materials being prepared for publication (a book). The US District Court of Texas, Austin Division, ruled that the Secret Service had violated Jackson's privacy under the PPA, and the US Fifth Circuit upheld the ruling on appeal. In effect, a person's intellectual property can't implicate them in something that might be a crime if published, prior to the actual commission of the crime (publication).

Cyber Promotions, Inc. v. America Online, Inc., 948 F. Supp. 436 (E.D. Pa. 1996).

CompuServe v. Cyber Promotions, Inc., 962 F. Supp. 1015 (S.D. Ohio, C2–96–1070, 1997).

While CDA, 230 protects ISPs from tort liability for UGC in ways that discourage ISPs from deep involvement with the actual content, ISPs must manage and block spam email lest the volume that would result brings their systems down and/or alienates their customers. These cases solidified the legality of ISP actions against bulk spam.

In both cases involving Cyber Promotions, a spam/bulk email distributor, District Courts in Ohio and Pennsylvania, respectively, found that Internet service providers (ISPs) CompuServe and AOL, respectively, have the right to block spam/bulk electronic mail sent using their proprietary systems. In *CompuServe*, property tort law was at the core of the Court's finding in that Cyber Promotions committed a kind of trespass against CompuServe's property. In the *AOL* case, the Court found that AOL's action was not a violation of Cyber Promotions' First Amendment rights (and was a proper expression of AOL's rights).

Smyth v. Pillsbury Corp., 914 F. Supp. 97 (E.D. Pa. 1996).

Employees who claim personal intellectual property rights over their email are on shaky legal ground, as shown by *Smyth v. Pillsbury Corp.*

Smyth v. Pillsbury Corp. helped establish the lack of privacy, for employees, in corporate electronic mail. Mr. Smyth worked for Pillsbury. Company policy promised that all electronic mail was private and would not be intercepted or used in action against employees. However, after a series of email exchanges with a supervisor, Smyth was fired based on comments contained in his electronic mail. Smyth claimed that Pennsylvania state privacy law protected him; the Court found no such protection for email. Two cases with similar, pro-employer findings, follow.

Shoars v. Epson America, Inc., No. SCWI 12749, Cal. Sup. Ct., Los Angeles Cty. (1989).

Shoars worked for Epson, implementing electronic mail systems, and was terminated for refusing to monitor employee email. He sued and lost.

Epson promised its employees that the email system was private, but instructed Shoars to monitor employee electronic mail. Shoars complained within the company and was fired as a result. Shoars sued, claiming that the company practice violated privacy law (and also that the firing was inappropriate). The Court upheld the termination, finding that the law did not protect electronic mail stored on the company servers.

Nieman v. Versuslaw, Inc., 512 F. App'x 635 (7th Cir. 2013).

The ubiquity of information on the WWW sometimes causes people to think that their intellectual property and privacy rights are violated. If there is a lot of material available about me that I did not offer purposely, I might think that the privacy of my persona is being misappropriated. *Nieman v. Versuslaw, Inc.* speaks to the "public" nature of some materials on the WWW by noting that records of court proceedings are not private, and the fact that such records appear in search results on major search engines and legal research websites does not give rise to privacy claims.

Plaintiff Nieman discovered that certain legal-search websites (such as *Lexis/ Nexis.com, Justia.com, Leagle.com*, and *VersusLaw.com*) linked copies of documents from a prior lawsuit to his name. That litigation involved a former employer and was settled. When Nieman encountered difficulty obtaining another insurance job, he suspected that potential employers had learned of his prior lawsuit online and so "blacklisted" him from employment opportunities. Nieman alleged that, in late 2011, he wrote to each of the defendants and asked them to delink his court cases from their online search results. The defendants declined. Google pointed out that it simply aggregates information already published on the Internet. VersusLaw responded that its publication of public records was protected by the First Amendment and that it would block links to public records only by court order.

Nieman asserted claims for (1) commercial misappropriation of his name, (2) intentional interference with current and prospective economic advantage,

(3) unjust enrichment/civil conspiracy, (4) retaliation under the Illinois Human Rights Act and 42 U.S.C. § 1981, (5) violation of the Racketeer Influenced and Corrupt Practices Act, and (6) violation of the Lanham Act.

The district court dismissed the complaint for failure to state a claim. The court held that Nieman failed to state a claim under any of his theories of relief and that all of his claims were barred by the First Amendment, which protects the publication of public records. Nieman's claims were premised on the fact that defendants' websites provided links to information and documents in the public record. Also, to the extent that Nieman's claims related to alleged invasions of privacy or defamation, the court held they were barred by CDA, 230 that provides limited liability protection for online services as a publisher or speaker of the content from websites they index. The Seventh Circuit affirmed the decision and noted that "[t]he First Amendment privileges the publication of facts contained in lawfully obtained judicial records, even if reasonable people would want them concealed."

GoDaddy.com, LLC v. Hollie Toups, 429 S.W.3d 752 (Tex. App. 2014).

Domain hosting company *GoDaddy.com* was found to be immune from class action litigation under CDA, 230 for merely hosting (but not creating) "revenge porn" websites.

Several women filed a class action lawsuit on behalf of a putative class of women who allege that defendants who operated two revenge porn websites published sexually explicit photographs of plaintiffs without their permission or consent. GoDaddy, as an interactive computer service provider, hosted the revenge porn websites. GoDaddy did not create the offensive material at issue. Plaintiffs argued that because GoDaddy knew of the content, failed to remove it, and then profited from the activity on the websites, GoDaddy was jointly responsible for plaintiffs' damages. Plaintiffs alleged that these revenge websites engaged in the publication of obscenity and child pornography in violation of Texas Penal Code. Plaintiffs further alleged that GoDaddy hosted the websites despite having knowledge that the developers were engaged in illegal activities. Plaintiffs further contend that:

> [b]y its knowing participation in these unlawful activities, GoDaddy has also committed the intentional Texas tort of invasion of privacy upon these Plaintiffs, as well as ... intrusion on Plaintiffs' right to seclusion, the public disclosure of their private facts, the wrongful appropriation of their names and likenesses, false light invasion of Plaintiffs' privacy, and a civil conspiracy ... to perpetrate these intentional state law torts.

The trial court denied GoDaddy's motion to dismiss. On appeal, the Texas Court of Appeals reversed the trial court and found GoDaddy to be immune from liability under CDA, 230. The Court stated that:

> [b]ecause GoDaddy acted only as an interactive computer service provider and was not an information content provider with regard to the material published on the websites, plaintiffs cannot maintain claims against GoDaddy that treat it as a publisher of that material. Moreover, plaintiffs cannot circumvent the statute by couching their claims as state law intentional torts.

Jones v. Dirty World Entm't Recordings LLC, 755 F.3d 398 (6th Cir. 2014).

Jones v. Dirty World further establishes that CDA, 230 bars state law claims against websites that solicit and encourage but do not materially contribute to the creation of content submitted by users to their sites. The case parses differences among various ways that ISPs and website providers can involve themselves with content when publishing and the ways that involvement relates to CDA, 230 immunity.

Nik Richie is employed as the manager of Dirty World, LLC ("Dirty World"), owners and operators of the website www.TheDirty.com. The website receives approximately six hundred thousand visits each day and eighteen million visits each month. Users of the site, who refer to themselves as "The Dirty Army," may submit "dirt"—i.e., content that may include text, photographs, or video about any subject. Users may also post comments about the content submitted by others. The vast majority of the content appearing on www.TheDirty.com is comprised of submissions uploaded directly by third-party users. Many, but not all, of the submissions and commentaries appearing on the website relate to stories, news, and gossip about local individuals who are not public figures. The site receives thousands of new submissions each day. Richie or his staff selects and edits approximately 150 to 200 submissions for publication each day. The editing of published submissions only consists of deletions. Richie or his staff briefly reviews each submission selected for publication to ensure that nudity, obscenity, threats of violence, profanity, and racial slurs are removed. Richie typically adds a short, one-line comment about the post with "some sort of humorous or satirical observation." Richie, however, does not materially change, create, or modify any part of the UGC, nor does he fact-check submissions for accuracy.

Sarah Jones, a schoolteacher and one-time cheerleader for the Cincinnati Bengals football team, became the unwitting subject of posts on the website. Initially, a visitor submitted a photograph of Jones, accompanied by the following post:

> THE DIRTY ARMY: Nik, here we have Sarah J, captain cheerleader of the playoff bound cinci bengals ... Most ppl see Sarah has [sic] a gorgeous cheerleader AND

highschool teacher … yes she's also a teacher … but what most of you don't know is … Her ex Nate … cheated on her with over 50 girls in 4 yrs … in that time he tested positive for Chlamydia Infection and Gonorrhea … so im sure Sarah also has both … whats worse is he brags about doing sarah in the gym … football field … her class room at the school she teaches at DIXIE Heights.

As was his custom on the website, Nik added his own commentary. He wrote: "Why are all high school teachers freaks in the sack?- nik." Additional posts/comments of this nature (from/by "The Dirty Army" followed).

Sarah Jones sued Richie and Dirty World for defamation, false light (a tort of right of privacy in the persona) and intentional infliction of emotional distress for user-generated posts that appeared on the website. Richie and Dirty World asserted that they were immune from suit under CDA, 230, but the trial court rejected the defense, finding that "a website owner who intentionally encourages illegal or actionable third-party postings to which he adds his own comments ratifying or adopting the posts becomes a 'creator' or 'developer' of that content and is not entitled to immunity." The case went to trial, and the jury returned a verdict in favor of Jones for $38,000 in compensatory damages and $300,000 in punitive damages.

Richie and Dirty World appealed. The Sixth Circuit vacated the judgment and reversed the district court's denial of Dirty World's and Richie's motion for judgment as a matter of law. In assessing whether CDA, 230 immunity held, the court applied what it called the "material contribution" test (as opposed to the district court's "encouragement" test) to determine whether an interactive computer service provider becomes a content provider. The court found that Dirty World and Richie did not author the statements at issue; however, they did select the statements for publication. But Richie and Dirty World cannot be found to have materially contributed to the illegal content of the statements, simply because those posts were selected for publication. Nor can they be found to have materially contributed to the illegal content through the decision not to remove the posts. Finally, the court found that the addition of Richie's own comments did not materially contribute to the illegal content.

Traditional Media Defamation Cases with New Media Implications

New York Times v. Sullivan, 39, 376 U.S. 254 (1964).

New York Times v. Sullivan established the "actual malice" standard in defamation cases involving public officials.

Consolidated and decided with *Abernathy v. Sullivan*, this case concerned a full-page ad in *The New York Times* that alleged that the arrest of the Rev. Martin Luther King, Jr., for perjury in Alabama was part of a campaign to destroy King's efforts to integrate public facilities and encourage blacks to vote. L. B. Sullivan, the Montgomery city commissioner, filed a libel action against the newspaper and four black ministers who were listed as endorsers of the ad, claiming that the allegations against the Montgomery police defamed him personally. Under Alabama law, and in state court in Montgomery, Sullivan did not have to prove that he had been harmed, and a defense claiming that the ad was truthful was unavailable, since the ad contained factual errors. Sullivan won a $500,000 judgment at the trial level. However, the *Times* appealed the ruling to the SCOTUS, and that body held that the First Amendment protects the publication of all statements—even false ones—about the conduct of public officials except when statements are made with actual malice (with knowledge that they are false or in reckless disregard of their truth or falsity). Under this new standard, Sullivan's case collapsed, the state judgment was overturned, and the ruling contributed to a positive climate for open public discussion, supported by the press, of issues of social importance regardless of whether they were "pleasant" for governmental leadership.

Hustler Magazine, Inc. v. Falwell, 485 U.S. 46 (1988).

In *Hustler v. Falwell*, the SCOTUS unanimously held that the First Amendment free-speech guarantee in most cases prohibits awarding damages to public figures to compensate for emotional distress intentionally inflicted upon them.

In order to qualify for such damages, public figures would have to prove that the statements were false and that the person who made them either knew they were false or acted with reckless disregard for the truth. The Court ruled that *Hustler Magazine*'s parody of Jerry Falwell did not reach either standard, and so reversed a jury verdict (and a $250,000 damage award) that had been in favor of Falwell.

Milkovich v. Lorain Journal Co., 497 U.S. 1 (1990).

The SCOTUS finding in *Milkovich v. Lorain Journal Co.* established that it is more difficult for publishers to avoid liability for defamation based on opinion if published statements are sufficiently factual.

A high school wrestling coach sued an author and a newspaper, for defamation, after respondents printed an article implying that the coach had lied under oath. The trial court granted summary judgment for the author and newspaper and the appellate court affirmed, holding that the article was an opinion and was protected by the First Amendment. The SCOTUS reversed, holding that the First Amendment did not prohibit the application of Ohio's libel laws to the alleged defamation. The Court said that there was no absolute privilege protecting opinion from the application of defamation laws. It said that the dispositive question was whether a reasonable fact finder could conclude that statements of the author and newspaper implied that the coach had perjured himself. The Court said that the connotation that the coach perjured himself was sufficiently factual to be susceptible of being proved true or false. It said that the coach had to show that the connotations were false and made with some level of fault.

Procter & Gamble Mfg. Co. v. Hagler, 880 S.W.2d 123, 128–29 (Tex. App. 1994).

Procter & Gamble Mfg. Co. v. Hagler clearly shows that publishing the truth is generally an adequate defense against claims of defamation.

In this case, the Texas Court of Appeals reversed a jury decision that would have awarded a Procter & Gamble employee over $15 million. Hagler, the employee and plaintiff in the case, claimed that the posting of his termination (for theft) on the company electronic bulletin board was defamatory. The Texas Court of Appeals reversed on the grounds that the posting was factual and lacked any actual malice on the part of Procter & Gamble.

Robert Thomas v. Bill Page et al., No. 04 LK 013, Circuit Court for the Sixteenth Judicial Circuit, Kane County, Ill. (2007).

Robert Thomas v. Bill Page reminds one that public officials can win defamation cases when they are able to support the higher, actual malice, standard.

In 2004, Illinois Supreme Court Chief Justice Robert Thomas, a former Chicago Bears place kicker, sued a newspaper for libel over a column (written by Page) that claimed the judge had traded a verdict/vote for political favors. A jury awarded Thomas $7 million after finding that the former columnist for the *Kane County Chronicle* had acted with malice when he wrote the article. Page claimed that the information had come from an anonymous source he would not identify, thereby making a defense based on the truth standard problematic. The trial judge reduced the verdict to $4 million and the parties later settled out of court after the newspaper filed a federal civil rights lawsuit against Justice Thomas and other members of the Illinois judiciary.

New Media–Related Cases in Defamation Law

Even prior to provision of defamation liability safe harbor in CDA, 230 (1996) and copyright safe harbor in the DMCA (1998), case outcomes indicated that ISPs might not be found to be liable for defamation arising from third-party content.

Cubby v. CompuServe Inc., No. 90 Civ. 6571. USDC (S.D.N.Y. Oct. 29, 1991).

Cubby v. CompuServe Inc. reminds us that since ISPs may not be aware of the content of material published on websites serviced by the ISP, they are not liable for alleged defamation contained in third-party postings.

This action for libel, business disparagement, and unfair competition was based on allegedly defamatory statements made in a publication carried on a computerized database delivered via CompuServe. The "Rumorville" electronic forum was one of hundreds hosted on CompuServe. Cubby, Inc., had started a forum ("Skuttlebut") that was competitive with Rumorville. Cubby alleged that Rumorville defamed Cubby/Skuttlebut by publishing untrue claims about Cubby/Skuttlebut on Rumorville. The Court found that CompuServe enjoyed the full protection of safe harbor in this case, as they would neither have been aware of, nor responsible for, materials published on sites they merely hosted.

Stratton Oakmont, Inc. v. Prodigy Services Co., 1995 WL 323710 (N.Y. Sup. Ct. 1995).

Stratton Oakmont, Inc. v. Prodigy Services provides a pre-CDA "alternative take" on the roles and responsibilities of ISPs and an indication that monitoring content raises the responsibility stakes for ISPs.

A poster to one of Prodigy's online forums made defamatory claims about the president (Daniel Porush) of the Stratton Oakmont securities firm. The Court found that Prodigy was liable for carrying the libel, largely because its promotional and marketing presentation of its online forum services carried an implied promise that it would monitor the sites it carried and would take down offensive materials. Despite the finding in the case, Porush was later found guilty (by the SEC and other agencies and entities) of a variety of illegal financial transactions, very much in support of the claims made in the defamatory comments. In this case, then, "truth" was not able to serve as defense against a claim of defamation; at the same time, ISPs were forewarned about the risks in making claims about monitoring the content carried in their networks.

Passage of the CDA (February 1996) provided safe harbor from third-party content articulated in Section 230. Legal justifications for ISP immunities from tort-relevant UGC, thereafter, are grounded in the CDA. Recall that the 1998 DMCA provides similar immunity from copyright infringement in third-party content. Remember that the two safe harbors are not interchangeable: the CDA, 230 does not provide immunity from copyright, patent, trademark, and/or trade secret infringements and the DMCA does not provide immunity from tort liabilities related to the persona.

Zeran v. America Online Inc., United States Court of Appeals, No. 97–1523 (4th Cir. 1997).

Zeran v. America Online Inc. is one of the first cases using the CDA safe harbor. Applying that safe harbor to defamation cases seemed, at first, to be questionable, as the law was intended, primarily, as a way to protect children from exposure to adult materials online.

Zeran had been the victim of a malicious Internet hoax when his identity was connected to advertising for items glorifying the Oklahoma City bombing. Zeran sued AOL for not taking down the defamatory materials. The trial court's decision that AOL was protected by the safe harbor provisions of the CDA was upheld by the appeals court, indicating that Section 230 applied to questions in addition to, and other than, online child protection.

Blumenthal v. Drudge, 992 F. Supp. 44 (D.D.C. 1998).

In *Blumenthal v. Drudge*, the US District Court for D.C. upheld the safe harbor provisions protecting ISPs from responsibility for materials provided through their networks.

Blumenthal, a Clinton White House operative, sued Matt Drudge and AOL for defamation over false claims about his marriage; Drudge retracted the claims two days after making them, claiming that his sources had misled him. The Court found in favor of Drudge and AOL, and Blumenthal eventually settled the matter by paying Drudge what was said to be a relatively small amount for having missed a deposition.

Dendrite International, Inc. v. John Doe No. 3., Superior Court of New Jersey, Appellate Division. 342 N.J. Super. 134 (2001).

Dendrite International, Inc. v. John Doe No. 3, was not, in itself, a defamation case. In order to bring legal action against an accused defamer, their identity must be known. Posters of online UGC are often anonymous or use a pseudonym. Plaintiffs sometimes initiate legal action against ISPs to discover the identity of potential defendants.

Dendrite, a financial services broker, wanted to sue three people who had been anonymous posters to an online message board. The messages brought into question the performance of Dendrite's stock. Dendrite sued to obtain the identities of the posters, particularly poster no. 3, against whom the company wanted to bring a defamation suit. The ISP, Yahoo!, provided the identities of nos. 1 and 2, but refused in the case of no. 3, as their policy specified that they would only give up identities in cases when their terms of service were violated or harm had been done to users. The Court agreed with Yahoo!'s assessment that poster no. 3 had done no harm, so the motion to provide the identity was denied. The decision was upheld on appeal.

Sue Scheff, Parents Universal Resource Experts vs. Carey Bock and Ginger Warbis, Case Number: 03–022937 (18), Circuit Court, Broward County, Fla. (Sept. 2006).

Sue Scheff, Parents Universal Resource Experts vs. Carey Bock and Ginger Warbis indicates that although ISPs are protected from liability for third-party content, the accused defamers themselves are not. Defamation can be as expensive in the online environment as it is in print.

Bock hired Scheff, a functionary in Parents Universal Resource Experts— PURE—to help Bock remove her sons from a boarding school in Costa Rica. Scheff put Bock in touch with a third party for assistance. Unhappy with the services provided, Bock published a negative review about Scheff (and PURE). Scheff and PURE sued Bock for defamation in Florida State Court. Bock appeared initially but then defaulted. The default judgment against her totaled $11.3 million.

McKee v. Laurion, 825 N.W.2d 725 (Minn. 2013).

McKee v. Laurion is an example of a spate of lawsuits against people who write and post, online, negative reviews about products or services. Negative online reviews provide fodder for significant amounts of defamation litigation.

In *McKee v. Laurion* the defendant had an encounter with the plaintiff doctor regarding the doctor's care and treatment of the defendant's father after the father suffered a stroke. Defendant thought that the doctor's care and treatment of his father was rude and insensitive. After learning of the son's online postings on various doctor review sites regarding that care and treatment, the doctor sued the son, claiming defamation *per se* and interference with business. By the time the case made its way up to the Minnesota Supreme Court, there were only six statements still at issue in the case:

Statement 1: Dr. McKee said he had to "spend time finding out if you [Kenneth Laurion] were transferred or died."

Statement 2: Dr. McKee said, "44% of hemorrhagic strokes die within 30 days. I guess this is the better option."

Statement 3: Dr. McKee said, "You [Kenneth Laurion] don't need therapy."

Statement 4: Dr. McKee said, "[I]t doesn't matter" that the patient's gown did not cover his backside.

Statement 5: Dr. McKee left the room without talking to the patient's family.

Statement 6: A nurse told Laurion that Dr. McKee was "a real tool!"

The Minnesota Supreme Court found that none of the six was actionable either (1) because there was no genuine issue of material fact as to the falsity of the statements (Statements 1, 2, and 4), or (2) because the statements were not capable of conveying a defamatory meaning that would harm the doctor's reputation and lower him in the estimation of the community (Statements 3, 5, and 6).

While an ultimate victory for the defendant, after two years of litigation that wound its way through two levels of appeals court, in hindsight, this defendant may not have appreciated the price tag for his online candor about his father's doctor.

In addition to filing lawsuits against accused defamers, members of prominent plaintiff classes that often engender negative reviews (doctors, restaurant and hotel owners, etc.) have developed codicils (non-disparagement clauses) seeking to limit negative reviews by consumers. Those actions have, in turn, led to additional litigation, and in some cases, legislation over free speech rights in online commentaries (Mason).

Intihar v. Citizens Info. Assocs., LLC, No. 2:13-cv-720 (M.D. Fla. Oct. 11, 2013).

Intihar v. Citizens Info. Assocs. is an example of an increasing trend of suits against companies that are exploiting the greater availability of criminal records and the general population's general interest in looking at such information.

Plaintiff brought a defamation lawsuit against a company that operates mugshotsonline.com, a website that publishes mug shots and other information pertaining to arrests and criminal charges. Plaintiff asserted that defendant published untrue statements about him, namely that he had been arrested for use of illegal drugs. Plaintiff alleged that defendant ignored his requests to remove the statements. Defendant moved to dismiss the suit on technical grounds that plaintiff failed to comply with a Florida law that required a plaintiff to give 5 days' written notice before filing suit relating to "publication or broadcast, in a newspaper, periodical, or other medium, of a libel or slander." The district court found that mugshotsonline.com fell into the category of "other medium" and thus, because plaintiff failed to allege that he had given the proper notice, the suit was dismissed without prejudice. As of press time, the plaintiff has filed an amended complaint and the case remains pending.

Johns-Byrne Company v. TechnoBuffalo LLC, No. 11 L 009161 (Cir. Court of Cook County, Illinois), Order, Jul. 13, 2012.

The question of whether bloggers are to be treated as reporters, and are thereby able to claim protection from revealing their sources under state shield laws, is a frequent issue in defamation cases. This issue further highlights the impact of new media outlets covering advances in technology. *Johns-Byrne Company v. TechnoBuffalo* arose in the context of a trade secret misappropriation case, rather than defamation, but illustrates treatment of bloggers as protected sources, a key factor in many online defamation cases.

Plaintiff was hired to print a manual for a new, not-yet-released Motorola smartphone. Plaintiff alleged that an unknown person captured images of the smartphone and submitted them to the defendant, a technology blog. Plaintiff asked the court to order defendant to unmask the identity of the source of the information that was posted on defendant's blog. Defendant asserted that it was protected under the Illinois Reporter's Privilege Act, which allows a reporter to protect the identity of his or her confidential sources unless the party seeking the information is able to meet a high burden for "divestiture" of the privilege. The court had originally held that the defendant blog was not protected by the Reporter's Privilege Act. Following a motion to reconsider, the judge found that the defendant blog fit the definition of "news medium" under the Act and was publishing "news" from a "source" and acting as a "reporter" under the Act. As a result, the court found that the defendant blog did not have to reveal the source of the leaked information.

Learning Objectives and Discussion Questions

Publicity
- Detail the right of publicity. Can you:
  - o Discuss important limitations and exceptions to the right of publicity, especially those related to constitutional free speech protections and the role of parody in intellectual property law?
- Detail ways that the traditional right of publicity appears to conflict with everyday new media practices. Can you:
  - o Describe factors that bring the right of publicity into conflict with CDA, 230 immunities;
  - o List conflicts between the public's right to know and the right of publicity;
  - o Describe circumstances that complicate the right of publicity involving celebrities;

o Note ways that ubiquitous images of private citizens in commercial environments have changed the right of publicity landscape;

o Appreciate the complexities involved when using social media accounts in the workplace;

o List ways that the right of publicity may empower everyday users to protect intellectual property, online, that is unprotected by other types of intellectual property law?

- Detail complexities that result from the lack of a uniform right of publicity. Can you:

o Detail ways that state right of publicity laws vary across states?

Privacy

- Describe factors that bring the right of privacy in the persona into conflict with CDA, 230 immunities. Can you:

o Discuss conflicts between the public's right to know and the right of privacy in the persona;

o List circumstances that complicate the right of privacy in the persona among public figures and celebrities?

- Detail effects on the right of privacy in the persona protection brought about by the changing socio-cultural environment. Can you:

o Discuss ways that ubiquitous images of private citizens in commercial environments have changed the right of privacy in the persona landscape;

o Describe the relationships among employment, electronic communication, and privacy of the persona?

Defamation

o List circumstances that complicate relationships among defamation and public figures and celebrities;

o Compare the actual malice standard for defamation, as applied to public figures, to lesser standards for cases involving common citizens;

o Discuss ways that authorizing bloggers as reporters might affect the outcomes of online defamation cases.

- Highlight ways that new media, especially the commercial character of the Internet and the data marketplace, reduce protections against defamation. Can you:

o Discuss factors that bring rights against defamation into conflict with CDA, 230 immunities?

CHAPTER EIGHT

International Intellectual Property Laws and Systems Cases

New Media Cases Illustrating International Intellectual Property Law

Jurisdiction over Foreign Trademark Infringers

Pebble Beach Co. v. Caddy, No. 04–15577, 2006 WL 1897091 (9ᵗʰ Cir. July 12, 2006).

International cases almost always raise jurisdiction questions. *Pebble Beach Co. v. Caddy* shows that using trademarks in countries other than where they are established (and/or registered) is contentious but still depends on the uses made of the mark(s).

The corporation behind the famous US golf course, Pebble Beach <www.pebblebeach.com>, filed suit against a small British inn named Pebble Beach Bed & Breakfast <www.pebblebeach-uk.com> for trademark infringement and dilution. The accused, Michael Caddy, moved to dismiss the case for lack of personal jurisdiction and insufficiency of service of process. Although Caddy could have simply stayed in England and refused to appear (in which case the Court might have found against him for non-appearance), he came to the United States and fought the claims. The trial court granted Caddy's motion to dismiss, noting that Caddy's business did not conflict with that of the Pebble Beach golf course because he did not direct his business toward the US or California. Pebble Beach appealed, and the Court of Appeals upheld the trial verdict, finding that Pebble Beach had not satisfied the three-factor "effects test" that would show that a defendant committed an intentional act expressly aimed at the state of jurisdiction that causes harm in the state of jurisdiction in order to be sued there. The Court further said that a non-interactive, "passive" website such as Caddy's was inadequate to establish jurisdiction. The appeals court also found that Caddy is not a cybersquatter because he had a legitimate business in England under the name he used there.

Google Finds Belgian Copyright Law to Be Less Friendly

Copiepresse v. Google, The Court of First Instance in Brussels, Nr. 06/10.928/C (Feb. 13, 2007).

When doing business overseas, Google (and other US-based new media firms) often face differing interpretations about intellectual property law. *Copiepresse v. Google* highlights that countries outside the US do not uniformly agree that Internet search, précis, and linking protocols are free from copyright violations.

Copiepresse (CP) is a Belgian collective rights management organization that represents Belgian newspapers. CP sued Google over the Google News service that copies headlines, the first sentence (or portion of sentence) of articles, and links, without prior permission from Belgian newspapers or the reporters who write the stories. Google argued (in a Belgian court) that their practice constitutes fair use, based on two exceptions: (1) that their use is an account of the news, and (2) that criticism or review of the news is fair use. However, the practical operation of Google News impedes their defense. The "accounts of news" exception usually applies to a commentary on the news, and Google News reproduces news without any commentary. Further, the "criticism or review" function requires careful examination of a collection of elements, and in Google's case, no human performs this task. Given the voluminous nature of the materials used, it is not practical for Google to get consent from reporters and writers. The end result? Google lost in Belgium.

Under US law (e.g., *Kelly v. Arriba Soft*), Google News would likely win, because its use would be considered "transformative" (and thereby protected as fair use). Under Belgian law, transformation of an underlying work is viewed negatively and as a violation of an author's moral rights. The Belgian court wrote that:

- [We] Conclude that Google may not claim any exception as stipulated in copyright law and related rights;

- Conclude that the activities of Google News (i.e. the reproduction and communication to the public of the titles of articles and the short extracts from articles) and the use of the Google "cache" (i.e. the registration accessible to the public of the so-called "cache" memory of articles and documents) breach copyright law;
- Order Google to remove from all these sites (specifically from Google News as well as the visible cache links in relation to the search engine Google web) all articles, photographs and graphic representation of authors for whom the voluntary third parties intervening justify that they hold the rights.

The court also levied fines. Copiepresse and Google have been in ongoing negotiations in an effort to reach a settlement, action that the Court finding against Google rather "forced" them into.

Google Hits a Bump in the Road over Its Gmail Mark in Germany

Google Inc. v. Daniel Giersch, Office for Harmonization in the Internal Market (Trade Marks and Designs), Second Board of Appeal R 252/2007–2 (Feb. 26, 2008).

Even large corporations can become the "junior" who proposes use of a trademark already belonging to a "senior." US trademark registration only counts in the US, as Google learned, in *Google Inc. v. Daniel Giersch*, when trying to protect Gmail overseas.

After losing court battles in Germany over the issue, Google filed cases in other European venues, including the Office for Harmonization in the Internal Market of Germany, against Daniel Giersch (of Monaco) for infringement of the "Gmail" trademark. Daniel Giersch started using the name "G-Mail" in 2000, four years prior to Google's use of it. Giersch's service scans messages, sends them via the Internet, then prints and hand delivers them at the receiving end. After Giersch became aware of Google's plan to offer Gmail in Germany, negotiations between the parties resulted in an impasse and, subsequently, Giersch sued Google for infringement. Giersch won both in multiple court cases and before the Office of Harmonization in Germany; his trademarks are registered there, in Switzerland, Monaco, and Norway (Mills).

European View of Privacy of the Person Does Not Mesh with US Approach

Google Spain v AEPD and Mario Costeja González, Court of Justice of the European Union, May 13, 2014.

When it comes to balancing privacy against freedom of speech, some European countries take a decidedly different view from the USA. Nowhere is this more evident than in the emerging case law involving the "right to be forgotten." The right to be forgotten poses the question of whether and to what degree individuals can control the information that is available about them online. *Google Spain v AEPD and Mario Costeja González* marks a "win" for the peoples' right to know about their own intellectual property.

In the *Costeja* case, a Spanish man requested the removal of a link to a digitized 1998 article in a Spanish newspaper about an auction for his foreclosed home, for a debt that he had subsequently paid. Google filed suit in Spanish courts, and the matter was referred to the Court of Justice of the European Union, which ruled in favor of the Spaniard and against Google. While the court found no valid reason for links to the story to remain in this particular case, the court noted "that would not be the case if it appeared, for particular reasons, such as the role played by the data subject in public life, that the interference with his fundamental rights is justified by the preponderant interest of the general public in having, on account of its inclusion in the list of results, access to the information in question." In essence, the court suggests that the question of privacy versus public interest must be weighed on a case-by-case basis. Since the ruling, Google has received thousands of requests to de-link stories. In addition to the implications for freedom of speech, the decision imposes a serious burden on search engines to engage in a rather vague balancing test to determine if information remains of interest to the general public.

Loss of Trade Secrets outside of the US

United States v. Aleynikov, 673 F.3d 71 (2nd Cir. 2012).

The global economy, multinational corporations, workforces from diverse geographic locations, and the ease of copying digital information "raise the stakes" for trade secrets. US legislators have "called the raise" with passage of the Economic Espionage Act (EEA) and the National Stolen Property Act (NSPA). However, those laws do not always convict suspects across multiple court proceedings.

During his employment with Goldman Sachs, Aleynikov was a member of a team of computer programmers responsible for developing and improving aspects of the Platform, Goldman Sachs's high volume trading software, including code for the Platform's interface with NASDAQ. On his last day of employment at Goldman, Aleynikov copied, compressed, encrypted, and transferred to an outside server in Germany, hundreds of thousands of lines of source code for the trading system, including trading algorithms that determine the value of stock options. The entity that operates the German server offers free and paid services to computer programmers who wish to store their source code projects. After transferring the source code to the German server, Aleynikov deleted the program he used to encrypt the files. He also deleted his "bash history," i.e., the history of his most recent computer commands. That evening, and in the days that followed, Aleynikov accessed the German server and downloaded the source code to his home computer, and from there to other home computers and to a portable flash drive. Aleynikov then flew to Chicago, Illinois, to meet with operatives from Teza Technologies, a firm that competes with Goldman. He brought with him a laptop computer and the flash drive containing source code for Goldman's trading system, including some of the source code that he copied and transferred to a German server.

Aleynikov was convicted by a jury on two counts of theft of trade secrets under the federal Economic Espionage Act and National Stolen Property Act (NSPA). He was sentenced to 97 months of imprisonment and ordered to pay a fine of $12,500.

The Second Circuit reversed the conviction and found that the theft and subsequent interstate transmission of purely intangible property (i.e., source code) is beyond the scope of the NSPA.

In the wake of the Aleynikov case, in order to strengthen the Economic Espionage Act, on January 14, 2013 Congress enacted the Theft of Trade Secrets Clarification Act of 2012 that allows for punishment of acts like the one Aleynikov committed. In addition, Congress passed the Foreign and Economic Espionage Penalty Enhancement Act of 2012, that further increases the maximum penalties for foreign economic espionage. For individuals, the penalties are increased from $500,000 to $5,000,000. For organizations, the penalties are increased from $10,000,000 to "the greater of $10,000,000 or 3 times the value of the stolen trade secret to the organization, including expenses for research and design and other costs of reproducing the trade secret that the organization has thereby avoided." Additionally, the United States Sentencing Commission will evaluate and amend the federal sentencing guidelines for foreign trade secret theft convictions.

Patents around the World

In re: BlackBerry Application No. 09159981.1 (Case No. T 1148/11 – 3.5.05). Board of Appeal of the European Patent Office, Aug. 7, 2014.

As if the patent laws in a single country are not complicated enough, imagine the exponentially complicated process of procuring patent rights in multiple countries under multiple filing frameworks and multiple different sets of "prior art."

In re: BlackBerry Application No. 09159981.1 is one example of a decision from the Board of Appeal of the European Patent Office relating to an application by

BlackBerry Limited. BlackBerry Limited was refused registration for an invention titled "Efficient Attachment of User-Selected Files to E-Mail from Handheld Device." The European Patent Office rejected the patent on the ground that it lacked an inventive step. The office cited an earlier patent, "Design and Implementation of a Wireless Internet Remote Access Platform." The Appeal Board agreed that the subject matter of claim 1 of this subject patent did not involve an inventive step having regard to the skilled person's common general knowledge. These are principles that are similar to those encountered in the US patent framework (i.e., "novelty," and "non-obviousness"). The case underscores the difficulties encountered when attempting to claim patent rights in a global sphere. Not only does the inventor have to show that its invention is new at home, but also abroad as well.

Learning Objectives and Discussion Questions

- Describe some of the most pressing, current, international, new media, intellectual property clashes in our primary areas of interest:
  o Copyright;
  o Patent;
  o Trademark;
  o Trade Secrets;
  o Torts of the Persona (right of publicity; privacy, defamation).

CHAPTER NINE

Digital Rights Management Cases

Cases Illustrating DRM

United States of America v. Elcomsoft Co., Ltd. and Dmitry Sklyarov, Case No. CR 01 20138 (N.D. Cal. 2002).

United States of America v. Elcomsoft Co., Ltd. and Dmitry Sklyarov was the first case that enacted criminal prosecution of a person under the DMCA. Sklyarov's acquittal was largely based on the grounds that the DMCA's provisions for DRM are confusing.

On July 16, 2001, a Russian programmer named Dmitry Sklyarov was arrested and charged with trafficking in circumvention software. Section 1204 of the DMCA defines criminal penalties for violation of sections 1201 and 1202, including no more than five years' imprisonment for the first offense and up to ten years for any subsequent offense (17 U.S.C. § 1204(a)). Sklyarov, a PhD student employed by a Russian software company named ElcomSoft, wrote a piece of software he called the Advanced eBook Processor Program (AEBPR), which reformats eBooks to allow viewing with software other than the proprietary eBook software. Sklyarov came to Las Vegas to present at the hacker conference DEF CON but was arrested as he was leaving his hotel to return to the airport and home (Electronic Frontier Foundation, "*United States v. Elcomsoft & Sklyarov* FAQ").

The Adobe eBook Reader, distributed free of charge by Adobe, displays eBook content sold by a number of third-party sellers. Sellers of eBooks use an Adobe Content server to generate unique vouchers that travel with the eBook and reside on the user's computer. The voucher provides permission to the eBook software to allow the book to be viewed on the screen. Specific book permissions can be customized so that, for example, one book may be printed in its entirety, while another can only be printed a page at a time, or a page per day, depending on the choice of the eBook publisher. As his DEF CON presentation (Sklyarov) and the court documents both describe, Sklyarov's AEBPR unlocked the contents of eBooks using the voucher intended to protect the contents, creating a Portable Document Format (PDF) version of the book with no restrictions on use:

> Thus, the restrictions imposed by the publisher are stripped away, leaving the ebook in a PDF format that is readily copyable, printable, and easily distributed electronically. The conversion accomplished by the AEBPR program enables a purchaser of an ebook to engage in fair use of an ebook without infringing the copyright laws by, for example, allowing the lawful owner of an ebook to read it on another computer, to make a back-up copy, or to print the ebook in paper form. The same AEBPR technology, however, also allows a user to engage in copyright infringement by making and distributing unlawful copies of the ebook. (*United States of America v. Elcomsoft Co., Ltd. and Dmitry Sklyarov*)

Some three weeks after his arrest, Sklyarov was released from jail, but the US Department of Justice continued with its prosecution of Sklyarov and ElcomSoft. The case went to a jury trial in December 2002, and both Sklyarov and ElcomSoft were acquitted. After the trial, at least one juror reported that the jury found that, while the product was clearly illegal according to the DMCA, the law itself was so confusing that they could well believe that the Russian company could have failed to understand that their product was breaking the law (Bowman).

The Chamberlain Group, Inc., v. Skylink Technologies, Inc., 02 C 6376 (2004).

One often thinks of the DMCA in relation to new media consisting of information, entertainment, and complex digital technologies. The provisions of the DMCA, as they relate to DRM, may also apply to more mundane technologies. In *Chamberlain Group, Inc., v. Skylink*, electronic garage door openers (and the software code that operates them) were at issue.

In late 2003, The Chamberlain Group, manufacturers of garage door openers, sued Skylink Technologies for violating the DMCA by selling a door-opening remote designed to interoperate with Chamberlain's door-opening system. Skylink, manufacturers of aftermarket remotes, had reverse engineered a device to defeat Chamberlain's rolling code system. With a rolling code, the code needed to open the door increments by three after each use, purportedly to prevent someone with a code grabber from recording the code during use, then returning to the garage later and gaining unauthorized access with the stolen code. Skylink's universal remote sent three codes in quick succession. If the first code failed to open the door, the second and third would reset the door opener, taking advantage of a resynchronization failsafe that measured two sequential failed codes to look for the appropriate increment of three between them. This resynchronizing feature was designed to allow an authorized user to reestablish a connection legitimately lost, for example, if the remote was pressed many times outside of the range of the receiver in the door opener. Chamberlain claimed that by allowing the user to effectively reprogram the door opener, Skylink was defeating the Technological Protection Measure built in to the opener's microchip, and was therefore in violation of the new 1201 provisions of the law.

Consumers Union (publishers of *Consumer Reports*) wrote in their amicus brief to the Court in support of Skylink: "This case presents the question of whether companies can use the anti-circumvention provisions of the Digital Millennium Copyright Act ("DMCA") to foreclose competition for after-market products (such as replacement parts) without an underlying claim of copyright infringement and in the absence of evidence that consumers were not authorized to use the products they had purchased" (Urban and Schultz). In other words, one of the key questions in the Skylink case was whether the language in the DMCA protecting technological protection measures applies when there is no underlying copyright question. Did Congress intend for the anti-trafficking provision to create a new economic right separate from copyright or only to offer additional protection to an underlying copyrighted work?

In fact, Chamberlain argues that the computer code itself, that is, the door-opening code protected by the rolling code, was copyrightable. In its request for summary judgment, Chamberlain revealed that it, too, offers for sale universally compatible remotes intended to work with openers sold by other companies, but that it draws the line at offering a remote capable of defeating the rolling code systems manufactured by its competitors, such as Genie. It is of interest that, in this same document, Chamberlain's discussion of the harm caused by Skylink centers around the damage caused to the market for Chamberlain's universal remotes, specifically recounting how Skylink undercut the exclusive aftermarket remote provider relationship Chamberlain had enjoyed with Lowe's home improvement stores.

In her ruling denying Chamberlain's request for summary judgment, District Court Judge Rebecca Pallmeyer found that there were significant noninfringing uses for the Skylink remotes beyond defeating the rolling code system, since Skylink remotes interoperate with a number of other garage door systems, not just

Chamberlain's. She also found that there were reasons to doubt whether Chamberlain had clearly demonstrated that the computer code was copyrighted. Although Chamberlain had filed registration papers with the US Copyright Office, the version of its code actually in use at the time it went to court against Skylink was different from that listed in the filed application. Furthermore, she found that owners of garage door openers are implicitly authorized to circumvent any protection measures on a number of grounds: that this is the established practice in the marketplace; that Chamberlain itself had participated in this market; and that Chamberlain had failed to notify consumers on product packaging or elsewhere that only Chamberlain-approved opening remotes could be used with their openers. She found, therefore, that Chamberlain had failed to meet another standard of section 1201(a), that access was effectively prohibited.

Chamberlain appealed, but the Federal Circuit upheld the lower court's decision. The Federal Circuit took a slightly different view of the case, namely that Chamberlain's claim had no merit because they had failed to prove any connection between the device and actual copyright infringement:

> The anti-circumvention and anti-trafficking provisions of the DMCA create new grounds of liability. A copyright owner seeking to impose liability on an accused circumventor must demonstrate a reasonable relationship between the circumvention at issue and a use relating to a property right for which the Copyright Act permits the copyright owner to withhold authorization—as well as notice that authorization was withheld. A copyright owner seeking to impose liability on an accused trafficker must demonstrate that the trafficker's device enables either copyright infringement or a prohibited circumvention. Here, the District Court correctly ruled that Chamberlain pled no connection between unauthorized use of its copyrighted software and Skylink's accused transmitter.

Even though, on its face, the case seems almost ridiculous and it is hard to imagine that Congress would have intended copyright law to be used to protect garage door openers, the appellate decision in the *Chamberlain v. Skylink* case seems to instruct us that liability for the act of circumvention can only be considered if there is an actual copyright violation as well. The ruling therefore ties the acts in section 1201(a) much more closely to the traditionally protected rights of the copyright holder than they would seem to be linked in a straightforward reading of the law. According to the logic applied in the Skylink case: if no unauthorized access and no copyright infringement, then no trafficking liability. This is a very different conclusion from the one drawn in other cases, such as *321 Studios*, where a software company was found to be in violation of the anti-trafficking provisions, when they were considered on their own and not in conjunction with any acts of unauthorized access or copyright infringement.

EFF v. Sony BMG, Cal. Sup. Ct. Los Angeles Cty. (2005).

One of the central problems with DRM is that it sometimes does not operate in line with expectations. DRM sometimes imposes onerous use restrictions, requires laborious effort on the part of users, or presents unexpected (and perhaps unintended) consequences. Especially troubling are DRM aspects that are buried in the background in ways that lack transparency. *EFF v. Sony BMG* illustrates many of these serious issues.

Throughout the first five years of the new millennium, the recording industry's distress about explosive growth of (often illegal) online music downloading and concurrent, multiyear losses in traditional album sales drove it to continue a feverish search for technical solutions to the piracy problem. The Recording Industry Association of America (RIAA) took a leading role in a number of legal battles with major peer-to-peer software providers and networks, and even took the step of bringing suits against individuals alleged to be major file traders. New media formats like the Super Audio CD (SACD) and Digital Audio Tape (DAT), which both had stronger copy protection than regular audio CDs, were effectively "dead on arrival," neither embraced nor adopted by consumers in sufficient numbers to create a real market. Initiatives like the Secure Digital Music Initiative (SDMI) failed to gather enough industry support to take off, possibly due to a lack of confidence in the DRM following its widely publicized defeat by Ed Felten and his team, although it is possible that licensing terms and standardization of devices would have been as daunting had the project matured.

In October 2005, programmer Mark Russinovich discovered a strange piece of software on his computer, and after some diligent research, he discovered it to be a "rootkit" that had been installed without his knowledge when he placed a Sony CD into his computer. The software cloaked certain files and directories on the computer to mask itself, and when Russinovich attempted to manually remove the offending code, it disabled his CD player (Russinovich). He posted a blow-by-blow account of his detective work, and the story quickly spread through mainstream media. Although it admitted being the source of the software, Sony was slow to release updates that effectively and easily reversed the effects of the rootkit, and at first released patches that actually put users at risk for further and more severe damage to their systems. In a widely quoted interview with National Public Radio, Sony executive Thomas Hesse perfectly epitomized the company's tepid response: "Most people, I think, don't even know what a rootkit is, so why should they care about it?" (Hesse). Within a few weeks of the discovery, malicious viruses exploiting the file-hiding features of the Sony software were discovered. "'This is no longer a theoretical vulnerability; it is a real vulnerability,' said Sam Curry, vice president of Computer Associates' eTrust Security Management division. 'This is no longer about digital rights management or content protection, this is about people having their PCs taken over'" (Borland).

The software Sony clumsily installed, called XCP and developed by a Sony partner, First4Internet, was originally intended to prevent users from burning unlimited CD copies of an original audio CD, and to require them to use a media player packaged with the CD rather than a player already present on the user's computer. Speaking to reporters about First4Internet's software in July 2005, prior to the detection of the rootkit problems, Thomas Hesse, president of global digital business for Sony BMG, said: "The casual piracy, the schoolyard piracy, is a huge issue for us. Two-thirds of all piracy comes from ripping and burning CDs, which is why making the CD a secure format is of the utmost importance" (Delahunty).

Within a few weeks of the initial news about XCP, news of another Sony DRM technology, MediaMax, surfaced. While not as difficult to get rid of or as potentially dangerous to users' computers as was XCP, MediaMax installed itself on the users' computers even if the user answered "no" to the user agreement. MediaMax was suspected of collecting and transmitting information about user activity back to Sony. In the news reports and the litigation that followed, Sony's vague and misleading End User License Agreements received the bulk of the criticism. The Electronic Frontier Foundation and the state attorneys general from Texas and California filed a class action suit against Sony, eventually settling for the cost of replacing CDs and for $622,000 in damages in the state cases. Speaking after the settlement, California Attorney General Bill Lockyer said, "Companies that want to load their CDs with software that limits the ability to copy music should fully inform consumers about it, not hide it, and make sure it doesn't inflict security vulnerabilities on computers" (Kelzer). Sony ceased the manufacture and distribution of audio CDs containing the XCP and the MediaMax technologies.

Gawronski v. Amazon.com, Inc., Case No. 2:09-cv-01084-JCC (W.D. Wash.), Dkt. No. 1, Jul. 30, 2009.

In a class action case that was quickly settled, *Gawronski v. Amazon.com, Inc.*, Amazon faced significant negative publicity and customer dissatisfaction for using DRM to remove, without prior notification, reading material from users' devices. The incident underscores some of the worst fears over DRM; that moving most media content to digital files opens the door to technologically mediated, external controls.

In mid-July 2009, Amazon used remote DRM to remove some eBooks from customers' Kindle e-readers. The books, including *1984*, were written by George Orwell. Amazon later returned the cost of the eBooks and said the removals were required when it learned that the publisher from whom they had acquired the texts did not have the proper rights to sell the books in the US (Jones, "Who Took My Book").

Subsequently (July 30, 2009), Justin Gawronski, a teenager from Michigan who was reading *1984* for a school assignment, and Antoine Bruguier of California, brought a class action lawsuit against Amazon.com in US District Court in the Western District of Washington. The plaintiffs:

> claimed that Amazon.com harmed them by taking away their property—the e-book files—and also claimed that they had lost valuable electronic marginal notes (such as "remember this paragraph for your thesis"), which were useless without the corresponding files. The complaint alleged that Amazon.com had breached its own terms of service by deleting the files. The complaint also claimed trespass to chattels and a violation of the Computer Fraud and Abuse Act. (Sanders 538–39)

Amazon settled the case before trial via an agreement that restored the margin notes to people who lost them via the file deletion. Amazon also paid the plaintiffs $150,000 in lawyer's fees; the lawyers donated a portion of the money to various causes associated with literacy and children (Sanders 538–39).

Learning Objectives and Discussion Questions

- Detail the legal structures that enforce digital rights management. Can you:
  o Discuss the distinction between acts and tools in terms of anti-circumvention regulation and implications for both consumers and rights holders;
  o Discuss specific cases where digital rights management has succeeded or failed?

CHAPTER TEN

Intellectual Property Law in Virtual Worlds and Games Cases

Cases Involving Virtual Worlds and Games

Bragg v. Linden Research, Inc. and Philip Rosedale, No. 06–4925, USDC (E.D. Pa., May 30, 2007).

Bragg v. Linden Research, Inc. and Philip Rosedale began as a dispute over virtual land, virtual property, and virtual value between Second Life (SL) proprietors Linden Lab (LL), and Bragg, a resident-entrepreneur. The case developed into a dispute about that property and over Linden Lab's terms of service (ToS) for SL.

    Bragg v. Linden began when LL excluded Mr. Bragg from SL and confiscated his virtual holdings for an alleged violation of the ToS. Mr. Bragg was accused of leveraging land sale auctions in SL to his advantage. His virtual property was taken/revoked, at an estimated value of about $5,000 US.[1] Bragg used the ToS to claim that (a) the ToS specified/assured that the virtual property was his, that (b) Linden Lab's in-world adjudication procedures were inadequate, such that (c) his virtual property was seized without due process.

    Bragg filed the case in a Pennsylvania state court in October 2006, but the case was moved to federal court in November 2006 and was heard by Judge Eduardo Robreno. In May 2007, Robreno ruled in favor of Bragg, and in doing so, virtually invalidated the ToS as legally binding, as well as agreeing that the internal appeal and adjudication procedures that Linden Lab uses in SL are woefully inadequate ("2nd Life: Judge Rules"). He defined the ToS as an unenforceable "contract of adhesion," so allowed the case (Bragg's claim that the ToS gave him ownership of his virtual property) to go forward (LL had asked for dismissal). Judge Robreno repeated his ruling on a second action (a LL motion to compel arbitration) by denying arbitration.

At least three things resulted (or may result) from this case: (1) LL settled with Bragg (undisclosed terms) for what was thought to be a return of his virtual property, (2) LL immediately changed its ToS to redefine ownership, making it clear that LL owns everything in and about SL. This illustrates the slippery slope within proprietary virtual environments. While the Court's action did have a short-term and limited effect (the value of Bragg's holdings was returned to him), the company merely went into its rules and changed them, in effect obviating the long-term outcome of the Court's ruling, and (3) in another way, this ruling could have a long-term effect if other courts use it as precedent for invalidating similar shrink wrap/click-through contracts and ToS—courts have often upheld software shrink wrap/click-through contracts and ToS as binding. However, "everyone knows" that virtually no one reads software fine print. With packaged goods, these agreements are contained within software packaging such that consumers can't read them before they've "agreed" by opening the package; online, the agreements often appear via pop-up windows through which users seldom read before clicking the "I agree" button so they can get on with their current/wanted activities. In almost all cases, the agreements consist of numerous lengthy paragraphs of overly legalistic technical terminology. There is a legal principle in contract law that holds that inaccessible contract terms may be less than legally binding. The rulings in *Bragg v. Linden* may provide fodder for judicial reinterpretations of the status of software and/or online shrink wrap/click-through contracts and ToS.

Eros, LLC, et al. v. Simon, et al., 1:07-cv-04447-SLT-JMA. USDC (E.D.N.Y. Oct. 24, 2007).

Eros, LLC v. Robert Leatherwood and John 1–10 Does, 8:2007cv01158. (M.D. Fla. July 3, 2007).

Copyrights can be compromised in virtual worlds that allow users to create content. *Eros, LLC, et al. v. Simon, et al.*, and *Eros, LLC v. Robert Leatherwood and John 1–10 Does* are cases featuring litigation by plaintiffs claiming that defendants infringed copyrights by making copies and selling protected content in SL.

Eros, LLC, et al. v. Simon, et al., 1:07-cv-04447-SLT-JMA. USDC (E.D.N.Y. Oct. 24, 2007).

Six SL content creators filed a lawsuit in the New York Federal District Court, claiming copyright and trademark infringement against Thomas Simon (and unnamed others). Simon (known as Rase Kenzo in SL) allegedly exploited a flaw in the SL software to duplicate thousands of copies of Eros's products. Simon settled the case for about $600.00 after initially turning down an offered settlement that would have cost him ten times that much (Dannenberg).

Eros, LLC v. Robert Leatherwood and John 1–10 Does, 8:2007cv01158. (M.D. Fla. July 3, 2007).

Eros LLC pursued another suit, this time against an SL resident known as Catteneo. Eros LLC accused Catteneo of illicitly copying and selling an animated "virtual sex" bed for as little as L$4,000, a price that sharply undercut Eros's price. On September 6, 2007, a motion to subpoena AT&T and Charter Communications for the RL identity of Catteneo was granted. Eros made similar requests of LL and PayPal. Eventually (via the subpoenas and detective work), Eros "established" that Catteneo was Robert Leatherwood of Texas; however, the nineteen-year-old denied being Catteneo for a time. A default judgment was entered against Leatherwood by the District Court for the Middle District of Florida, as through his denials of being Catteneo he did not attend the hearings.

By March 2008, Leatherwood admitted owning the account and settled with Eros. The terms were not announced but were thought to be a mere agreement to cease and desist from further commerce using the materials that Eros had created.

Estavillo v. Sony Computer Entertainment America, 2009 WL 3072887 (N.D. Cal. Sept. 22, 2009).

Venue is a crucial legal issue, as are claims about constitutional protection of First Amendment free speech rights. *Estavillo v. Sony Computer Entertainment America* made clear that courts do not yet treat virtual worlds as real places (no jurisdiction applies), such that private game companies cannot violate free speech by removing players from their games, forums, or networks.

Eric Estavillo was removed from Sony's PlayStation 3 network; Sony accused him of violating their ToS in some forum posts. Plaintiff sued for violation of his First Amendment free speech rights and for some contract claims. The court granted Sony's request for dismissal, indicating that Sony's virtual game network is not a governmental entity, therefore, Estavillo did not have a valid First Amendment cause for action (Goldman, "Online Game Network").

Abreu v. Slide, Inc., 12 0042 WHA (N.D. Cal.; July 12, 2012).

Although a small number of cases (including the previously cited *Bragg v. Linden*) indicate that courts are willing to rule that ToS and EULAs may be overly broad or unfair, generally ToS, EULAs, shrink wrap, and click-through contracts survive and empower game proprietors. *Abreu v. Slide, Inc.* is an example of many cases where aspects of ToS are upheld in ways that strongly advantage game companies.

SuperPoke is a game developed by Slide (later purchased by Google). Players took care of virtual pets; virtual coins enabled commerce and reward systems. Christalee Abreu sued on behalf of a potential class of players whose accounts were nullified after Google closed the game. The class claimed to have invested "hundreds or thousands" of dollars in virtual goods that lost value after the game was closed. At one point in the filings, Google claimed that players' losses might amount (when totaled) to more than $5 million. Plaintiffs sought the right to litigate against Google rather than be forced into the arbitration procedures specified in the ToS.

US District Court judge William Alsup ruled that any members in the class wanting judicial relief would have to adhere to the arbitration proceedings laid out in the ToS.

Hart v. Electronic Arts, 717 F.3d 141 (3rd Cir. 2013).

In re NCAA Student–Athlete Name & Likeness Licensing Litig., 724 F.3d 1268 (9th Cir. 2013).

These two cases illustrate a number of intellectual property principles as they relate to games and virtual worlds. First, they speak to the right of publicity, asking important questions about who controls those rights. Second, they speak to the right of publicity as it relates to virtual depictions of celebrity players, asking important questions about the degree of exactness in representation required to invoke a right of publicity. These cases are also part of a much broader set of issues than celebrity athletes' right of publicity within games and virtual worlds. The cases involve the rights of the NCAA and game companies to contract over, market, and benefit from, athletes' images after the players graduate from the college programs that control their images while they are students.

Recall that two right of publicity cases reflect on some of the issues considered here. *Cardtoons, L.C. v. Major League Baseball Players' Ass'n* established that appropriation of images is sometimes not an infringement, for example, when celebrity depictions on non-licensed baseball cards are parodies, because the parody earns both fair use and First Amendment protections. *CBC Distribution and Marketing, Inc. v. Major League Baseball Adv. Media* established that players' names and reports/records of their accomplishments (statistics) are not protectable via copyright. Neither of these cases makes comment as to the status of using, without the direct permission of the subject, visually similar characterizations in non-parodies, nor do these cases speak to the anti-trust issues that are raised by the NCAA's procurement and commercial, for-profit, use of those images.

The two cases at hand illustrate that courts in the US are not uniform or clear about relationships among the right of publicity in games and virtual worlds and the very same right in more traditional mediated entertainment and/or information contexts. According to Ochoa ("Rationalizing"):

> the fact that courts cannot yet articulate a consistent First Amendment standard that distinguishes between the literal depiction of a celebrity in a sports-simulation videogame and the literal depiction of a celebrity in a more traditional work of entertainment strongly suggests that courts simply do not place the same value on the videogame medium as they do on more traditional media.

Hart v. Electronic Arts, 717 F.3d 141 (3rd Cir. 2013).

In *Hart v. Electronic Arts*, a former college football player sued a game developer for using his likeness in a video game. The trial court decided that the company's use was protected by the First Amendment; the appellate court overruled, finding in favor of the plaintiff's right of publicity.

Ryan Hart played quarterback for the Rutgers football team and was depicted in an EA college football video game. Hart sued, claiming that the use infringed his right of publicity. As a matter of fact, there was little doubt that the depiction was based on Hart; EA used his (and other players') likeness to promote (and people) their game. EA claimed that the First Amendment protects the depiction; the trial court agreed. However, the Third Circuit Court of Appeals disagreed and reversed the ruling, setting the precedent that the First Amendment does not give game developers the right to appropriate images, regardless of the level of celebrity of the model.

In re NCAA Student-Athlete Name & Likeness Licensing Litig., 724 F.3d 1268 (9th Cir. 2013).

In re NCAA Student-Athlete Name & Likeness Licensing Litig. combines litigation brought by Sam Keller, Ed O'Bannon, and others and is part of a long-running series of litigation brought by former NCAA athletes. The cases involved a number of legal issues, including right of publicity, First Amendment rights, antitrust issues, and a number of other technical legal questions. At the base of these, however, are fundamental questions about the abilities of so-called student athletes to control their images and to profit from that control.

As was the case in *Hart v. Electronic Arts*, there is no material disagreement over the fact that former NCAA players were represented by avatars in video games enabling gamers to virtually become well-known former star athletes. The games were based and marketed around drawing fans from particular schools to play the game through the virtual actions of their college heroes.

The contentious issues focused on the fact that players are not compensated for their appearance in the video games. The NCAA, and its member schools, forbids players from profiting from activities during their time at school; prior to the decision in *Hart v. Electronic Arts*, those rights were also claimed for graduates as long as the representation was of their college persona. Neither the NCAA nor EA claimed the right to use Ed O'Bannon's persona dressed in a post-graduation uniform of, say, the New Jersey Nets, but they did continue to show the virtual O'Bannon dressed in a UCLA Bruin uniform long past the time that O'Bannon graduated and stopped playing college basketball. Plaintiffs claimed that these ongoing actions violated their right of publicity. They also claimed that the practices constitute collusion on the part of the NCAA and its member schools; the anti-trust aspect of the case has yet to be fully litigated.

Following the precedent in the *Hart v. Electronic Arts*, the trial court held that EA is not protected by the First Amendment; the decision was affirmed by the Ninth Circuit Court of Appeals.

Learning Objectives and Discussion Questions

- Detail the complexities inherent in applying terrestrial law to games and virtual worlds. Can you:
  - o Make arguments in favor of or against players' First Amendment free speech rights and in favor of and/or against game developers' First Amendment free speech rights in games and virtual worlds;
  - o Describe the multiple considerations when establishing jurisdiction over litigation involving games and virtual worlds;
  - o Discuss intellectual property ownership, rights assignment and management, and the multiple parties involved in games and virtual worlds?

- Detail the legal aspects that may require special treatment in games and virtual worlds or that may suggest the need for new laws. Can you:
  - o Represent the variety of positions concerning the roles of EULA, ToS, shrink wrap and click-through agreements (contract laws) as controlling vehicles in games and virtual worlds;
  - o Describe why providers of games and virtual worlds continue to claim safe harbor under the DMCA given the large amount of content they produce?

Notes

Chapter Three

1. Note that the system works—and is unforgiving. While investigating Amazon.com's site, one of the authors clicked the 1-click® button, and an unwanted book was on its way.
2. An example of such a standard-setting organization is the Universal Serial Bus (USB) Implementers Forum, an industry-standards body incorporating leading companies from the computer and electronics industries. Notable members have included Apple Computer, Hewlett-Packard, NEC, Microsoft, Intel, and Agere. USB is a serial bus standard to interface devices. It was designed for computers such as PCs and the Apple Macintosh; now, because of its popularity, it is used in numerous electronic devices such as video game consoles, PDAs, and cell phones.
3. In an appeal of *Apple Inc. v. Samsung Elecs. Co*, the Federal District Court in Northern California denied Apple's request for an injunction against certain models of Samsung's smartphones, even though Apple won patent infringement cases and received over $119M in damages. See Chen.

Chapter Seven

1. On appeal, although the Court of Appeals for the Ninth Circuit affirmed the finding that the defendant was entitled to summary judgment, the Court did so after it held that the defendant was not an "information content provider" as contemplated under the CDA, and

thus was immune from liability. See *Carafano v. Metrosplash.com, Inc.*, 339 F.3d 1119 (9th Cir. 2003).

Chapter Ten

1. That gamers look for exploits in games that improve users' performance and outcomes is almost gospel in the gaming community. In some ways, it's remarkable that Linden Lab found Bragg's behavior to be problematic. However, in this case, the outcome—Lindens—are a form of gaming credit that can be negotiated for real currency, so "rigging" the bidding process in land auctions was thought to be a serious violation and threat to the common order.

Glossary

1. Terms appearing in the glossary are not fully defined within the texts.

Works Cited

1. The Works Cited list appears in, and applies to, both volumes in the 2nd edition.

Cases

1. The case list appears in, and applies to, both volumes in the 2nd edition.

Glossary[1]

Legal Terminology

Answer: After the plaintiff files and serves a complaint, the defendant is granted a limited amount of time to answer each of the allegations in the complaint.

Anti-Circumvention: Legal constraints against "going around" (or hacking) the access, usage, and copy restrictions embedded within digital media content.

Briefs: The legal memoranda prepared by the parties and submitted to the court. Briefs contain the factual basis and legal theories of the parties' positions.

Click-Through Agreement: Presentation of Terms of Service and/or End-User License Agreement via automated buttons that enable the user to indicate awareness of, and agreement to, the contractual arrangements. Click-Through Agreements appear interactively in digital environments.

Common Law: Laws developed via judicial, rather than legislative, actions. Common laws are based on court rulings, decisions, and precedents.

Compulsory License: Governmental requirement that holders of certain kinds of intellectual property rights must grant use to others, generally in exchange for a royalty (but in the case of music in the US, the royalty is only required based on sales, not recording).

Concurring Opinion: Individual judges on appellate panels will, from time to time, issue their own concurring opinions when they feel a need to expound on a point of law or make a distinction of law that is not otherwise noted in the majority opinion. A concurrence does not have the force of law of a majority opinion, but it may help a particular judge establish a principle that may, in future cases, be built into a majority opinion.

Cybersquatting: Acquiring and holding a URL for the purpose of extracting payments for its use from parties with a more legitimate claim to the URL than the cybersquatter.

Default Judgment: Judgment in favor of the plaintiff when the defendant fails to appear before a court (or answer a summons).

Digital Rights Management (*DRM*): Technology that enforces a restriction on the use of digital content.

Dissenting Opinion: One or more judges in the minority may choose to write a dissenting opinion that elaborates on the reasons why the minority believes the majority opinion is incorrect. While some dissenting opinions read a bit like "sour grapes," not infrequently, as the law evolves, what started as a minority opinion may in later times shift to become the majority opinion of an appellate court.

Doctrine of Equivalents: In patent law, an infringement need not be an "exact" or "word-for-word" copy in order to be "equivalent" and infringe.

End-User License Agreement (*EULA*): Contractual stipulation and specification for the ownership relationships inherent in the use of technologies. Generally specifies ways that the company retains ownership while the consumer is allowed to use the technology under certain conditions.

Fifth Amendment Rights: Against self-incrimination; sets out the rules for grand jury indictments.

First Amendment Rights: Include freedom of speech, freedom of the press, freedom of religion, right to assemble peaceably, right to petition the government.

Fourth Amendment Rights: Against unreasonable search and seizure.

"Magic Circle" Test: Deciding whether a virtual world is so much a "game" that it is, or should be, protected from intrusion by "out-of-game" elements (such as laws).

Majority: In appellate courts, which generally contain panels of judges (three to nine), when there is not unanimity in decision-making, the majority of justices who agree issue a majority opinion that becomes the binding law (stands as precedent).

Minority: As noted above, the minority is the portion of an appellate panel that has fewer votes for its position and, ultimately, does not prevail in setting new law.

Natural Rights: The concept of a universal right inherent in the nature of living beings. An idea developed by Thomas Hobbes and others, natural rights are taken as not contingent upon beliefs or laws. Some cultures consider intellectual property rights to have natural rights foundations.

Personal Jurisdiction: The inherent power of a court to compel a litigant to appear before it. The rules concerning personal jurisdiction are complex and, at times, inconsistent, but they center around whether a party (usually a defendant) has had sufficient contact with the forum where the court is located to allow the court to compel the defendant to appear.

Postmortem Right: A right that adheres (to the deceased or the person's estate) after death.

Prosecution History Estoppel: Patent applicants who make amendments to their applications (to avoid infringing previous patents) cannot make infringement claims based on the pre-amendment patent terms (that were later amended).

Public Domain: Materials that are not owned or controlled by anyone and that may be freely used by all. Sometimes referred to as "the Commons," as the material is held "in common" by the people of a given area, government, or jurisdiction.

Shrink-Wrap Agreements: Presentation of Terms of Service and/or End-User License Agreement via declarations of the contractual arrangements. Shrink-Wrap Agreements are printed on or within software packaging and generally are effective after "breaking the seal" or opening the package.

Subject Matter Jurisdiction: In addition to having power to compel parties to appear, courts must also have jurisdiction to hear the subject matter of the dispute. In certain types of intellectual property disputes, patents and copyrights for example, the federal courts (as opposed to state courts) have exclusive subject matter jurisdiction to hear these types of cases.

Termination: Curtailing rights. In the case of copyright, the process for certain creators to recover rights they gave up early in their careers.

Terms of Service (ToS): Contractual stipulations and specifications for using technologies.

Tort: A civil wrong that causes someone to suffer a loss or damage. Tort infractions are sometimes less than fully intentional; negligence can produce tort liabilities, as can intentional harms. Criminal acts can include tort liabilities, but the tort aspects are adjudicated in civil, not criminal, courts and cases.

Triennial Rulemaking: Every three years the US Copyright Office reexamines exemptions from the Copyright Act and (especially), the DMCA portions.

Media and New Media Terminology

Anti-Circumvention: Prohibitions against technologies for defeating digital rights management.

Cache: Temporary storage area in a computer's memory system where frequently accessed data can be kept for rapid access. Various cache locations contain copies of information, limiting the need to retrieve new originals.

Commons: The "space" where materials in "the Public Domain" reside. Citizens share ownership and control of the materials in "the Commons."

Creative Commons: Organization, website, and protocols that enable content creators (copyright holders) to parse their rights, thereby indicating acceptable ways for others to use the materials.

Hacker/Hacking: Discovering vulnerabilities and/or exploiting them within computing systems and networks via technological skill and creativity.

Inworld: Term designating the presence of the user or content within a game or virtual world. Sometimes contrasted to being in the "real world," "off line," or "meatspace."

Machinima: Real-time videos capturing activities on computer screens. Often developed by game or virtual world participants, or fans, as a way to capture game play or to tell stories cinematically.

Massively Multiplayer Online Role-Playing Game (MMORPG): Computer-based role-playing games featuring a large number of players interacting in an online virtual space.

Media Commodification: The notion that commercial media turn members of the audience into "the product" via the process of setting a value on their media consumption and then "selling" them to advertisers based on the size or features of the potential or actual audience for a given media item.

Peer-to-Peer Networks (P2P): Distributed computer networks (usually between "lay" participants rather than governmental or formal businesses) using diverse connectivity and cumulative bandwidth rather than centralized servers and network facilities. Uses peer nodes rather than "clients" and "servers." P2P networks are generally facilitated by special software.

Prosumers: Citizen new media participants who produce media content in addition to consuming it.

RAM: Random access memory is the writable and, generally, volatile memory in computers and storage devices.

Reverse Engineering: Discovering the (inner) workings of (patented) devices by disassembly, observation, and trial-and-error.

Works Cited[1]

"About ARIPO." *African Regional Intellectual Property Organization.* <http://www.aripo.org/index.php/about-aripo>. WEB 24 July, 2014.

"About Google Patent Search." *Google.* <https://support.google.com/faqs/answer/2539193?hl=en>. WEB 15 December, 2013.

"A Call to Improve Intellectual Property Rights of Developing Countries." *Science in Africa,* October, 2002. <http://scienceinafrica.com/policy/call-improve-intellectual-property-rights-developing-countries>. WEB 14 July, 2014.

ADNDRC: Asian Domain Name Dispute Resolution Centre. <http://www.adndrc.org/>. WEB 25 November, 2013.

Ahmed, Azam. "Former Goldman Programmer Gets 8-year Jail Term for Code Theft." *New York Times,* March 18, 2011. <http://dealbook.nytimes.com/2011/03/18/ex-goldman-programmer-sentenced-to-8-years-for-theft-of-trading-code/>. WEB 24 February, 2014.

Almeling, David S. "Seven Reasons Why Trade Secrets Are Increasingly Important." *Berkeley Technology Law Journal* 27 (2012): 1091–1118. <http://btlj.org/data/articles/27_2/1091_1118_Almeling_WEB_110612.pdf>. WEB 24 February, 2014.

"A Long Way to Privacy Safeguards." *New York Times,* May 11, 2014. <http://www.nytimes.com/2014/05/12/opinion/a-long-way-to-privacy-safeguards.html>. WEB 15 April, 2015.

"Alternative Dispute Resolution." *World Intellectual Property Organization.* <http://www.wipo.int/amc/en/index.html>. WEB 25 November, 2013.

Ambrosi, Alain, Valérie Peugeot, and Daniel Pimienta. *Word Matters: Multicultural Perspectives on Information Societies.* Caen, France: C & F Éditions, 2005. Print.

American Law Institute. "Definition of Trade Secret." *Restatement (Third) of Unfair Competition Current through June 2009*. Chapter 4. Appropriation of Trade Values Topic 2. Trade Secrets § 39. <http://www.wipo.int/wipolex/en/text.jsp?file_id=194019#LinkTarget_471>. WEB 1 September, 2014.

———. "Overview, Institute Projects." <http://www.ali.org/index.cfm?fuseaction=about.instituteprojects>. WEB 16 November, 2013.

———. *Restatement of the Law of Torts*: As Adopted and Promulgated by the American Law Institute. Washington, DC, 1939. Print.

———. *Restatement of the Law Second, Torts:* As Adopted and Promulgated by the American Law Institute. Washington, DC, 1965. Print.

———. *Restatement of the Law (3d) of Unfair Competition:* As Adopted and Promulgated by the American Law Institute. Washington, DC, 1995. Print.

American Library Association. "Appeals Court Shoots Holes in FCC's Broadcast Flag Rule." *American Libraries* 36.6 (2005): 17. Print.

Anderson, Chris. "The Long Tail." *Wired* October, 2004: 170–77. Print.

Anderson, Nate. "How a Mayor's Quest to Unmask a Foul-Mouthed Twitter User Blew up in His Face." *ars technica*, May 13, 2014. <http://arstechnica.com/tech-policy/2014/05/how-a-mayors-quest-to-unmask-a-foul-mouthed-twitter-user-blew-up-in-his-face/>. WEB 16 May, 2014.

_____. "Piracy Problems? US Copyright Industries Show Terrific Health." *ars technica*, November 2, 2011. <http://arstechnica.com/tech-policy/2011/11/piracy-problems-us-copyright-industries-show-terrific-health/>. WEB 16 November, 2013.

_____. "Pirate Bay Verdict: Guilty, with Jail Time." *ars technica*, April 17, 2009. <http://arstechnica.com/tech-policy/2009/04/the-pirate-bay-verdict-guilty-with-jail-time/>. WEB 16 November, 2013.

_____. "US Government Finally Admits Most Piracy Estimates Are Bogus." *ars technica*, April 13, 2010. <http://arstechnica.com/tech-policy/2010/04/us-government finally-admits-most-piracy-estimates-are-bogus/>. WEB 16 November, 2013.

"Apple Inc." *Wikipedia*. <http://en.wikipedia.org/wiki/Apple_Computer#Notable_litigation>. WEB 16 November, 2013.

"Ask Patents." *Stack Exchange*. <https://patents.stackexchange.com/tour>. WEB 31 August, 2014.

Bailey, Jonathan. "The Messy World of Fan Art and Copyright." *Plagiarism Today*, May 3, 2010. <https://www.plagiarismtoday.com/2010/05/13/the-messy-world-of-fan-art-and-copyright/>. WEB 14 August, 2014.

Balasubramani, Venkat. "1st Circuit Reinstates $675,000 File-Sharing Award against Tenenbaum — Sony BMG v. Tenenbaum." *Technology & Marketing Law Blog*. September 20, 2011. <http://blog.ericgoldman.org/archives/2011/09/1st_circuit_rei.htm>. WEB 24 November, 2013.

_____. "First Sale Doctrine Doesn't Allow Resale of Digital Songs – Capitol Records v. ReDigi." April 5, 2013. *Technology & Marketing Law Blog*. <http://blog.ericgoldman.org/archives/2013/04/first_sale_doct.htm>. WEB 26 November, 2013.

Baron, Steven L., Edward Lee Lamoureux, and Claire Stewart. *Case Analyses for Intellectual Property Law and New Media*. New York, NY: Peter Lang, 2015. Print.

Barry, Chris, Ronen Arad, Landan Ansell, and Evan Clark. "2013 Patent Litigation Study." <http://www.pwc.com/en_US/us/forensic-services/publications/assets/2013-patent-litigation-study.pdf>. WEB 31 December, 2013.

Beebe, Barton. "An Empirical Study of U.S. Copyright Fair Use Opinions, 1978–2005. *University of Pennsylvania Law Review* 156.3 (2008): 549–624. Print.

Berlin Declaration. October, 2003. <http://openaccess.mpg.de/286432/Berlin-Declaration>. WEB 15 July, 2014.

Bessler, Abigail. "Obama Signs Bill 'Unlocking' Cell Phones." *CBS News*, August 1, 2014. <http://www.cbsnews.com/news/obama-signs-bill-unlocking-cellphones/>. WEB 5 October, 2014.

Bethesda Statement on Open Access Publishing. June, 2003. <http://legacy.earlham.edu/~peters/fos/bethesda.htm>. WEB 15 July, 2014.

Black, Sharon. *Telecommunications Law in the Internet Age*. San Francisco, CA: Morgan Kaufmann Publishers/Academic Press, 2002. Print.

Blank, Rebecca M., and David J. Kappos. *Intellectual Property and the U.S. Economy: Industries in Focus*. Economics and Statistics Administration and United States Patent and Trademark Office. March 2012. <http:/www.uspto.gov/news/publications/IP_Report_March_2012.pdf>. WEB 3 July, 2014.

Blankenhorn, Dana. "Apps Versus Applications." *ZDNet*. April 16, 2010. <http://www.zdnet.com/blog/open-source/apps-versus-applications/6286>. WEB 16 November, 2013.

Blascovich, Jim, and Jeremy Bailenson. *Infinite Reality: Avatars, Eternal Life, New Worlds, and the Dawn of the Virtual Revolution*. New York, NY: Harper/Collins, 2011. Print.

The Bluebook: A Uniform System of Citation. 19th ed. The Harvard Law Review Association, (2010). Print.

Blum, Andrew. *Tubes: A Journey to the Center of the Internet*. New York, NY: HarperCollins Publishers, 2012. Print.

"Blurring the Lines: IP in a Virtual World." *World Intellectual Property Review*, January 9, 2013. <http://www.worldipreview.com/article/blurring-the-lines-ip-in-a-virtual-world>. WEB 23 March, 2015.

Bohn, Roger, and James Short. "Measuring Consumer Information." *International Journal of Communication* 6 (2012): 980–1000. <http://ijoc.org/index.php/ijoc/article/viewFile/1566/743>. WEB 16 November, 2013.

Bollier, David. *Public Assets, Private Profits: Reclaiming the American Commons in an Age of Market Enclosure*. Washington, DC: New America Foundation, 2001. Print.

Borland, John. "'Bots' for Sony CD Software Spotted Online." *CNet.com*, November 10, 2005. <http://news.cnet.com/Bots-for-Sony-CD-software-spotted-online/2100-1029_3-5944643.html>. WEB 23 November, 2013.

Bowman, Lisa M. "Elcomsoft Verdict: Not Guilty." *CNet.com*, December 17, 2002. <http://news.cnet.com/2100-1023-978176.html>. WEB 23 November, 2013.

Boyette, Randi. "Words that Hurt—And Kill." *ADL.org*. <http://archive.adl.org/ADL_Opinions/Education/20071213-op-ed.htm>. WEB 23 November, 2013.

Branscomb, Anne Wells. "Cyberspaces: Familiar Territory or Lawless Frontiers." *Journal of Computer-Mediated Communication* 2.1 (June, 1996). <http://onlinelibrary.wiley.com/doi/10.1111/j.1083-6101.1996.tb00053.x/full>. WEB 12 October, 2014.

Bray, Hiawatha. "Hackers Go One Up." *The Boston Globe*, October 26, 2000. 3rd ed., sec. Business. Print.

Bright, Peter. "Driven by Necessity, Mozilla to Enable HTML5 DRM in Firefox." *ars technica*, May 14, 2014. <http://arstechnica.com/information-technology/2014/05/driven-by-necessity-mozilla-to-enable-html5-drm-in-firefox/>. WEB 7 October, 2014.

Brinckerhoff, Courtenay C. "A Look at the USPTO Backlog Statistics." September 19, 2013. <http://www.foley.com/a-look-at-the-uspto-backlog-statistics-09-19-2013/>. WEB 15 December, 2013.

Brodkin, Jon. "How Linux Defenders Attack Bad Software Patents before They're Approved." *ars technica*, September 17, 2013. <http://arstechnica.com/tech-policy/2013/09/how-linux-defenders-attack-software-patents-before-theyre-approved/>. WEB 28 September, 2014.

_____. "In World of Copyright Craziness, BitTorrent, Inc. Soars to New Heights." *ars technica*, February 9, 2012. <http://arstechnica.com/gadgets/2012/02/in-world-of-copyright-craziness-bittorrent-inc-soars-to-new-heights/>. WEB 23 November, 2013.

Brown, Melissa A. "Copyright Exceptions for Libraries in the Digital Age: U.S. Copyright Office Considers Reform of Section 108, Highlights of the Symposium." *College & Research Libraries News* 74.4 (2013): 199–214. Print.

Budapest Open Access Initiative. *Read the Budapest Open Access Initiative*. February 14, 2002. <http://www.budapestopenaccessinitiative.org/read>. WEB 15 July, 2014.

Buedel, Matt. "ACLU Details Suit against City; Ardis Exploring Counter Legal Action." *Journal Star*, June 12, 2014. <http://www.pjstar.com/article/20140612/NEWS/140619670>. WEB 16 June, 2014.

Bunker, Matthew D. "Eroding Fair Use: The 'Transformative' Use Doctrine after Campbell." *Communication Law and Policy* 7 (2002): 1–24. Print.

Busch, Richard. "Artists to Labels: 'HASTA LA VISTA, BABY!'" *Forbes*, March 5, 2012. <http://www.forbes.com/sites/richardbusch/2012/03/05/artists-to-labels-hasta-la-vista-baby/>. WEB 25 November, 2013.

_____. "Battle over Copyright Termination—and the First Round Goes to ..." *Forbes*, June 12, 2012. <http://www.forbes.com/sites/richardbusch/2012/06/12/the-battle-over-copyright-termination-and-the-first-round-goes-to/>. WEB 25 November, 2013.

Caplan, Brian D. "Navigating US Copyright Termination Rights." *wipo.int*. August, 2012. <http://www.wipo.int/wipo_magazine/en/2012/04/article_0005.html>. WEB 15 September, 2014.

Carroll, John. "Intellectual Property Rights in the Middle East: A Cultural Perspective." *Fordham Intellectual Property, Media and Entertainment Law Journal* 11.3 (2001): 555–600. <http://ir.lawnet.fordham.edu/cgi/viewcontent.cgi?article=1222&context=iplj>. WEB 25 July, 2014.

Castronova, Edward. *Exodus to the Virtual World: How Online Fun Is Changing Reality*. New York, NY: Palgrave Macmillan, 2007. Print.

————. *Synthetic Worlds: The Business and Culture of Online Games*. Chicago, IL: University of Chicago Press, 2005. Print.

CBC News. "$675K Music-Sharing Fine Left Intact By U.S. Top Court." *cbcnews*, May 21, 2012. <http://www.cbc.ca/news/arts/story/2012/05/21/riaa-lawsuit-copyright-filesharing-p2p.html>. WEB 23 November, 2013.

Centanni, Jillian A. "Trade Secrets Litigation: DuPont Wins Property from U.S. Subsidiary as Part of Its $920M Damages Award against the Parent." *Gibbons IP Law Alert*, April 16, 2013. <http://www.iplawalert.com/2013/04/articles/trade-secret/trade-secrets-litigation-dupont-wins-property-from-u-s-subsidiary-as-part-of-its-920m-damages-award-against-the-parent/>. WEB 24 February, 2014.

Center for Media & Social Impact. "Best Practices in Fair Use of Dance-Related Materials." (2009). <http://www.cmsimpact.org/fair-use/best-practices/best-practices-fair-use-dance-related-materials>. WEB 15 September, 2014.

————. "Code of Best Practices in Fair Use for Academic and Research Libraries." (2012). <http://www.cmsimpact.org/fair-use/best-practices/code-best-practices-fair-use-academic-and-research-libraries>. WEB 15 September, 2014.

————. "Code of Best Practices in Fair Use for Media Literacy Education." (2009). <http://www.cmsimpact.org/fair-use/best-practices/code-best-practices-fair-use-media-literacy-education>. WEB 15 September, 2014.

————. "Code of Best Practices in Fair Use for Online Video." (2008). <http://www.cmsimpact.org/fair-use/best-practices/code-best-practices-fair-use-online-video>. WEB 15 September, 2014.

————. "Code of Best Practices in Fair Use for OpenCourseWare." (2009). <http://www.cmsimpact.org/fair-use/best-practices/code-best-practices-fair-use-opencourseware>. WEB 15 September, 2014.

————. "Code of Best Practices in Fair Use for Poetry." (2011). <http://www.cmsimpact.org/fair-use/best-practices/code-best-practices-fair-use-poetry>. WEB 15 September, 2014.

————. "Code of Best Practices in Fair Use for Scholarly Research in Communication." (2010). <http://www.cmsimpact.org/fair-use/best-practices/code-best-practices-fair-use-scholarly-research-communication>. WEB 15 September, 2014.

————. "Documentary Filmmakers' Statement of Best Practices in Fair Use." (2005). <http://www.cmsimpact.org/fair-use/best-practices/documentary-filmmakers-statement-best-practices-fair-use>. WEB 15 September, 2014.

————. "Report on Orphan Works Challenges: For libraries, Archives, and Other Memory Institutions." (2013). <http://www.cmsimpact.org/fair-use/related-materials/documents/report-orphan-works-challenges-libraries-archives-and-other-mem>. WEB 15 September, 2014.

————. "Set of Principles in Fair Use for Journalism." (2013). <http://www.cmsimpact.org/fair-use/best-practices/set-principles-fair-use-journalism>. WEB 15 September, 2014.

————. "Society for Cinema and Media Studies' Statement of Best Practices in Fair Use in Teaching for Film and Media Educators." (2008). <http://www.cmsimpact.org/fair-use/best-practices/society-cinema-and-media-studies-statement-best-practices-fair-use-teaching->. WEB 15 September, 2014.

———. "Society for Cinema and Media Studies' Statement of Fair Use Best Practices for Media Studies Publishing." *n.d.* <http://www.cmsimpact.org/fair-use/best-practices/society-cinema-and-media-studies-statement-fair-use-best-practices-media-stu>. WEB 15 September, 2014.

———. "Statement of the Fair Use of Images for Teaching, Research, and Study." *n.d.* <http://www.cmsimpact.org/fair-use/best-practices/statement-fair-use-images-teaching-research-and-study>. WEB 15 September, 2014.

Center for the Study of the Public Domain, Duke Law School. "Orphan Works Analysis and Proposal." Duke Law School, 2005. <http://www.law.duke.edu/cspd/pdf/cspdproposal.pdf>. WEB 24 November, 2013.

Chang, Steve. "The Ten Most Important Video Game Patents." *Gamasutra.* <http://www.gamasutra.com/view/feature/130152/the_ten_most_important_video_game_.php>. WEB 10 August, 2014.

Chen, Brian X. "Apple Appeals Judge's Decision to Deny a Ban on Samsung Products." *New York Times,* August 29, 2014. <http://bits.blogs.nytimes.com/2014/08/29/apple-appeals-judges-decision-to-deny-a-ban-on-samsung-products/>. WEB 15 April, 2015.

Cheng, Roger. "Tablets Expected to Surpass Desktop, Laptop Sales by 2015." *CNET.com,* April 4, 2013. <http://news.cnet.com/8301-1035_3-57577905-94/tablets-expected-to-surpass-desktop-laptop-sales-by-2015/>. WEB 10 August, 2014.

Cohen, Adam. "One Friend Facebook Hasn't Made Yet: Privacy Rights." *New York Times,* February 18, 2008. <http://www.nytimes.com/2008/02/18/opinion/18mon4.html>. WEB 15 April, 2015.

"Coke Secrets Plot Woman Is Jailed." *BBC News,* May 23, 2007. <http://news.bbc.co.uk/2/hi/americas/6685299.stm>. WEB 27 January, 2014.

Coldewey, Devin. "America's Media Consumption so High It's Measured in Zettabytes." *NBCNEWS.com.* August 17, 2012. <http://www.nbcnews.com/technology/americasmedia-consumption-so-high-its-measured-zettabytes-950292>. WEB 24 November, 2013.

Commerce Committee. *Committee Report 2 of 3—House Report 105–551—Digital Millennial Copyright Act of 1998.* Commission on Intellectual Property Rights; "Integrating Intellectual Property Rights and Development Policy." October, 2002. <http://www.iprcommission.org/papers/pdfs/final_report/CIPR_Exec_Sumfinal.pdf>. WEB 14 July, 2014.

Consalvo, Mia. "There Is No Magic Circle." *Games and Culture* 4.4 (2009): 408–417. <http://www.bendevane.com/VTA2012/wpcontent/uploads/2012/01/mia_2009.pdf>. WEB 6 August, 2014.

Cotropia, Christopher Anthony, Cecil D. Quillen, Jr., and Ogden H. Webster. "Patent Applications and the Performance of the U.S. Patent and Trademark Office." February 26, 2013. Richmond School of Law Intellectual Property Institute Research Paper No. 2013–01. <http://papers.ssrn.com/sol3/Delivery.cfm/SSRN_ID2225781_code345316.pdf?abstractid=2225781&mirid=1>. WEB 15 December, 2013.

"Court Locator," United States Courts. <http://www.uscourts.gov/court_locator.aspx.>. WEB 25 November, 2013.

CPR: International Institute for Conflict Prevention & Resolution. <http://www.cpradr.org>. WEB 25 November, 2013.

Crain, Matthew. *The Revolution Will Be Commercialized: Finance, Public Policy, and the Construction of Internet Advertising.* Diss. University of Illinois, 2013. Print.

Craver, Scott, Patrick McGregor, Min Wu, Bede Liu, Adam Stubblefield, Ben Swartzlander, Dan S. Wallach, and Edward W. Felten. "Reading between the Lines: Lessons from the SDMI Challenge." 10th USENIX Security Symposium. Washington, DC: USENIX, 2001. Print.

———. "SDMI Challenge FAQ." 2000. <http://www.cs.princeton.edu/sip/sdmi/faq.html>. WEB 6 October, 2014.

Creative Commons. *creativecommon.org. n.d.* <http://creativecommons.org/>. WEB 15 September, 2014.

———. "Explore the Creative Commons Licenses." *creativecommon.org. n.d.* <https://creativecommons.org/choose/>. WEB 15 September, 2014.

———. "Which Creative Commons License Is Right for Me—Poster?" *creativecommon.org. n.d.* <http://creativecommons.org.au/content/licensing-flowchart.pdf>. WEB 15 September, 2014.

Crews, Kenneth D. "The Law of Fair Use and the Illusion of Fair-Use Guidelines." *Ohio State Law Journal* 62 (2001): 599–702. Print.

Crouch, Dennis. "USPTO Takes Action to Reduce RCE Backlog." March 28, 2013. *patentlyo.com.* <http://www.patentlyo.com/patent/2013/03/uspto-takes-action-to-reduce-rce-backlog.html>. WEB 15 December, 2013.

Cummings, Alex Sayf. *Democracy of Sound: Music Piracy and the Remaking of American Copyright in the Twentieth Century.* New York, NY: Oxford UP, 2013. Print.

Czarnota, Jedrzej P. "The Benefits and Practice of Harnessing Players as a QA Resource: Lessons from Open Source Software and EVE Online." *Hounds of Synthetic*, February 27, 2014. <http://jedrzej czarnota.squarespace.com/blog/2014/2/27/the-benefits-and-practice-of-harnessing-players-as-a-qa-resource-lessons-from-open-source-software-development-and-eve-online-case>. WEB 12 August, 2014.

Dannenberg, Ross. "Case: Eros v. Simon (SETTLED 2007) — Second Life." *patentarcade.com.* April 7, 2008. <http://www.patentarcade.com/2008/04/case-eros-v-simon-settled-2007-second.html>. WEB April 12, 2015.

"Data Brokers: A Call for Transparency and Accountability." *Federal Trade Commission*, May, 2014. <http://www.ftc.gov/system/files/documents/reports/data-brokers-call-transparency-accountability-report-federal-trade-commission-may-2014/140527databrokerreport.pdf>. WEB June 8, 2014.

DeBoer, Clint. "MPA Wins China DVD Lawsuit." *Audioholics.com*, March 6, 2008. <http://www.audioholics.com/news/mpa-wins-china-dvd-lawsuit>. WEB 25 July, 2014.

Delahunty, James. "Sony BMG Test 'Sterile Burning' Copy Protection." *afterdawn.com*, May 30, 2005. <http://www.afterdawn.com/news/article.cfm/2005/05/30/sony_bmg_test_sterile_burning_copy_protection>. WEB 12 October, 2014.

DeSantis, Nick. "NCAA Reaches $20-Million Settlement with Plaintiffs in Video-Game Lawsuit." *The Chronicle of Higher Education*, June 9, 2014. <http://chronicle.com/blogs/ticker/ncaa-reaches-20-million-settlement-with-plaintiffs-in-video-game-lawsuit/79403>. WEB 10 August, 2014.

Devaiah, Vishwas. "A History of Patent Law." *Alternative Law Forum.* <http://www.altlawforum.org/PUBLICATIONS/document.2004-12-18.0853561257>. Accessed via the Internet

Archive/WaybackMachine, May 27, 2009. <http://web.archive.org/web/20090527045230/http://www.altlawforum.org/PUBLICATIONS/document.2004-12-18.0853561257>. WEB 24 December, 2013.

"Directive 2011/77/EU of the European Parliament and of the Council of 27 September 2011 Amending Directive 2006/116/EC on the Term of Protection of Copyright and Certain Related Rights." September, 2011. <http://eurlex.europa.eu/LexUriServ/LexUriServ.do?uri=OJ:L:2011:265:0001:0005:en:PDF>. WEB 23 November, 2013.

Doctorow, Cory. "VLC Will Play iTunes Music Store Tracks." *BoingBoing.net*, March 26, 2004. <http://www.boingboing.net/2004/03/26/vlc-will-play-itunes.html>. WEB 6 October, 2014.

———. "When Love Is Harder to Show Than Hate." May 13, 2009. *The Guardian*. <http://www.theguardian.com/technology/2009/may/13/cory-doctorow-copyright>. WEB 24 September, 2014.

Duranske, Benjamin Tyson. *Virtual Law*. Chicago, IL: American Bar Association, 2008. Print.

Dyer, Mitch. "GameSpy Multiplayer Shutting Down, Hundreds of Games at Risk." *IGN*, April 3, 2014. <http://www.ign.com/videos/2014/04/03/gamespy-multiplayer-shutting-down-games-at-risk>. WEB 5 October, 2014.

Electronic Frontier Foundation. *About EFF*. <https://www.eff.org/about>. WEB 29 November, 2013.

———. *Apple v. Does*. <https://www.eff.org/node/873/873>. WEB 29 November, 2013.

———. *A Better Way Forward: Voluntary Collective Licensing of Music File Sharing. 'Let the Music Play Whitepaper.'* April, 2008. <https://www.eff.org/pages/better-way-forward-voluntary-collective-licensing-music-file-sharing>. WEB 27 November, 2013.

———. *DRM* <https://www.eff.org/issues/drm>. WEB 29 November, 2013.

———. *Patent Busting Project* <https://www.eff.org/patent-busting>. WEB 15 December, 2013.

———. "Unintended Consequences: Sixteen Years under the DMCA." September 16, 2014. <https://www.eff.org/wp/unintended-consequences-16-years-under-dmca>. WEB 2 October, 2014.

———. "Unintended Consequences: Twelve Years under the DMCA." March 3, 2010. <https://www.eff.org/wp/unintended-consequences-under-dmca>. WEB 1 December, 2013.

———. *US v. Elcomsoft & Sklyarov FAQ*. <https://w2.eff.org/IP/DMCA/US_v_Elcomsoft/us_v_sklyarov_faq.html>. WEB 29 November, 2013.

Elkin-Koren, Niva. "Public/Private and Copyright Reform in Cyberspace." *Journal of Computer-Mediated Communication* 2.1, Part 2, June, 1996. <http://jcmc.indiana.edu/vol2/issue2/index.html>. WEB 11 August, 2014.

Niva Elkin-Koren. "Public/Private and Copyright Reform in Cyberspace." *Journal of Computer-Mediated Communication* 2.2 (September, 1996). <http://onlinelibrary.wiley.com/doi/10.1111/j.1083-6101.1996.tb00059.x/full>. WEB 12 October, 2014.

Entertainment Software Association. "Entertainment Software. In-Game Advertising." <http://www.theesa.com/games-improving-what-matters/advertising.asp>. WEB 11 August, 2014.

———. "Sales, Demographic and Usage Data: Essential Facts about the Computer and Video Game Industry." <http://www.theesa.com/facts/pdfs/esa_ef_2013.pdf>. WEB 5 August, 2014.

Europa. Activities of the European Union, Summaries of Legislation: Audiovisual and Media. "Television Broadcasting Activities: Television without Frontiers" (TVWF) Directive.

<http://europa.eu/legislation_summaries/audiovisual_and_media/l24101_en.htm>. WEB 14 July, 2014.

Expenditure Trends in ARL Libraries 1985–2012. Washington, DC: Association of Research Libraries, 2013. <http://www.arl.org/storage/documents/expenditure-trends.pdf>. Web 27 August, 2014.

"Fair Use Checklist." Columbia University Libraries. March 14, 2008. <http://copyright.columbia.edu/copyright/files/2009/10/fairusechecklist.pdf>. WEB 20 October, 2014.

"Fan Fiction." *Chilling Effects. n.d.* <https://www.chillingeffects.org/fanfic/?print=yes>. WEB 14 August, 2014.

Farivar, Cyrus. "Dept. of Commerce Takes Tiny Step Towards Restoring Right to Unlock Cellphones." *ars technica*, September 17, 2013. <http://arstechnica.com/tech-policy/2013/09/dept-of-commerce-takes-tiny-step-towards-restoring-right-to-unlock-cellphones/>. WEB 30 November, 2013.

_____. "EFF Wants $30,000 to Defeat a Podcasting Patent Troll." *ars technica*, May 30, 2013. <http://arstechnica.com/tech-policy/2013/05/eff-wants-30000-to-defeat-a-ridiculous-podcasting-patent-troll/>. WEB 31 December, 2013.

_____. "European Court of Human Rights Unanimously Rejects Pirate Bay Appeal." *ars technica*, March 13, 2013. <http://arstechnica.com/tech-policy/2013/03/european-court-of-human-rights-unanimously-rejects-pirate-bay-appeal/>. WEB 24 November, 2013.

_____. "Exporting Copyright: Inside the Secretive Trans-Pacific Partnership." *ars technica*, May 17, 2012. <http://arstechnica.com/tech-policy/2012/05/trans-pacific-partnership-could-be-acta-plus-legal-experts-fear/>. WEB 25 July, 2014.

_____. "Germany Wants Google to Pay for News Citations, Passes Re-Publishing Bill." *ars technica*, March 1, 2013. <http://arstechnica.com/tech-policy/2013/03/germany-wants-google-to-pay-for-news-citations-passes-re-printing-bill/>. WEB 9 July, 2014.

_____. "Judge Denies MPAA Attempt to Seize Profits from Copyright Infringement." *ars technica*, February 7, 2013. <http://arstechnica.com/tech-policy/2013/02/judge-denies-mpaa-attempt-to-seize-profits-from-copyright-infringement/>. WEB 9 July, 2014.

_____. "Minnesota File-Sharing Case Finally Ends after Six Years—$222,000 Ruling Stands." *ars technica*, March 18, 2013. <http://arstechnica.com/tech-policy/2013/03/minnesota-file-sharing-case-finally-ends-after-six-years-222000-ruling-stands/>. WEB 24 November, 2013.

_____. "'Six Strikes' Enforcement Policy Debuts." *ars technica*, February 25, 2013. http://arstechnica.com/tech-policy/2013/02/six-strikes-enforcement-policy-debuts/. WEB 26 July, 2014.

Faughnder, Ryan. "Privacy Group Calls for FTC Investigation of Jay-Z App." *latimes.com*, July 13, 2013. <http://articles.latimes.com/2013/jul/15/entertainment/a-et-ct-privacy-group-calls-for-ftc-investigation-of-jayz-app-20130715>. WEB 24 November, 2013.

Faulkner, Michael, and Eric Goldman. "The Battle over UNIX: SCO v. Linux, AIX and the Open Source Community." June 14, 2004. <http://www.ericgoldman.org/Articles/scovunix.pdf>. WEB 29 September, 2014.

Felten, Ed. "What Is a Speedbump?" *Freedom-to-Tinker.com*, April 26, 2004. <https://freedom-to-tinker.com/blog/felten/what-speedbump/>. WEB 6 October, 2014.

Ferrera, Gerald R., Stephen D. Lichenstein, Margo E.K. Rader, Ray August, and William T. Schiano. *CyberLaw: Text and Cases*. Cincinnati, OH: South-Western College Publishing/Thompson Learning, 2001. Print.

Fink, Steven. *Sticky Fingers: Managing the Global Risk of Economic Espionage*. Chicago, IL: Dearborn Trade, 2002. Print.

"First Amendment—Invasion of Privacy." *n.d. Legal Information Institute at Cornell University*. <http://www.law.cornell.edu/anncon/html/amdt1dfrag7_user.html>. WEB September 12, 2014.

Fisk, Margaret Cronin. "Ten Top U.S. Intellectual-Property Verdicts Doubled to $4.6 Billion in '11." *Bloomberg News*, January 30, 2012. <http://www.bloomberg.com/news/2012-01-31/top-ten-ip-verdicts-hit-4-6-billion-in-2011-almost-twice-previous-year.html>. WEB 24 February, 2014.

Fitzpatrick, Kathleen. "On Open Access Publishing." *plannedobsolesence.net*, March 26, 2011. <http://www.plannedobsolescence.net/on-open-access-publishing/>. WEB 30 September, 2014.

Flaherty, Scott. "Jury Favors Music Site in Antitrust Row with Denver Nightclub." July 12, 2013. *Law360*. <http://www.law360.com/articles/457080/jury-favors-music-site-in-antitrust-row-with-denver-nightclub>. WEB 2 September, 2014.

Foresman, Chris. "DRM Licensing Group Presses on with Plan to Plug Analog Hole." *ars technica*, June 11, 2009. <http://arstechnica.com/gadgets/2009/06/drm-licensing-group-presses-on-with-plan-to-plug-analog-hole/>. WEB 6 October, 2014.

"France Mulls Culture Tax on Smartphones." *BloombergBusinessweek/AP News*, May 13, 2013. <http://www.businessweek.com/ap/2013-05-13/france-mulls-culture-tax-on-smartphones>. WEB 25 July, 2014.

GAO. *Intellectual Property: Observations on Efforts to Quantify the Economic Effects of Counterfeit and Pirated Goods*. US Government Accountability Office. April, 2010. <http://www.gao.gov/new.items/d10423.pdf>. WEB 3 July, 2014.

Garcia, Louis. "12 Unbelievable Video Game Patents You Didn't Know Existed." *games radar*, May 20, 2014. <http://www.gamesradar.com/12-unbelievable-video-game-patents/>. WEB 10 August, 2014.

Garfinkel, Simson L. "Patently Absurd." *Wired*, July, 1994. <http://www.wired.com/wired/archive/2.07/patents.html?topic=&topic_set=l>. WEB 15 December, 2013.

Garner, Bryan A., ed. *Black's Law Dictionary*. 8th ed. St. Paul, MN: Thompson-West Group, 2004. Print.

Gartner. "Gartner Says Worldwide Video Game Market to Total $93 Billion in 2013." October 29, 2013. <https://www.gartner.com/newsroom/id/2614915>. WEB 5 August, 2014.

Gerson, Rebecca M. "Celebrity Trademark Rights: Images v. Innuendos." *Ohio State Bar Association*, November 27, 2013. <https://www.ohiobar.org/forpublic/resources/lawyoucanuse/pages/lawyoucanuse-268.aspx>. WEB 6 January, 2014.

Geuss, Megan. "University of California to Allow Open Access to New Academic Papers." *ars technica*, August 3, 2014. <http://arstechnica.com/tech-policy/2013/08/university-of-california-to-allow-open-access-to-new-academic-papers/>. WEB 28 September, 2014.

Gidda, Mirren. "Edward Snowden and the NSA Files—Timeline." *The Guardian*, July 25, 2013. <http://www.guardian.co.uk/world/2013/jun/23/edward-snowden-nsa-files-timeline>. WEB 24 November, 2013.

Gillett, Frank. "Why Tablets Will Become Our Primary Computing Device." *forrester.com*. April 23, 2012. <http://blogs.forrester.com/frank_gillett/12-04-23-why_tablets_will_become_our_primary_computing_device>. WEB 24 November, 2013.

Gladstone, Julia Alpert. "Determining Jurisdiction in Cyberspace: The 'Zippo' Test or the 'Effects' Test?" I^nSite Proceedings, 2003 meeting of the Informing Science Institute, Pori, Finland. Santa Rosa, CA: Informing Science Institute. <http://proceedings.informing-science.org/IS2003Proceedings/docs/029Glads.pdf>. WEB 25 July, 2014.

Glater, Jonathan D. "Judge Reverses His Order Disabling Web Site." *The New York Times*. March 1, 2008. <http://www.nytimes.com/2008/03/01/us/01wiki.html>. WEB 15 April, 2015.

Goldman, Eric. "California's New Law Shows It's Not Easy to Regulate Revenge Porn." *Forbes*, October 8, 2013. <http://www.forbes.com/sites/ericgoldman/2013/10/08/californias-new-law-shows-its-not-easy-to-regulate-revenge-porn/>. WEB 10 June, 2014.

_____. "11th Circuit Freaks Out about Metatags—*North American Medical v. Axiom*." *Technology & Marketing Law Blog*, April 8, 2008. <http://blog.ericgoldman.org/archives/2008/04/11^th_circuit_fr.htm>. WEB 26 November, 2013.

_____. "Important Ninth Circuit Ruling on Keyword Advertising, Plus Recaps of the Past 4 Months of Keyword Ad Decisions." *Technology & Marketing Law Blog*, March 9, 2011. <http://blog.ericgoldman.org/archives/2011/03/important_ninth.htm>. WEB 3 January, 2014.

_____. "Online Game Network Isn't Company Town—Estavillo v. Sony." *Technology & Marketing Law Blog*, October 1, 2009. <http://blog.ericgoldman.org/archives/2009/10/online_game_net.htm>. WEB 12 October, 2014.

_____. "Rationalizing (?) the Hart and Keller v. EA Sports Publicity Rights Rulings." *Technology & Marketing Law Blog*, August 5, 2013. <http://blog.ericgoldman.org/archives/2013/08/a_futile_attemp.htm>. WEB 6 April, 2014.

_____. "The State Attorneys General Want to Eviscerate a Key Internet Immunity." *Forbes*, June 26, 2013. <http://www.forbes.com/sites/ericgoldman/2013/06/26/the-state-attorneys-general-want-to-eviscerate-a-key-internet-immunity/>. WEB 5 April, 2014.

_____. "Supreme Court's Kirtsaeng Ruling Is Good News for Consumers, but the First Sale Doctrine Is Still Doomed–Kirtsaeng v. John Wiley." *Technology & Marketing Law Blog*, March 26, 2013. <http://blog.ericgoldman.org/archives/2013/03/the_supreme_cou.htm>. WEB 26 November, 2013.

_____. "Want to Avoid Defaming Someone Online? Link to Your Sources. *Forbes*, October 23, 2013. <http://www.forbes.com/sites/ericgoldman/2013/10/23/want-to-avoid-defaming-someone-online-link-to-your-sources/>. WEB 19 June, 2014.

Goldstein, Paul. *Copyright's Highway: From Gutenberg to the Celestial Jukebox*. Stanford, CA: Stanford UP, 2003. Print.

Gordon, Wendy J. "Fair Use as Market Failure: A Structural and Economic Analysis of the Betamax Case and Its Predecessors." *Columbia Law Review* 82.8 (1982): 1600–57. Print.

Governo, David M., and Corey M. Dennis. "Social Media Defamation Victories Assist Companies in Fighting Reputational Attacks." *Governo Law Firm, LLC*, January 9, 2013. <http://www.governo.com/TheFirm/News.asp?NewsID=670>. WEB 19 June, 2014.

Gullo, Karen. "Ex-Dow Scientist Who Stole Secrets Gets 7 Years, 3 Months Prison." *Business week.com*. December 21, 2011. <http://www.bloomberg.com/news/2011-12-21/ex-dow-scientist-gets-more-than-seven-years-in-prison-for-stealing-secrets.html>. WEB 24 February, 2014.

Hamblen, Matt. "App Economy Expected to Double by 2017 to $151B." *Computerworld*, July 15, 2013. <http://www.computerworld.com/s/article/9240794/App_economy_expected_to_double_by_2017_to_151B?source=CTWNLE_nlt_pm_2013-07-15>. WEB 24 November, 2013.

Hassanien, Mohamed R. "Bilateral WTO-Plus Free Trade Agreements in the Middle East: A Case Study of OFTA in the Post-TRIPS Era." *Wake Forest Intellectual Property Law Journal* 8.2. (2008): 161–95. <http://ipjournal.law.wfu.edu/files/2009/09/issue.8.2.pdf>. WEB 25 July, 2014.

Hassett, Rob. "Rights of Privacy and Publicity in Interactive Media." <http://www.internetlegal.com/articles/rightsof.htm>. WEB 17 March, 2014.

Hefflinger, Mark. "Chinese Movie Download Service Jeboo Sues MPA." *digitalmediawire.com*. May 22, 2008. <http://www.dmwmedia.com/news/2008/03/25/chinese-movie-download-service-jeboo-sues-mpa>. WEB 25 July, 2014.

———. "Walmart to End Support for DRM-Wrapped Songs in October." *Digitalmediawire*, June 1, 2009. <http://www.dmwmedia.com/news/2009/06/01/walmart-to-end-support-for-drm-wrapped-songs-in-october>. WEB 5 October, 2014.

Hesse, Thomas. Interview. "Sony Music CD's under Fire from Privacy Advocates." *Morning Edition*, National Public Radio, Broadcast. November 4, 2005. <http://www.npr.org/templates/story/story.php?storyId=4989260>. WEB 6 October, 2014.

Heydary Hamilton, PC. "Troubling Global Trends Emerging in Online Defamation." *n.d.* <http://www.heydary.com/publications/online-defamation-laws.html>. WEB 19 June, 2014.

Hirtle, Peter. "Copyright Term and the Public Domain in the United States." January 1, 2014. <http://copyright.cornell.edu/resources/publicdomain.cfm>. WEB 25 August, 2014.

———. "Research, Libraries, and Fair Use: The Gentlemen's Agreement of 1935." *Journal of the Copyright Society of the U.S.A.* (2006): 545–74. Print.

Hoffman, Chris. "Android Is Based on Linux, but What Does That Mean?" *How-to Geek*, May 12, 2014. <http://www.howtogeek.com/189036/android-is-based-on-linux-but-what-does-that-mean/>. WEB 28 September, 2014.

Hollman, Steven P., and Jennifer D. Brechbill. "Political Trademarks in the 2012 Presidential Election." *Intellectual Property Today*, June, 2012. <http://www.iptoday.com/issues/2012/06/political-trademarks-in-2012-presidential-election.asp>. WEB 15 March, 2015.

Hovey, Craig. *The Patent Process: A Guide to Intellectual Property for the Information Age.* New York, NY: John Wiley & Sons, 2002. Print.

Huizinga, Johan. Homo *Ludens: A Study of the Play-Element in Culture.* London, UK: Routledge & Kegan Paul, 1949. Print.

Hurst, Nathan. "How the America Invents Act Will Change Patenting Forever." *Wired.com*, March 15, 2013. <http://www.wired.com/design/?p=146445>. WEB 24 November, 2013.

Intellectual Property Office. "The 18ᵗʰ Century." *ipo.gov.uk*. <http://www.ipo.gov.uk/types/patent/p-about/p-whatis/p-history/p-history-18century.htm>. WEB 24 December, 2013.

———. "History of Patents." <http://www.ipo.gov.uk/types/patent/p-about/p-whatis/p-history.htm>. WEB 24 December, 2013.

———. "Tudors and Stuarts." <http://www.ipo.gov.uk/types/patent/p-about/p-whatis/p-history/p-history-tudor.htm>. WEB 24 December, 2013.

International Intellectual Property Alliance. <http://www.iipa.com/>. WEB 24 November, 2013.

———. "IIPA's New Economic Study Reveals the Copyright Industries Remain a Driving Force in the U.S. Economy." Press Release. January 30, 2007: 1. <http://www.iipa.com/pdf/IIPA2006CopyrightIndustriesReportPressReleaseFINAL01292007.pdf>. WEB 21 March, 2015.

International Trade Administration, Office of Trade and Economic Analysis, US Department of Commerce. *U.S. Export Fact Sheet.* February 6, 2014. <http://trade.gov/press/press-releases/2014/export-factsheet-february2014-020614.pdf>. WEB 21 March, 2015.

International Trade Statistics, 2012. *World Trade Organization.* <http://www.wto.org/english/res_e/statis_e/its2012_e/its2012_e.pdf>. WEB 3 July, 2014.

Internet Corporation for Assigned Names and Numbers. "New Generic Top-Level Domains, About the Program." *icann.org.* <http://newgtlds.icann.org/en/about/program>. WEB 27 January, 2014.

———. "New Generic Top-Level Domains, Delegated Strings." *icann.org.* <http://newgtlds.icann.org//en/program-status/delegated-strings>. WEB 27 January, 2014.

———. "Timeline for the Formulation and Implementation of the Uniform Domain-Name Dispute-Resolution Policy." *icann.org.* <http://www.icann.org/udrp/udrp-schedule.htm>. WEB 21 March, 2015.

———. "Uniform Domain Name Dispute Resolution Policy." *icann.org*, Oct 24, 1999. <http://www.icann.org/udrp/udrp-policy-24oct99.htm>. WEB 15 March, 2015.

———. "Who Runs the Internet?" *icann.org*, Feb 3, 2013. <http://www.icann.org/en/about/learning/factsheets/governance-06feb13-en.pdf>. WEB 24 November, 2013.

Jaffe, Adam B., and Josh Lerner. *Innovation and Its Discontents: How Our Broken Patent System Is Endangering Innovation and Progress, and What to Do about It.* Princeton, NJ: Princeton UP, 2004. Print.

Jaszi, Peter. "Copyright Term Extension Act of 1995." Testimony at Hearing before Committee on the Judiciary, United States Senate. Washington, DC, September 20, 1995. Hathi Trust, Digital Library <http://babel.hathitrust.org/cgi/pt?id=pst.000031265782;view=1up;seq=1>. WEB 7 January, 2014.

Jenkins, Henry. *Convergence Culture: Where Old and New Media Collide.* New York, NY: New York UP, 2006. Print.

Jobs, Steve. "Thoughts on Music." February 6, 2007. <http://macdailynews.com/2007/02/06/apple_ceo_steve_jobs_posts_rare_open_letter_thoughts_on_music/>. WEB 6 October, 2014.

Johnsen, Andreas, Ralf Christensen, and Henrik Moltke. *Good Copy Bad Copy.* <https://www.youtube.com/watch?v=WEKl5I_Q044>. WEB 16 July, 2014.

Johnson, David R. "Due Process and Cyberjurisdiction." *Journal of Computer-Mediated Communication* 2.1 (June, 1996). <http://onlinelibrary.wiley.com/doi/10.1111/j.1083-6101.1996.tb00181.x/full>. WEB 12 October, 2014.

Jones, Ashby. "Do Gene Sequences Deserve Patent Protection?" *The Wall Street Journal* Law Blog, December 10, 2009. <http://blogs.wsj.com/law/2009/12/10/science-and-the-law-do-gene-sequences-deserve-patent-protection>. WEB 31 December, 2013.

———. "Who Took My Book? E-Book Readers Kindle Debate over Digital Rights." *The Wall Street Journal* Law Blog, July 23, 2009. <http://blogs.wsj.com/law/2009/07/23/who-took-my-book-e-book-reader-kindles-debate-over-digital-rights/>. WEB 20 October, 2014.

Jordan, Robert. "The New Patent Law: End of Entrepreneurship?" *Forbes*, November 13, 2012. <http://www.forbes.com/sites/robertjordan/2012/11/13/the-new-patent-law-end-of-entrepreneurship/>. WEB 27 December, 2013.

Kaergard, Chris, and Nick Vlahos. "Word on the Street: An Open Letter to Peoria Mayor Jim Ardis on Twittergate." *Journal Star*, June 16, 2014. <http://www.pjstar.com/article/20140615/NEWS/140619392>. WEB 16 June, 2014.

Kain, Erik. "If You Thought SOPA Was Bad, Just Wait Until You Meet ACTA." *Forbes*, January 23, 2012. <http://www.forbes.com/sites/erikkain/2012/01/23/if-you-thought-sopa-was-bad-just-wait-until-you-meet-acta/>. WEB 1 December, 2013.

Keen, Andrew. *Digital Vertigo: How Today's Online Social Revolution Is Dividing, Diminishing, and Disorienting Us.* New York, NY: St. Martin's Press, 2012. Print.

Kelzer, Gregg. "Sony Settles Rootkit CD Suit with Texas, California." *InformationWeek* December 20, 2006. <http://www.informationweek.com/sony-settles-rootkit-cd-suit-with-texas-california/d/d-id/1050108?>. WEB 21 March, 2015.

Kennedy, John. "YouTube Goes Pro—Buys Next New Networks for US$50m." August 3, 2011. *Siliconrepublic.com.* <http://www.siliconrepublic.com/business/item/20788-youtube-goes-pro-buys-nex>. WEB 24 November, 2013.

Kim, Nancy, S. *Wrap Contracts: Foundations and Ramifications.* Oxford, UK: Oxford UP, 2013. Print.

Klapow, Mark. "Litigation Forecast 2013: What Corporate Counsel Need to Know for the Coming Year." Crowell & Moring, LLP, 2013. <http://www.crowell.com/files/crowell-moring-litigation-forecast-2013.pdf>. WEB 24 February, 2014.

Kling, Rob, Lisa Spector, and Joanna Fortuna. "The Real Stakes of Virtual Publishing: The Transformation of E-Biomed into Pubmed Central." *Journal of the American Society for Information Science and Technology* 55.2: 127–48. Print.

Kravets, David. "Copyright Lawsuits Plummet in Aftermath of RIAA Campaign." *Wired.com*, May 18, 2010. <http://www.wired.com/threatlevel/2010/05/riaa-bump/>. WEB 24 November, 2013.

———. "US Signs ACTA." *ars technica*, October 4, 2011. <http://arstechnica.com/tech-policy/2011/10/us-signs-international-anti-piracy-accord/>. WEB 25 July, 2014.

Krazit, Tom. "Beatles Judge Finds Itunes Nothing to Get Hung About." *CNET News*, May 8, 2006. <http://news.cnet.com/Beatles-judge-finds-iTunes-nothing-to-get-hung-about/2100-1027_3-6069490.html>. WEB 25 November, 2013.

Kross, Nancy. "The Film and Entertainment Industry: Reel in the Profits." *Bidness Etc.*, January 21, 2014. <http://www.bidnessetc.com/20818-film-entertainment-industry-reel-profits/>. WEB 8 July, 2014.

Kucklich, Julian. "Precarious Playbour: Modders and the Digital Games Industry." *The Fiberculture Journal* 5 (2005). <http://five.fibreculturejournal.org/fcj-025-precarious-playbour-modders-and-the-digital-games-industry/>. WEB 12 August, 2014.

Kudon, Jeremy. "Form over Function: Expanding the Transformative Use Test for Fair Use." *Boston University Law Review* 80 (2000): 579–612. Print.

Ladas & Parry, LLP. "A Brief History of the Patent Law of the United States." <http://www.ladas.com/Patents/USPatentHistory.html>. WEB 26 December, 2013.

Lamoureux, Edward Lee. *Privacy, Surveillance, and the New Media You*. New York, NY: Peter Lang, 2016. Print.

Lamoureux, Edward Lee, Steven L. Baron, and Claire Stewart. *Intellectual Property Law and Interactive Media: Free for a Fee*. New York, NY: Peter Lang, 2009. Print.

Lattman, Peter. "Court Overturns Conviction of Ex-Goldman Programmer." *New York Times*, February 17, 2012. <http://dealbook.nytimes.com/2012/02/17/court-overturns-conviction-of-ex-goldman-programmer/>. WEB 24 February, 2014.

Lauder, Gary. "New Patent Law Means Trouble for Tech Entrepreneurs." *Forbes*, September 20, 2011. <http://www.forbes.com/sites/ciocentral/2011/09/20/new-patent-law-means-trouble-for-tech-entrepreneurs/>. WEB 27 December, 2013.

"Leahy-Smith America Invents Act Revises U.S. Patent Law Regime." *Harvard Law Review* 125.5 (March, 2012): 1290–97. <http://www.harvardlawreview.org/issues/125/march12/Recent_Legislation_9058.php> and <http://cdn.harvardlawreview.org/wp-content/uploads/pdfs/vol125_leahy_smith_america_invents_act.pdf>. WEB 14 March, 2015.

Lee, Timothy B. "Court Rules Book Scanning Is Fair Use, Suggesting Google Books Victory." *ars technica*, October 10, 2012. <http://arstechnica.com/tech-policy/2012/10/court-rules-book-scanning-is-fair-use-suggesting-google-books-victory/>. WEB 24 November, 2013.

_____. "French Copyright Cops: We're Swamped with 'Three Strikes' Complaints." *ars technica*, July 14, 2011. <http://arstechnica.com/tech-policy/2011/07/french-agency-were-swamped-with-three-strikes-complaints/>. WEB 1 December, 2013.

_____. "Publishers Abandon Fight against Google Book Scanning." *ars technica*, October 4, 2012. <http://arstechnica.com/tech-policy/2012/10/publishers-abandon-fight-against-google-book-scanning/>. WEB 24 November, 2013.

_____. "Study Suggests Patent Office Lowered Standards to Cope with Backlog." *ars technica*, April 7, 2013. <http://arstechnica.com/tech-policy/2013/04/study-suggests-patent-office-lowered-standards-to-cope-with-backlog/>. WEB 15 December, 2013.

Legal Information Institute. <http://www.law.cornell.edu/supct/>. WEB 20 October, 2014.

_____. "CRS Annotated Constitution: Fourth Amendment." <http://www.law.cornell.edu/anncon/html/amdt4toc_user.html>. WEB 25 November, 2013.

———. "Listing by Jurisdiction." <http://www.law.cornell.edu/states/listing.html>. WEB 20 October, 2014.

———. US Code. <http://www.law.cornell.edu/uscode/text>. WEB 25 November, 2013.

"Legal Proceedings." Apple Computer, Inc. Annual Report Pursuant to Section 13 or 15(D) of the Securities Exchange Act of 1934 for the Fiscal Year Ended September 24, 2005. <http://www.sec.gov/Archives/edgar/data/320193/000110465905058421/a05-20674_110k.htm>. WEB 25 November, 2013.

"Legislative Fact Sheet—Trade Secrets Act." *Uniform Law Commission, the National Conference of Commissioners on Uniform State Laws.* <http://www.uniformlaws.org/LegislativeFact-Sheet.aspx?title=Trade%20Secrets%20Act>. WEB 17 February, 2014.

Lessig, Lawrence. *Code: And Other Laws of Cyberspace.* New York, NY: Basic Books, 1999. Print.

———. *Free Culture: How Big Media Uses Technology and the Law to Lock Down Culture and Control Creativity.* New York, NY: Penguin Press, 2004. Print.

———. *Future of Ideas: The Fate of the Commons in a Connected World.* New York, NY: Random House, 2002. Print.

———. "Jail Time in the Digital Age." *New York Times,* 30 July 2001. <http://www.nytimes.com/2001/07/30/opinion/30LESS.html>. WEB 24 November, 2013.

———. "Little Orphan Artworks." *New York Times.* May 20, 2008. <http://www.nytimes.com/2008/05/20/opinion/20lessig.html>. WEB 24 November, 2013.

Leval, Pierre N. "Toward a Fair Use Standard." *Harvard Law Review* 103 (1990): 1105–36. Print.

Levy, Steven. *Crypto: How the Code Rebels Beat the Government—Saving Privacy in the Digital Age.* New York, NY: Penguin Books, 2001. Print.

"Life of a Patent: From Application to Issuance and Beyond." *Patents+TMS.* <http://blog.patents-tms.com/?p=197>. WEB 16 December, 2013.

Lipson, Ashley Saunders, and Robert D. Brain. *Computer and Video Game Law: Cases, Statutes, Forms, Problems & Materials.* Durham, NC: Carolina Academic Press, 2009. Print.

Lister, Martin, Jon Dovey, Seth Giddings, Iain Grant, and Kieran Kelly. *New Media: A Critical Introduction.* 2nd ed. London, UK: Routledge, 2009. Print.

Litman, Jessica. "Copyright Legislation and Technological Change." *Oregon Law Review* 68 (1989): 275–361. Print.

———. *Digital Copyright.* Amherst, NY: Prometheus Books, 2001. Print.

———. *Law 760: Trademarks & Unfair Competition.* <http://www-personal.umich.edu/~jdlitman/classes/tm/handout.pdf>. WEB 25 November, 2013.

———. "Lawful Personal Use." *Texas Law Review* 85 (2007): 1871–1920. Print.

Loren, Lydia Pallas. "Redefining the Market Failure Approach to Fair Use in an Era of Copyright Permission Systems." *Journal of Intellectual Property Law Association* 5 (Fall 1997): 1–58. Print.

MacManus, Christopher. "SimCity Launch a Complete Disaster." *CNet.com,* March 7, 2013. <http://www.cnet.com/news/simcity-launch-a-complete-disaster/>. WEB 5 October, 2014.

Madison, Michael J. "Rewriting Fair Use and the Future of Copyright Reform." *Cardozo Arts and Entertainment Law Journal* 23 (2005): 391–418. Print.

Magid, Larry. "What Are SOPA and PIPA and Why All the Fuss?" *Forbes*, January 18, 2012. <http://www.forbes.com/sites/larrymagid/2012/01/18/what-are- sopa-and-pipa-and-why-all-the-fuss/>. WEB 1 December, 2013.

"Majority Views NSA Phone Tracking as Acceptable Anti-terror Tactic." Pew Research Center for the People & the Press, June 10, 2013. <http://www.people-press.org/2013/06/10/majority-views-nsa-phone-tracking-as-acceptable-anti-terror-tactic/>. WEB 25 November, 2013.

"Make Unlocking Cell Phones Legal." whitehouse.gov. <https://petitions.whitehouse.gov/petition/make-unlocking-cell-phones-legal/1g9KhZG7>. WEB 30 November, 2013.

Makuch, Eddie. "GOG Celebrates Six Years of Advancing the 'DRM-Free Movement.'" *GameSpot*, September 8, 2014. <http://www.gamespot.com/articles/gog-celebrates-six-years-of-advancing-the-drm-free/1100-6422150/>. WEB 5 October, 2014.

Maltz, Tamir. "Customary Law & Power in Internet Communities." *Journal of Computer-Mediated Communication* 2.1 (June, 1996). <http://onlinelibrary.wiley.com/doi/10.1111/j.1083-6101.1996.tb00182.x/full>. WEB 12 October, 2014.

Masnick, Mike. "Lawsuit Filed to Prove Happy Birthday Is in the Public Domain; Demands Warner Pay Back Millions of License Fees." *techdirt.com*, June 13, 2013.<http://www.techdirt.com/articles/20130613/11165823451/filmmaker-finally-aims-to-get-court-to-admit-that-happy-birthday-is-public-domain.shtml>. WEB 25 November, 2013.

———. "RIAA Spent $17.6 Million in Lawsuits … to Get $391,000 in Settlements?" *techdirt.com*, July 14th, 2010. <http://www.techdirt.com/articles 20100713/17400810200.shtml>. WEB 24 November, 2013.

Mason, Melanie. "Gov. Jerry Brown Signs Bill Protecting Consumers' Online Reviews." *Los Angeles Times*, September 9, 2014. <http://www.latimes.com/local/political/La-me-pc-brown-bill-signing-20140909-story.html>. WEB 21 September, 2014.

Matlack, Carol. "France's 'Culture Tax' Could Hit YouTube and Facebook." *BloombergBusinessweek*. December 26, 2013. <http://www.businessweek.com/articles/2013-12-26/frances-culture-tax-could-hit-youtube-and-facebook>. WEB 25 July, 2014.

May, Christopher. *The Global Political Economy of Intellectual Property Rights: The New Enclosures*. 2nd ed. New York, NY: Routledge, 2000. Print.

Mazumdar, Anandashankar. "President Signs Bill Restoring Consumer Right to Unlock Mobile Handsets." *Bloomberg BNA*, August 6, 2014. <http://www.bna.com/president-signs-bill-n17179893361/>. WEB 6 October, 2014.

McGonagle, John J., and Carolyn M. Vella. *The Manager's Guide to Competitive Intelligence*. Westport, CT: Praeger, 2003. Print.

McLaughlin, Kathy. "Mother Fights Record Companies' Lawsuit on Her Own." *USA Today.com*, December 25, 2005. <http://usatoday30.usatoday.com/news/nation/2005-12-25-download-suit_x.htm>. WEB 25 November, 2013.

McLeod, Kembrew. *Owning Culture: Authorship, Ownership, & Intellectual Property Law*. New York, NY: Peter Lang, 2001. Print.

McLuhan, Marshall. *The Gutenberg Galaxy: The Making of Typographic Man*. Toronto, Canada: University of Toronto Press, 1962. Print.

McLuhan, Marshall. *Understanding Media: The Extensions of Man*. New York, NY: McGraw-Hill, 1964. Print.

Merges, Robert P., Peter S. Menell, and Mark A. Lemley. *Intellectual Property in the New Technological Age*. 2nd ed. Gaithersburg, VA: Aspen Law & Business, 2000. Print.

"Michael S. Hart." *n.d. Project Gutenberg*. <http://www.gutenberg.org/wiki/Michael_S._Hart>. WEB 15 July, 2014.

"Microsoft Computing Safety Index Shows Consumers Do Little to Change Online Habits Despite Multiple Risks." *Microsoft.com*, February 4, 1013. <http://www.microsoft.com/en-us/news/press/2013/feb13/02-04sid13pr.aspx>. WEB 26 August, 2014.

Micucci, Emily. "Patent Law Change to 'First To File' System Poses Hurdle for Entrepreneurs." *Worcester Business Journal Online*, April 1, 2013. <http://www.wbjournal.com/article/20130401/PRINTEDITION/303299986>. WEB 27 December, 2013.

Milligan, Robert B., and Daniel Joshua Salinas. "Top 10 Developments/Headlines in Trade Secret, Computer Fraud, and Non-Compete Law in 2012." January 3, 2013. <http://www.seyfarth.com/publications/MATS010313>. WEB 24 February, 2014.

Mills, Elinor. "Google Loses Gmail Trademark Appeal in Europe." *Cnet.com*, March 20, 2008. <http://www.cnet.com/news/google-loses-gmail-trademark-appeal-in-europe/>. WEB 1 November, 2014.

"MLB Advanced Media Awarded United States Patent for Online Geolocation Technology." *mlb.com*, May 14, 2009. <http://mlb.mlb.com/news/press_releases/press_release.jsp?ymd=20090514&content_id=4729922&vkey=pr_mlbcom&fext=.jsp&c_id=mlb>. WEB 6 October, 2014.

Montano, Natalie H. "Hero with a Thousand Copyright Violations: Modern Myth and an Argument for Universally Transformative Fan Fiction." *Northwestern Journal of Technology and Intellectual Property* 11.7 (2013). <http://scholarlycommons.law.northwestern.edu/cgi/viewcontent.cgi?article=1206&context=njtip>. WEB 14 August, 2014.

Moore, Steven. "A Fractured Fairy Tale: Separating Fact & Fiction on Patent Trolls." *IPWatchdog*, July 29, 2013. <http://www.ipwatchdog.com/2013/07/29/a-fractured-fairy-tale-separating-fact-fiction-on-patent-trolls/id=43697/>. WEB 1 September, 2014.

———. "Probing 10 Patent Troll Myths—A Fractured Fairytale Part 2." *IPWatchdog*, July 30, 2013. <http://www.ipwatchdog.com/2013/07/30/probing-10-patent-troll-myths-a-fractured-fairytale-part-2/id=43754/>. WEB 1 September, 2014.

———. "A Fractured Fairytale Part 3: More Patent Troll Myths." *IPWatchdog*. July 31, 2013, <http://www.ipwatchdog.com/2013/07/31/a-fractured-fairytale-part-3-more-patent-troll myths/id=43755/>. WEB 1 September, 2014.

———. "A Fractured Fairytale Part 4: More Patent Troll Myths." *IPWatchdog*, August 1, 2013. <http://www.ipwatchdog.com/2013/08/01/a-fractured-fairytale-part-4-more-patent-troll-myths/id=43758/>. WEB 1 September, 2014.

———. "Patent Troll Epilogue—A Fractured Fairy Tale Part 5." *IPWatchdog*, August 2, 2013. <http://www.ipwatchdog.com/2013/08/02/patent-troll-epilogue-a-fractured-fairy-tale-part-5/id=43630/>. WEB 1 September, 2014.

Morrison, Heather Grace. *Freedom for Scholarship in the Internet Age* (Thesis). Communication, Art & Technology: School of Communication. November 21, 2012. <http://summit.sfu.ca/item/12537#310>. WEB 17 September, 2014.

Mullin, Joe. "Authors, Composers Want 3.4% of Every Belgian's Internet Bill." *ars technica*, May 1, 2013. <http://arstechnica.com/apple/2013/05/authors-composers-want-3-4-of-every-belgians-internet-bill/>. WEB 15 July, 2014.

———. "Filmmaker Picks a Copyright Fight with 'Happy Birthday.'" *ars technica*, June 14, 2013. <http://arstechnica.com/tech-policy/2013/06/filmmaker-picks-a-copyright-fight-with-happy-birthday/>. WEB 25 November, 2013.

———. "French Media to Google: Pay Us for News Searches." *ars technica*, October 19, 2012. <http://arstechnica.com/tech-policy/2012/10/google-threatens-to-cut-french-media-out-of-news-search/>. WEB 15 July, 2014.

———. "How ISPs Will Do 'Six Strikes': Throttled Speeds, Blocked Sites." *ars technica*, November 16, 2012. < http://arstechnica.com/tech-policy/2012/11/how-isps-will-do-six-strikes-throttled-speeds-blocked-sites/>. WEB 1 December, 2013.

———. "'Patent Troll' Claiming Playlists and Podcasts Scores License with SanDisk." *ars technica*, September 12, 2013. <http://arstechnica.com/tech-policy/2013/09/patent-troll-claiming-playlists-and-podcasts-scores-license-with-sandisk/>. WEB 31 December, 2013.

———. "Second Anti-Patent-Troll Bill Shows up, and Splits Emerge on the First." *ars technica*, November 18, 2013. <http://arstechnica.com/tech-policy/2013/11/second-anti-patent-troll-bill-shows-up-as-splits-emerge-on-the-first/>. WEB 2 December, 2013.

———. "Study of French "Three Strikes" Piracy Law Finds No Deterrent Effect." *ars technica*, January 23, 2014. <http://arstechnica.com/tech-policy/2014/01/study-of-french-three-strikes-piracy-law-finds-no-deterrent-effect/>. WEB 26 July, 2014.

———. "Web's Longest Nightmare Ends: Eolas' Patents Are Dead on Appeal." *ars technica*, July 22, 2013. <http://arstechnica.com/tech-policy/2013/07/the-webs-longest-nightmare-ends-eolas-patents-are-dead-on-appeal/>. WEB 15 December, 2013.

———. "White House Calls for Cell Phone Unlocking Ban to Be Overturned; Obama Refutes Library of Congress, Calls Unlocking Crucial for Consumer Choice." *ars technica*, March 4, 2013. <http://arstechnica.com/tech-policy/2013/03/white-house-calls-for-cell-phone-unlocking-ban-to-be-overturned/>. WEB 30 November, 2013.

Murch, Angela. "Video Games—Intellectual Property Protection in the U.S.A." *Intellectual Property Today*, August, 2013. <http://www.iptoday.com/issues/2013/08/video-games-intellectual-property-protection-in-usa.asp>. WEB 7 August, 2014.

Murphy, John. "Intellectual Property & Development." *Latin Business Chronicle* 28 (April, 2008). <http://www.latinbusinesschronicle.com/app/article.aspx?id=2328>. WEB 14 July, 2014.

Murray, Janet H. *Hamlet on the Holodeck: The Future of Narrative in Cyberspace.* New York, NY: Free Press, 1997. Print.

"Music Piracy Suit against N.Y. Family Is Settled for $7,000." *Associated Press*, April 27, 2009. *nytimes.com.* <http://www.nytimes.com/2009/04/28/business/media/28piracy.html?_r=0>. WEB 25 November, 2013.

Najjar, Jared. "Patent Infringement Litigation and the Commercial General Liability Insurance Policy: Are Insurers Obligated to Indemnify and Defend under 'Advertising Injury' Provisions?" *DULR ON*, February 13, 2013. <http://www.denverlawreview.org/online-articles/2013/2/13/patent-infringement-litigation-and-the-commercial-general-li.html>. WEB 31 December, 2013.

National Arbitration Forum. <http://www.adrforum.com/default.aspx>. WEB 25 November, 2013.

Nazer, Daniel. "The Copyright Alert System FAQ." *Electronic Freedom Forum*, February 28, 2013. <https://www.eff.org/deeplinks/2013/02/six-strikes-copyright-alert-system-faq>. WEB 26 July, 2014.

Neal, James G. *Hearing on Preservation and Reuse of Copyrighted Works, Statement of James G. Neal*. Washington, DC: n. pag., 2014. <http://judiciary.house.gov/index.cfm/2014/4/hearing-preservation-and-reuse-of-copyrighted-works>. WEB 27 August, 2014.

Nimmer, David. *Copyright: Sacred Text, Technology, and the DMCA*. The Hague, The Netherlands: Kluwer Law International, 2003, p. 396–99. Print.

Nimmer, Melville B., and David Nimmer. *Nimmer on Copyrights: A Treatise on the Law of Literary, Musical and Artistic Property, and the Protection of Ideas*. New York, NY: Matthew Bender, 2005. Print.

Nordqvist, Christian. "Human Genes May Not Be Patented, US Supreme Court Ruled Today." *Medical News Today*, June 13, 2013. <http://www.medicalnewstoday.com/articles/261945.php>. WEB 31 December, 2013.

Oberding, Juliet M. "A Separate Jurisdiction for Cyberspace?" *Journal of Computer-Mediated Communication* 2.1 (June, 1996). <http://onlinelibrary.wiley.com/doi/10.1111/j.1083-6101.1996.tb00186.x/full>. WEB 12 October, 2014.

O'Brien, Danny. "Lowering Your Standards: DRM and the Future of the W3C." Electronic Frontier Foundation, October 2, 2013. <https://www.eff.org/deeplinks/2013/10/lowering-your-standards>. WEB 5 October, 2014.

Ochoa, Tyler T. "Rationalizing (?) the Hart and Keller v. EA Sports Publicity Rights Rulings." *Technology & Marketing Law Blog*, August 5, 2013. <http://blog.ericgoldman.org/archives/2013/08/a_futile_attemp.htm>. WEB 13 October, 2014.

———. "Who Owns an Avatar? Copyright, Creativity, and Virtual Worlds." *Vanderbilt Journal of Entertainment and Technology Law* 14.4,(2012): 959–91. <http://www.jetlaw.org/wp-content/journal-pdfs/Ochoa.pdf>. WEB 29 June, 2012.

OECD. *Magnitude of Counterfeiting and Piracy of Tangible Products: An Update*. Organization for Economic Cooperation and Development. November 2009. <http://www.oecd.org/sti/ind/44088872.pdf>. WEB 3 July, 2014.

Ogi, Tetsuro, Toshio Yamada, Michitaka Hirose, and Kenji Suzuki. "Live Video Integration for High Presence Virtual World." *Proceedings of INET2001* (2001). <http://lab.sdm.keio.ac.jp/ogi/papers/SCI2001paper.pdf>. WEB 15 August, 2014.

Ogi, Tetsuro, Toshio Yamada, Ken Tamagawa, and Michitaka Hirose. "Video Avatar Communication in a Networked Virtual Environment." *Proceedings of INET2000* (2000). <https://www.isoc.org/inet2000/cdproceedings/4c/4c_3.htm>. WEB 15 August, 2014.

Okerson, Ann, and Kendon Stubbs. "The Library 'Doomsday Machine.' (Sharp Price Increases for Scholarly Journals)." *Publishers Weekly*, 238.8 (February 8, 1991): 36+. Print.

Online Policy Group. "Issue: Digital Defamation." <http://www.onlinepolicy.org/defamation. htm>. WEB 8 June, 2014.

Open Access Directory. *Timeline*. <http://oad.simmons.edu/oadwiki/Timeline>. WEB 15 July, 2014.

"Open at the Source." *Apple.com. n.d.* <https://www.apple.com/opensource/>. WEB 28 September, 2014.

Open Source Initiative. *Frequently Answered Questions.* <http://opensource.org/faq>. WEB 14 July, 2014.

———. *The Open Source Definition (Annotated).* <http://opensource.org/osd-annotated>. WEB 14 July, 2014.

Oppenheim, Matthew J. "Letter to Professor Felten from Recording Industry Association of America. April 9, 2001. <http://www.cs.princeton.edu/sip/sdmi/riaaletter.html>. WEB 6 October, 2014.

Oswald, Ed. "Orphaned Works Legislation Faces Pushback from Artists." *BetaNews*, May 13, 2008. <http://www.betanews.com/article/Orphaned_Works_legislation_faces_pushback_from_artists/1210704196>. WEB 25 August, 2014.

"Overview of IP in Video Games." *IGDA. n.d.* <http://wiki.igda.org/IP_Rights_SIG/Overview_of_IP_in_Video_Games>. WEB 10 August, 2014.

Palazzolo, Joe. "First Amendment Doesn't Distinguish between Bloggers and Press, Court Says." *Wall Street Journal*, January 17, 2014.< http://blogs.wsj.com/law/2014/01/17/first-amendment-doesnt-distinguish-between-bloggers-and-press-court-says/>. WEB 15 April, 2015.

Paradise, Paul R. *Trademarks Counterfeiting, Product Piracy, and the Billion Dollar Threat to the U.S. Economy.* Westport, CT: Quorum Books, 1999. Print.

Parmentier, Guy. "Orchestrating Innovation with User Communities in the Creative Industries." *Technology Forecasting and Social Change* 83 (2014): 40–53. DOI: 10.1016/j.techfore.2013.03.007. <http://halshs.archives-ouvertes.fr/docs/00/84/88/61/PDF/Orchestrationcommunities.pdf>. WEB 12 August, 2014.

Patterson, Lyman Ray. *Copyright in Historical Perspective.* Nashville, TN: Vanderbilt University Press, 1968. Print.

Paul, Ryan. "Controversial Amazon 1-Click Patent Survives Review." *ars technica*, March 10, 2010.<http://arstechnica.com/tech-policy/2010/03/controversial-amazon-1-click-patent-survives-review/>. WEB 18 March, 2014.

———. "*Minecraft* Developer Sued by Aggressive Litigator over DRM Patent." *ars technica*, July 21, 2012. <http://arstechnica.com/gaming/2012/07/minecraft-developer-sued-by-aggressive-litigator-over-drm-patent/>. WEB 8 October, 2014.

———. "'Unethical' HTML Video Copy Protection Proposal Draws Criticism from W3C reps." *ars technica*, February 23, 2012. <http://arstechnica.com/business/2012/02/unethical-html-video-copy-protection-proposal-criticized-by-standards-stakeholders/>. WEB 7 October, 2014.

Pelton, Eric & Associates, PLLC. "Nearly All of the Top 10 in the FORBES® CELEBRITY 100 LIST (WORLD'S MOST POWERFUL CELEBRITIES) Own Registered Trademarks." May 24, 2011. <http://www.erikpelton.com/2011/05/24/celebrities-are-trademarks-too-nine-of-the-top-10-in-forbes-celebrity-100-list-have-registered-trade-marks/>. WEB 6 January, 2014.

Peters, Marybeth. "The Importance of Orphan Works Legislation." *copyright.gov*, September 25, 2008. <http://www.copyright.gov/orphan/OWLegislation/>. WEB 15 September, 2014.

Policy on Enhancing Public Access to Archived Publications Resulting from NIH-Funded Research. February 3, 2005. <http://grants.nih.gov/grants/guide/notice-files/NOT-OD-05-022.html>. WEB 15 July, 2014.

———. *Recommendation of the Register of Copyrights in Rm. 2005–11; Rulemaking on Exemptions from Prohibition on Circumvention of Copyright Protection Systems for Access Control Technologies.* 2006. <http://www.copyright.gov/1201/docs/1201_recommendation.pdf>. WEB 21 March, 2015.

Ponte, Lucille. "The Emperor Has No Clothes: How Digital Sampling Infringement Cases Are Exposing Weaknesses in Traditional Copyright Law and the Need for Statutory Reform." *American Business Law Journal* 43 (2006): 515–60. Print.

Post, David G., and David R. Johnson. "The Great Debate—Law in the Virtual World." *First Monday* 11.2 (2006). <http://firstmonday.org/ojs/index.php/fm/article/view/1311/1231>. WEB 12 October, 2014.

"Public Opinion on Privacy." Electronic Privacy Information Center. <http://epic.org/privacy/survey/>. WEB 25 November, 2013.

Quinn, Gene. "The RCE Backlog: A Critical Patent Office Problem." *IPwatchdog*, February 14, 2013. <http://www.ipwatchdog.com/2013/02/14/the-rce-backlog-a-critical-patent-office-problem/id=35431/>. WEB 15 December, 2013.

Ramos, Andy, Laura López, Anxo Rodríguez, Tim Meng, and Stan Abrams. "The Legal Status of Video Games: Comparative Analysis in National Approaches." *WIPO*, July 29, 2013. <http://www.wipo.int/export/sites/www/copyright/en/activities/pdf/comparative_analysis_on_video_games.pdf>. WEB 5 August, 2014.

Redman, Christopher, and Thomas Sancton. "We Are Not an Average Nation: An Exclusive Talk with Jacques Chirac." *Time* 146.24 (December 11, 1995): 59.

Reid, Brad. "Courts Affirm Bloggers' First Amendment Protections." *Huffington Post*, February 6, 2014. <http://www.huffingtonpost.com/brad-reid/courts-affirm-bloggers-fi_b_4738174.html>. WEB 17 March, 2014.

Report of the Register of Copyrights on the General Revision of the U.S. Copyright Law. July, 1961. <http://www.copyright.gov/reports/annual/archive/ar-1961.pdf>. WEB 26 August, 2014.

"Reverse Engineering." *Chillingeffects.org*. <http://www.chillingeffects.org/reverse/>. WEB 25 August, 2014.

Revised Policy on Enhancing Public Access to Archived Publications Resulting from NIH-Funded Research. January 11, 2008. <http://grants.nih.gov/grants/guide/notice-files/NOT-OD-08-033.html>. WEB 15 July, 2014.

"Right of Publicity: An Overview." *Legal Information Institute.* <http://www.law.cornell.edu/wex/publicity>. WEB 7 September, 2014.

Risen, Tom. "The U.S. Gives the Internet to the World." *U.S. News & World Report*, March 17, 2014. <http://www.usnews.com/news/articles/2014/03/17/the-us-gives-the-internet-to-the-world>. WEB 8 July, 2014.

Rivette, Kevin G., and David Kline. *Rembrandts in the Attic: Unlocking the Hidden Value of Patents.* Boston, MA: Harvard Business School Press, 2000. Print.

Rodriguez, Juan Carlos. "Ex-Dow Scientist Gets 5 Years for Selling Secrets." *Law360*, January 13, 2012. <http://www.law360.com/articles/300068/ex-dow-scientist-gets-5-years-for-selling-secrets>. WEB 24 February, 2014.

Rohter, Larry. "A Copyright Victory, 35 Years Later." *New York Times*, September 10, 2013. <http://www.nytimes.com/2013/09/11/arts/music/a-copyright-victory-35-years-later.html?_r=3&>. WEB 25 November, 2013.

"Ron Paul 2012 v. Does 1–10." *Digital Media Law Project*, January 20, 2012. <http://www.dmlp.org/threats/ron-paul-2012-v-does-1-10#description>. WEB 6 January, 2014.

Roseneor, Jonathan. *CyberLaw: The Law of the Internet.* New York, NY: Springer, 1997. Print.

Roth, Daniel. "Open Source Tycoons." *Wired*, April 2008: 122. Print.

RPX Corporation. *NPE Litigation Report, 2013.* <http://www.rpxcorp.com/wp-content/uploads/2014/01/RPX-2013-NPE-Litigation-Report.pdf.> WEB 16 October, 2014.

Russinovich, Mark. "Sony, Rootkits and Digital Rights Management Gone Too Far." *Mark Russinovich's Blog*, October 31, 2005. <http://blogs.technet.com/b/markrussinovich/archive/2005/10/31/sony-rootkits-and-digital-rights-management-gone-too-far.aspx>. WEB 6 October, 2014.

Russolillo, Steven. "St. Jude Awarded $2.3 Billion in Trade-Secrets Case." *Wall Street Journal*, April 26, 2011. <http://online.wsj.com/news/articles/SB10001424052748703778104576287192660243186>. WEB 24 February, 2014.

Ryan, Johnny. *A History of the Internet and the Digital Future.* London: Reaktion Books. 2010.

Sadun, Erica. "Apple, Labels Both Win with DRM-Free Itunes, Tiered Pricing." *ars technica*, January 6, 2009. <http://arstechnica.com/apple/2009/01/apple-labels-both-win-with-drm-free-itunes-tiered-pricing/>. WEB 6 October, 2014.

Salen, Katie, and Eric Zimmerman. *Rules of Play: Game Design Fundamentals.* MIT Press, 2003. Print.

Samuels, Julie. "Podcasting Community Faces Patent Troll Threat; EFF Wants to Help." February 5, 2013. <https://www.eff.org/deeplinks/2013/02/podcasting-community-faces-patent-troll-threat-eff-wants-help>. WEB 31 December, 2013.

Samuelson, Pamela. "Anti-Circumvention Rules: Threat to Science." *Science* 293.5537 (2001): 2028–31. Print.

Sanders, Alicia C. "Restraining Amazon.com's Orwellian Potential: The Computer Fraud and Abuse Act as Consumer Rights Legislation." *Federal Communications Law Journal* 63.2.(March, 2011): 535–52. Print.

Scacchi, Walt. "Computer Game Mods, Nodders, Modding, and the Mod Scene." *First Monday* 15.5 (May 3, 2010). <http://firstmonday.org/article/view/2965/2526>. WEB 12 August, 2014.

Schaefers, Scott. "Scott Schaefers Discussing Employee Social Media Privacy—How Employers Can Strike the Necessary Balance." *Trading Secrets*, April 18, 2014. <http://www.tradese-cretslaw.com/2014/04/articles/trade-secrets/scott-schaefers-discussing-employee-social-media-privacy-how-employers-can-strike-the-necessary-balance>. WEB 15 April, 2015.

Schroeder, Ralph. "Defining Virtual Worlds and Virtual Environments." *Journal of Virtual Worlds Research* 1.1 (July 2008): 2–3. <https://journals.tdl.org/jvwr/index.php/jvwr/article/view/294/248>. WEB 5 August, 2014.

"2nd Life: Judge Rules against 'One-sided' TOS in Bragg Lawsuit." *mmosite.com* (via Reuters), May 2, 2007. <http://news.mmosite.com/content/2007-06-02/20070602235243962.shtml>. WEB 12 October, 2014.

The Section 108 Study Group Report. US Copyright Office and the National Digital Information Infrastructure and Preservation Program of the Library of Congress. March, 2008. <http://www.section108.gov/docs/Sec108StudyGroupReport.pdf>. WEB 18 November, 2013.

Seidel, Arthur H. *What the General Practitioner Should Know about Trademarks and Copyrights.* Philadelphia, PA: American Law Institute, 1976. Print.

SelectUSA. "The Media & Entertainment Industry in the United States." US Department of Commerce. <http://selectusa.commerce.gov/industry-snapshots/media-entertainment-in-dustry-united-states>. WEB 19 March, 2015.

"Senator Coons Introduces Legislation to Help Companies Protect Their Trade Secrets." July 17, 2012. <http://www.coons.senate.gov/newsroom/releases/release/senator-coons-intro-duces-legislation-to-help-companies-protect-their-trade-secrets->. WEB 17 February, 2014.

"Sending a DMCA Takedown Notice." *n.d. dmca-info.com.* <http://www.dmca-info.com/send-ing-a-dmca-takedown-notice.html>. WEB 26 August, 2014.

Shanley, Mia, and Sandra Maler. "Pirate Bay Co-Founder Arrested in Sweden to Serve Copyright Violation Sentence." *Reuters*, May 31, 2014. <http://www.reuters.com/arti-cle/2014/05/31/us-sweden-piratebay-idUSKBN0EB0XF20140531>. WEB 26 July, 2014.

Shirky, Clay. *Cognitive Surplus: Creativity and Generosity in a Connected Age.* New York, NY: Penguin Press, 2010. Print.

Simons, Barbara. "The ACM Declaration in *Felten v. RIAA*." *Communications of the ACM* 44.10 (2001): 23. Print.

Sinclair, Brendan. "Patented Game Mechanics that Might Surprise You." *Gamespot.com*, April 3, 2012. <http://www.gamespot.com/articles/patented-game-mechanics-that-might-surprise-you/1100-6369027/>. WEB 12 August, 2014.

Singel, Ryan. "Open Season on Patents Starts Thursday, Thanks to Crowdsourced Platform." *wired.com*, September 20, 2013. <http://www.wired.com/threatlevel/2012/09/patent-bust-ing-crowdsourced/>. WEB 15 December, 2013.

Singer, Natasha. "Under Code, Apps Would Disclose Collection of Data." *NYT.com*, July 25, 2013. <http://www.nytimes.com/2013/07/26/technology/under-code-apps-would-disclose-collection-of-data.html>. WEB 24 November, 2013.

Siwek, *Copyright Industries in the U.S. Economy: The 2011 Report.* Economists Incorporated, 2011. <http://www.iipa.com/pdf/2011CopyrightIndustriesReport.PDF>. WEB 25 June, 2014.

Sklyarov, Dimitry. "ElcomSoft—Ebooks Security—Theory and Practice." DEF CON Nine. Las Vegas, NV, 2001. <http://www.cs.cmu.edu/~dst/Adobe/Gallery/ds-defcon2/ds-defcon.html>. WEB 6 October, 2014.

Smedinghoff, Thomas J., ed. *Online Law: The SPA's Legal Guide to Doing Business on the Internet.* Reading, MA: Addison-Wesley Developers Press, 1996. Print.

Smith, Eric H. "Letter to Mr. Stanford McCoy ('Identification of Countries Under Section182 of the Trade Act of 1974: Request for Public Comments')." February 11, 2008. <http://www.iipa.com/pdf/2008SPEC301COVERLETTER.pdf>. WEB 29 September, 2014.

Solove, Daniel J. *The Digital Person: Technology and Privacy in the Information Age.* New York, NY: New York UP, 2004. Print.

_____. *Future of Reputation: Gossip, Rumor, and Privacy on the Internet.* New Haven, CT: Yale UP, 2007. Print.

_____. *Nothing to Hide: The False Tradeoff between Privacy and Security.* New Haven, CT: Yale UP, 2011. Print.

Spears, Victoria Prussen. "The Case that Started It All: *Roberson v. The Rochester Folding Box Company.*" *Privacy & Data Security Law Journal* (November 2008): 1043–50. <http://meyerowitzcommunications.com/pdf/roberson-vs-the-rochester.pdf>. WEB 20 March, 2013.

Stallman, Richard. "About the GNU Project." May 14, 2014. <https://www.gnu.org/gnu/thegnuproject.html>. WEB 14 July, 2014.

———. "Initial Announcement—GNU Project." September 27, 1983. <https://www.gnu.org/gnu/initial-announcement.html>. WEB 14 July, 2014.

———. "RMS Lecture at KTH (Sweden)." Lecture, October 20, 1986. Stockholm, Sweden. <https://www.gnu.org/philosophy/stallman-kth.html>. WEB 14 July, 2014.

———. "Words to Avoid." *Free Society: Selected Essays of Richard M. Stallman.* Boston, MA: GNU Press, 2002: 191–96. Print.

Straumsheim, Carl. "Arguments over Open Access." *Inside Higher Ed,* January 6, 2014. <https://www.insidehighered.com/news/2014/01/06/historians-clash-over-open-access-movement>. WEB 30 September, 2014.

Streitfeld, David. "Carpet Bombing: How One Business Is Trying to Get Rid of Bad Reviews." *New York Times,* January 16, 2014. <http://bits.blogs.nytimes.com/2014/01/16/carpet-bombing-how-one-business-is-trying-to-get-rid-of-bad-reviews/.WEB 15 April, 2015.

Suber, Peter. "Green/Gold OA and Gratis/Libre OA." *Open Access News,* August 2, 2008. <http://www.earlham.edu/~peters/fos/2008/08/greengold-oa-and-gratislibre-oa.html>. WEB 20 December, 2011.

Sullivan, Jessica. "Personal Audio Announces San Disk License Agreement." Personal Audio, press release, September 12, 2013. <http://personalaudio.net/wp content/uploads/2013/09/2013-09-13-Sandisk-Press-Release.pdf>. WEB 31 December, 2013.

"Summaries of Fair Use Cases." Stanford University Library. *n.d.* <http://fairuse.stanford.edu/overview/fair-use/cases/>. WEB 15 September, 2014.

Supreme Court of the United States (SCOTUS). <http://www.supremecourtus.gov>). WEB March 21, 2015.

Tajitsu, Naomi. "Kim Dotcom: New Mega Site Is Legal, Not Revenge for Megaupload Saga." *Huffington Post/Reuters*, January 19, 2013. <http://www.huffingtonpost.com/2013/01/19/kim-dotcom-new-mega-site_n_2511783.html>. WEB 26, July, 2014.

Talacko, Paul. "Towards a Piracy High Watermark: Copyright Protection: Paul Talacko Looks at the Initiative to Create Secure Music Standards and the Digital Watermarking Technology." *Financial Times*, Inside Track, December 29, 2000. Print.

Tedford, Thomas L., and Dale A. Herbeck. *Freedom of Speech in the United States*. 7th ed. State College, PA: Strata Publishing, Inc., 2013. Print.

Tehranian, John. "Infringement Nation: Copyright Reform and the Law/Norm Gap." *Utah Law Review* 3 (2007): 537–50. Print.

Terdiman, Daniel. "Curious Case of Lawsuit over Value of Twitter Followers Is Settled." *c/net*, December 3, 2012. <http://www.cnet.com/news/curious-case-of-lawsuit-over-value-of-twitter-followers-is-settled/>. WEB 30 July, 2014.

"Termination Rights—Explained." *Association of Independent Music Publishers—AIMP*. <http://www.aimp.org/copyrightCorner/2/Termination_Rights_-_Explained>. WEB 25 November, 2013.

"Terms of Service." *Linden Lab*. <http://lindenlab.com/tos>. WEB 11 August, 2014.

Top 500 Supercomputer Site. <http://www.top500.org/statistics/details/osfam/1>. WEB 28 September, 2014.

Trimble, Marketa. "The Problem of "International Orphan Works." *Technology and Marketing Law Blog*, January 3, 2013. <http://blog.ericgoldman.org/archives/2013/01/the_problem_of.htm>. WEB 28 September, 2014.

Turow, Joseph. *The Daily You: How the New Advertising Industry Is Defining Your Identity and Your Worth*. New Haven, CT: Yale UP, 2011. Print.

United States Code, Office of the Law Revision Council. <http://uscode.house.gov/search/criteria.shtml>. WEB November 25, 2013.

United States Copyright Office. "The Computer Software Rental Amendments Act of 1990: The Nonprofit Library Lending Exemption to the 'Rental Right': Executive Summary." September 15, 1994. <http://www.copyright.gov/reports/software_ren.html>. WEB 29 November 2013.

———. *Copyright Basics*. May, 2012. <http://www.copyright.gov/circs/circ1.pdf > or <http://www.copyright.gov/circs/circ01.pdf>. WEB 7 March, 2015.

———. *Copyright Restoration under the URAA*. January, 2013. <http://www.copyright.gov/circs/circ38b.pdf>. WEB 21 October, 2014.

———. *Duration of Copyright*. August, 2011. <http://www.copyright.gov/circs/circ15a.pdf>. WEB 21 October, 2014.

———. *How to Investigate the Copyright Status of a Work*. January, 2012. <http://www.copyright.gov/circs/circ22.pdf>. WEB 21 October, 2014.

———. *Report on Orphan Works: A Report of the Register of Copyrights*. Washington, DC, January 2006. <http://www.copyright.gov/orphan/orphan-report-full.pdf>. WEB 18 November, 2013.

————. "Rulemaking on Exemptions from Prohibition on Circumvention of Technological Measures that Control Access to Copyrighted Works." July 26, 2010. <http://www.copyright.gov/1201/2010/>. WEB 30 November, 2013.

————. "Section 1201: Exemptions to Prohibition against Circumvention of Technological Measures Protecting Copyrighted Works." October 26, 2012. <http://copyright.gov/1201/2012/>. WEB 3 October, 2014.

United States Court of Appeals, 7th Circuit. <http://www.ca7.uscourts.gov>. WEB November 25, 2013.

United States Courts. <http://www.uscourts.gov>. WEB November 25, 2013.

United States Department of Labor. "Definition of Trade Secret." <http://www.osha.gov/pls/oshaweb/owadisp.show_document?p_table=STANDARDS&p_id=10103>.

United States District Court, Northern District of Illinois. <http://www.ilnd.uscourts.gov>. WEB November 25, 2013.

United States Government Accountability Office. *Intellectual Property: Observations on Efforts to Quantify the Economic Effects of Counterfeit and Pirated Goods.* April, 2010. <http://www.gao.gov/new.items/d10423.pdf>. WEB 3 July, 2014.

United States House of Representatives, Committee on the Judiciary. *Copyright Law Revision, House Report 94-1476.* 1976. <http://copyright.gov/history/law/clrev_94-1476.pdf>. WEB 27 August, 2014.

United States Patent and Trademark Office (USPTO). Patent Process Overview. <http://www.uspto.gov/patents/process/ppo_textonly.jsp>. WEB 15 December, 2013.

————. "Patents, What Is a Patent?" <http://www.uspto.gov/patents/>. WEB 21 October, 2014.

————. *Performance and Accountability Report, Fiscal Year 2011.* <http://www.uspto.gov/about/stratplan/ar/USPTOFY2011PAR.pdf>. WEB 5 January, 2014.

————. *Performance and Accountability Report, Fiscal Year 2012.* <http://www.uspto.gov/about/stratplan/ar/USPTOFY2012PAR.pdf>. WEB 5 January, 2014.

————. *Section 1(a) Timeline: Application Based on Use in Commerce.* <http://www.uspto.gov/trademarks/process/tm_sec1atimeline.jsp>. WEB 5 January, 2014.

Urban, Jennifer M., and Jason Schultz, for Consumers Union. "Brief of Amicus Curiae Consumers Union in Support of Appellee." *The Chamberlain Group, Inc., v. Skylink Technologies, Inc.* <https://www.eff.org/files/filenode/Chamberlain_v_Skylink/20040408_skylink_amicus_brief.pdf>. WEB 21 October, 2014.

"Usage Statistics and Market Share of Unix for Websites." *W³Techs.* <http://w3techs.com/technologies/details/os-unix/all/all>. WEB 28 September, 2014.

"US Phone Unlocking Deadline Expires." *BBC News,* Technology. January 28, 2013. <http://www.bbc.co.uk/news/technology-21200566>. WEB November 30, 2013.

Vaidhyanathan, Siva. *Copyrights and Copywrongs: The Rise of Intellectual Property and How It Threatens Creativity.* New York, NY: New York UP, 2001. Print.

Van Gelder, Stéphane. "Think ICANN Will End up Rolling in New gTLD Cash? Think Again!" *CircleID,* January 2, 2014. <http://www.circleid.com/posts/20140102think_icann_will_end_up_rolling_in_new_gtld_cash_think_again/>. WEB 5 January, 2014.

von Lohman, Fred Hinze, and Gwen Hinze. *DMCA Triennial Rulemaking: Failing the Digital Consumer.* December 1, 2005. San Francisco, CA: Electronic Frontier Foundation.

<https://www.eff.org/document/dmca-triennial-rulemaking-failing-digital-consumer>. WEB 6 October, 2014.

Warner, Brian. "How Much Money Has Pat Riley Made Off His 'Three-peat' Trademark?" *Celebrity Networth*, June 23, 2013. <http://www.celebritynetworth.com/articles/entertainment-articles/how-much-money-has-pet-riley-made-off-his-three-peat-trademark/>. WEB 6 January, 2014.

Warr, Philippa. "GOG's Managing Director: Gamer Resistance to DRM Is Stronger Than Ever." *wired.co.uk*, December 31, 2013. <http://www.wired.co.uk/news/archive/2013-12/31/gog-qa>. WEB 7 October, 2014.

Warren, Samuel D., and Louis D. Brandeis. "The Right to Privacy." *Harvard Law Review* 4 (1890–91): 193–220. <http://www.law.louisville.edu/library/collections/brandeis/node/225>. WEB 17 March, 2014.

Waxer, Barbara, and Marsha L. Baum. *Internet Surf and Turf Revealed: The Essential Guide to Copyright, Fair Use, and Finding Media*. Boston, MA: Thompson Course Technology, 2006. Print.

Weber, Steven. *Success of Open Source*. Cambridge, MA: Harvard University Press, 2004. <http://site.ebrary.com/lib/alltitles/docDetail.action?docID=10328787>. WEB 17 September, 2014.

Webster, Tom. "The Infinite Dial 2011—Navigating Digital Platforms." *edisonresearch.com*, April 5, 2011. <http://www.edisonresearch.com/home/archives/2011/04/the_infinite_dial_2011.php>. WEB 24 November, 2013.

Wheeler, David A. "History of Unix, Linux, and Open Source/Free Software." *Secure Programming for Linux and Unix HOWTO*. <http://www.dwheeler.com/secure-class/Secure-Programs-HOWTO/history.html>. WEB 29 September, 2014.

Wolf, Christopher. "Standards for Internet Jurisdiction." *findlaw.com*, March 26, 2008. <http://library.findlaw.com/1999/Jan/1/241482.html>. WEB 24 November, 2013.

Wolford, Josh. "Media Consumption Booming in America." *Webpronews.com*, April 13, 2011. <http://www.webpronews.com/media-consumption-booming-in-america-2011-04>. WEB 24 November, 2013.

Wolverton, Brad. "Settlement in Video-Game Case Could Benefit Current NCAA Athletes." *The Chronicle of Higher Education*, June 1, 2014. <http://chronicle.com/blogs/ticker/settlement-in-video-game-case-could-benefit-current-ncaa-athletes/79023>. WEB 10 August, 2014.

World Intellectual Property Organization. WIPO Statistics Data Center: Direct Application Patents Filed, Total Count by Filing Office, 2011, United States. <http://ipstats.wipo.int/ipstatv2/>. WEB 31 August, 2014.

WTO. *International Trade Statistics, 2012*. World Trade Organization. <http://www.wto.org/english/res_e/statis_e/its2012_e/its2012_e.pdf>. WEB 3 July, 2014.

Xia, Jingfeng, Sarah B. Gilchrist, Nathaniel X. P. Smith, Justin A. Kingery, Jennifer R. Radecki, Marcia L. Wilhelm, Keith C. Harrison, Michael J. Ashby, and Alyson J. Mahn. "A Review of Open Access Self-Archiving Mandate Policies." *Portal: Libraries and the Academy* 12.1 (2012): 85–102. <https://www.press.jhu.edu/journals/portal_libraries_and_the_academy/portal_pre_print/current/articles/12.1xia.pdf>. WEB 18 September, 2014.

Xie, Yun. "Redefining Privacy in the Era of Personal Genomics." *ars technica*, February 23, 2010. <http://arstechnica.com/science/2010/02/dna-data-sharing-a-privacy-conundrum>. WEB 10 June, 2014.

Yegulalp, Serdar. "Berners-Lee and W3C Approve HTML5 Video DRM Additions." *InfoWorld*, October 4, 2013. <http://www.infoworld.com/article/2612478/html5/berners-lee-and-w3c-approve-html5-video-drm-additions.html>. WEB 5 October, 2014.

Yeh, Brian T. *An Overview of the "Patent Trolls" Debate*. Congressional Research Service, April 16, 2013. <http://www.fas.org/sgp/crs/misc/R42668.pdf>. WEB 28 December, 2013.

Zetter, Kim. "Judge Acquits Lori Drew in Cyberbullying Case, Overrules Jury." *Wired*, July 2, 2009. <http://www.wired.com/2009/07/drew_court/>. WEB 8 June, 2014.

Zolkos, Rodd. "Commercial Insurance Is Limited for Patent Infringement." *Business Insurance*, September 2, 2012. <http://www.businessinsurance.com/article/20120902/NEWS06/309029983>. WEB 31 December, 2013.

Cases[1]

A&M Records, Inc. v. Napster, Inc., 239 F. 3d 1004 (9ᵗʰ Cir. 2001).

Abdul-Jabbar v. Gen. Motors, 85 F.3d 407, 415–16 (9ᵗʰ Cir. 1996).

Abreu v. Slide, Inc., 12 0042 WHA (N.D. Cal., July 12, 2012).

Acuff-Rose Music Inc. v. Campbell, 972 F.2d 1429 (6ᵗʰ Cir. 1992).

Alice Corp. Pty. Ltd. v. CLS Bank Int'l, 134 S. Ct. 2347 (2014).

Almeida v. Amazon.com, Inc., 456 F.3d 1316 (11ᵗʰ Cir. 2006).

Amazon.com v. Barnesandnoble.com, 239 F.3d 1343 (Fed. Cir. 2001).

American Broadcasting Cos., Inc., et al. v. Aereo, Inc., f/k/a Bamboom Labs, Inc., 13 US 461 (2013).

Apple Inc. v. Samsung Elecs. Co., Case No.: 11-CV-01846-LHK, U.S. Dist. LEXIS 117494 (N.D. CA., August 20, 2014).

Art of Living Found. v. Doe, 2012 U.S. Dist. LEXIS 61582, 2012 WL 1565281 (N.D. Cal. May 1, 2012).

Ascend Health Corp. v. Wells, Case No. 4:12-CV-83-BR, 2013 U.S. Dist. LEXIS 35237 (E.D.N.C. 2013).

Association for Molecular Pathology v. Myriad Genetics, 133 S. Ct. 2107; 186 L. Ed. 2d 124; 2013.

Authors Guild v. Google Inc., 954 F. Supp. 2d 282, 2013 (S.D.N.Y.).

Authors Guild, Inc. v. HathiTrust, 755 F.3d 87 (2ⁿᵈ Cir. 2014).

Baker v. Selden, 101 U.S. 99 (1879).

Bally Total Fitness Holding Corp. v. Faber, 29 F. Supp. 2d 1161 (C.D. Cal. 1998).

Banks v. Unisys Corp., 228 F.3d 1357, 1359 (Fed. Cir. 2000).

Bartnicki v. Vopper, 532 U.S. 514 (2001).

Berger v. New York, 388 U.S. 41 (1967).

Big O Tire Dealers, Inc. v. Goodyear Tire & Rubber Co., 561 F.2d 1365 (10th Cir. 1977).

Bilski v. Kappos, 130 S. Ct. 3218 (2010).

Blumenthal v. Drudge, 992 F. Supp. 44 (D.D.C. 1998).

Board of Trustees of the Leland Stanford Junior University v. Roche Molecular Systems, Inc., et al., 583 F. 3d 832 (Fed. Cir. 2009), *affirmed* 1s31 S. Ct. 2188 (2011).

Bolger v. Youngs Drug Prods. Corp., 463 U.S. 60 (1983).

Bosley v. Wildwett.com, 310 F. Supp. 2d 914 (N.D. Ohio 2004).

Bowers v. Baystate Techs., Inc., 320 F.3d 1317 (Fed. Cir., 2003).

Bragg v. Linden Research, Inc. and Philip Rosedale, No. 06–4925, USDC (E.D. Pa., May 30, 2007).

Bridgeport Music v. Dimension Films, 410 F.3d 792 (6th Cir. 2005).

Brown v. ACMI Pop, 873 N.E.2d 954 (Ill. App. 1st Dist. 2007).

Campbell v. Acuff-Rose Music, Inc., 510 U.S. 569, 579 (1994).

Carafano v. Metrosplash.com, Inc., 339 F.3d 1119 (9th Cir. 2003).

Cardtoons, L.C. v. Major League Baseball Players' Ass'n, 95 F.3d 959 (10th Cir. 1996).

Carson v. Here's Johnny Portable Toilets, Inc., 698 F.2d 831, 835 (6th Cir. 1983).

Cartoon Network LP, LLLP v. CSC Holdings, Inc. (Cablevision), 536 F.3d 121 (2nd Cir. 2008).

Castle Rock Entertainment v. Carol Publ'g Group, 150 F.3d 132 (2nd Cir. 1998).

CBC Distribution and Marketing, Inc. v. Major League Baseball Adv. Media, L.P., F.3d (8th Cir. 2007).

Christian Louboutin S.A. v. Yves Saint Laurent Am. Holdings, Inc., 696 F.3d 206, (2nd Cir. 2012).

Christou et al. v. Beatport, LLC, 849 F. Supp. 2d 1055 (D. Colo. 2012).

Columbia Pictures Industries, Inc. v. Fung, 710 F.3d 1020 (9th Cir. 2013).

CompuServe v. Cyber Promotions, Inc., 962 F. Supp. 1015 (S.D. Ohio, C2–96–1070, 1997).

Computer Associates Int'l v. Altai, 982 F.2d 693 (2d Cir. 1992).

Copiepresse v. Google, The Court of First Instance in Brussels, Nr. 06/10.928/C (Feb. 13, 2007).

Corporate Techs., Inc. v. Harnett, 731 F.3d 6 (1st Cir. 2013).

Cubby v. CompuServe Inc., No. 90 Civ. 6571. USDC (S.D.N.Y. Oct. 29, 1991).

Cyber Promotions, Inc. v. America Online, Inc., 948 F. Supp. 436 (E.D. Pa. 1996).

Dendrite International, Inc. v. John Doe No. 3, Superior Court of New Jersey, Appellate Division. 342 N.J. Super. 134 (2001).

Dr. Seuss Enterprises, L.P. v. Penguin Books USA, Inc., 109 F.3d 1394 (9th Cir. 1997).

DVD Copy Control Assn., Inc. v. Bunner, 116 Cal. App. 4th 241, 10 Cal. Rptr. 3d 185, 69 U.S.P.Q.2d 1907 (Cal. Ct. App. 2004).

eBay Inc. v. MercExchange, L.L.C., 547 U.S. 388, 126 S.Ct. 1837 (2006).

EF Cultural Travel BV v. Explorica, Inc., 274 F.3d 577 (1st Cir. 2001).

EFF v. Sony BMG, Cal. Sup. Ct., Los Angeles Cty. (2005).

E.K.D. v. Facebook, Inc., 885 F. Supp. 2d 894 (S.D. Ill. 2012).

Eldred v. Ashcroft, 537 U.S. 186 (2003).

Eolas Technologies, Inc. v. Adobe Systems Inc., Case No. 6:09-CV-446 (E.D. Texas, Feb. 2012).

Eolas Techs. v. Microsoft Corp., 399 F.3d 1325 (Fed. Cir. 2005).

Eros, LLC, et al. v. Simon, et al., 1:07-cv-04447-SLT-JMA. USDC (E.D.N.Y. Oct. 24, 2007).

Eros, LLC v. Robert Leatherwood and John 1–10 Does, 8:2007cv01158. (M.D. Fla. July 3, 2007).

Estavillo v. Sony Computer Entertainment America, 2009 WL 3072887 (N.D. Cal. Sept. 22, 2009).

Feist Publications, Inc. v. Rural Telephone Service Co., 499 U.S. 340 (1991).

Festo Corp. v. Shoketsu Kinzoku Kogyo Kabushiki Co., 535 U.S. 722 (2002).

Field v. Google Inc., 412 F. Supp. 2d 1106 (D. Nev. 2006).

Folsom v. Marsh, 9 F.Cas. 342, 6 Hunt Mer. Mag. 175, 2 Story 100, No. 4901 (1841).

Fox News v. TVEYES, Inc., 13 Civ. 5315 (S.D. NY Sept. 9, 2014).

Fox Television Stations, Inc., et al., v. Filmon X Llc, et al., U.S. Dist. Lexis 188351. (USDC, November 26, 2013).

Fraley v. Facebook, Inc., 830 F. Supp. 2d 785 (N.D. Cal. 2011).

Free Software Fdn., Inc. v. Cisco Sys., Inc., No. 1:08-CV-10764 (S.D.N.Y. Dec. 11, 2008).

Gawronski v. Amazon.com, Inc., Case No. 2:09-cv-01084-JCC (W.D. Wash.), Dkt. No. 1, Jul. 30, 2009.

GoDaddy.com, LLC v. Hollie Toups, 429 S.W.3d 752 (Tex. App. 2014).

Golan v. Holder, 132 S. Ct. 873 (2012).

Goldman v. United States, 316 U.S. 129 (1942).

Google Inc. v. Daniel Giersch, Office for Harmonization in the Internal Market (Trade Marks and Designs), Second Board of Appeal R 252/2007–2 (Feb. 26, 2008).

Google Spain v. AEPD and Mario Costeja González, Court of Justice of the European Union, May 13, 2014.

Graham v. John Deere, 383 U.S. 1 (1966).

Grand Upright Music, Ltd v. Warner Bros. Records Inc., 780 F. Supp. 182 (S.D.N.Y. 1991).

Graver Tank & Mfg. Co. v. Linde Air Products, Co., 339 U.S. 605 (1950).

Griswold v. Connecticut, (No. 496) 151 Conn. 544, 200 A.2d 479, reversed by *Griswold v. Connecticut,* 381 U.S. 479, 85 S.Ct. 1678 (1965).

Haelan Laboratories, Inc. v. Topps Chewing Gum. Inc., 202 F.2d 866 (2nd Cir. 1953).

Harper & Row v. Nation Enterprises Case Media, 471 U.S. 539 (1985).

Hart v. Electronic Arts, 717 F.3d 141 (3rd Cir. 2013).

Henley v. Dillard Department Stores, 46 F. Supp. 2d 587 (N.D. Tex. 1999).

Hustler Magazine, Inc. v. Falwell, 485 U.S. 46 (1988).

Hustler Magazine, Inc., v. Moral Majority, Inc., Old Time Gospel Hour, Jerry Falwell, 606 F. Supp.1526 (C.D. Cal. Apr. 23, 1985).

IDX Systems Corp. v. Epic Systems, Corp., 285 F.3d 581 (7th Cir. 2002).

In re: Blackberry Application No. 09159981.1 (Case No. T 1148/11 – 3.5.05). Board of Appeal of the European Patent Office, Aug. 7, 2014.

In re NCAA Student-Athlete Name & Likeness Licensing Litig., 724 F.3d 1268 (9th Cir. 2013).

International Public Prosecution Office, Stockholm, v. Pirate Bay, (Stockholm District Court, *Verdict B 13301-06),* 2009.

Intihar v. Citizens Info. Assocs., LLC, No. 2:13-cv-720 (M.D. Fla. Oct. 11, 2013).

Inwood Labs., Inc. v. Ives Labs, 456 U.S. 844 (1982).

Ip Innovation LLC v. Red Hat, Inc., 705 F. Supp. 2d 687 (E.D. Tex. 2010).

IPXL Holdings, L.L.C. v. Amazon.com, Inc., 430 F.3d 1377 (Fed. Cir. 2005).

Jacobsen v. Katzer, 535 F.3d 1373, 1381 (Fed. Cir. 2008).

Jane Doe v. Friendfinder Network, Inc. and Various, Inc., Civil No. 07-cv-286 Opinion No. 2008 DNH 058 (2008).

Johns-Byrne Company v. TechnoBuffalo LLC, No. 11 L 009161 (Cir. Court of Cook County, Illinois), Order, Jul. 13, 2012.

Jones v. Dirty World Entm't Recordings LLC, 755 F.3d 398 (6th Cir. 2014).

Jordan v. Jewel, 743 F.3d 509 (7th Cir. 2014).

Joude v. WordPress Found., 2014 U.S. Dist. LEXIS 91345, 2014 WL 3107441 (N.D. Cal. July 3, 2014).

Kalem Co. v. Harper Bros., 222 U.S. 55 (1911).

Katz v. Chevaldina, (S.D. Fla. June 17, 2014).

Katz v. United States, 389 U.S. 347 (1967).

Kelly v. Arriba Soft Corp., 336 F.3d 811 (9th Cir. 2003).

Kewanee Oil Co. v. Bicron Corp., 416 U.S. 470; 94 S. Ct. 1879 (1974).

KNB Enters. v. Matthews, 78 Cal. App. 4th 362 (Cal. Ct. App. 2000).

KSR Int'l Co. v. Teleflex Inc., 550 U.S. 398, 127 S.Ct. 1727 (2007).

March Madness Athletic Ass'n v. Netfire, Inc., 2005 U.S. App. LEXIS 1475 (5th Cir. Jan. 24, 2005).

Marcus v. Rowley and San Diego Unified School District, 695 F.2d 1171 (9th Cir. 1983).

Markman v. Westview Instruments Inc., 517 U.S. 370 (1996).

Mazer v. Stein, 347 U.S. 201 (1954).

McIntyre v. Ohio Elections Commission, 514 U.S. 334 (1995).

McKee v. Laurion, 825 N.W.2d 725 (Minn. 2013).

McRoberts Software Inc. v. Media 100 Inc., 329 F.3d 557 (7th Cir. 2003).

MDY Indus., LLC v. Blizzard Entm't, Inc., 629 F.3d 928 (9th Cir. 2010).

Metro-Goldwyn-Mayer Studios Inc. v. Grokster, Ltd., (04–480) 545 U.S. 913 (2005).

Michaels v. Internet Entm't Group, Inc., 5 F. Supp. 2d 823 (C.D. Cal. 1998).

Microsoft Corporation v. i4i Limited Partnership, 131 S. Ct. 2238 (2011).

Microsoft v. TomTom, 2:09-cv-00247 (W. Dist. Wash. Apr. 2, 2009).

Milkovich v. Lorain Journal Co., 497 U.S. 1 (1990).

Monster Communications, Inc. v. Turner Broadcasting Sys. Inc., 935 F. Supp. 490 (S.D. N.Y. 1996).

Moseley v. Victoria's Secret Catalogue, Inc., (01–1015) 537 U.S. 418 (2003).

National Association for the Advancement of Colored People v. Alabama, 357 U.S. 449 (1958).

Network Automation, Inc. v. Advanced Sys. Concepts, Inc., 638 F.3d 1137 (9th Cir. 2011).

Newcombe v. Adolph Coors Co., 157 F.3d 686 (9th Cir. 1998).

New York Times v. Sullivan, 39, 376 U.S. 254 (1964).

Nieman v. Versuslaw, Inc., 512 F. App'x 635 (7th Cir. 2013).

Nixon v. Administrator of General Services, 433 U.S. 425 (1977).

Northland Family Planning Clinic v. Center for Bio-Ethical Reform, No: SACV 11-731 JVS (C.D. Cal. June 15, 2012).

NTP, Inc. v. Research in Motion, Ltd., 418 F.3d 1282 (Fed. Cir. 2005).

O'Grady v. Superior Court, 139 Cal. App. 4th 1423 (Ct. App. 2006).

Olmstead v. United States, 277 U.S. 438 (1928).

1-800 Contacts, Inc. v. WhenU.Com, Inc., 414 F.3d 400 (2nd Cir. 2005).

Oracle Am., Inc. v. Google Inc., 2012 U.S. App. LEXIS 25335 (Fed. Cir. Dec. 10, 2012).

Palladium Music, Inc. v. EatSleepMusic, Inc., 398 F.3d 1193, 1200 (10ᵗʰ Cir. 2005).

Panavision Int'l, L.P. v. Toeppen, 141 F.3d 1316 (9ᵗʰ Cir. 1998).

Paramount Pictures Corporation v. Carol Publishing Group, et al., USDC (S.D.N.Y. 1998).

Pebble Beach Co. v. Caddy, No. 04–15577, 2006 WL 1897091 (9ᵗʰ Cir. July 12, 2006).

PepsiCo Inc. v. Redmond, 54 F.3d 1262 (7ᵗʰ Cir. 1995).

Perfect 10, Inc. v. Amazon.com, Inc., 508 F.3d 1146 (9ᵗʰ Cir. 2007).

Perfect 10, Inc. v. CCBill LLC, 481 F.3d 751 (9ᵗʰ Cir. 2007).

Perkins v. LinkedIn Corp., 2014 U.S. Dist. LEXIS 81042 (N.D. Cal. June 12, 2014).

Personal Audio, LLC v. Apple, Inc. et al (2011) 2011 U.S. Dist. LEXIS 157778.

Pesina v. Midway Mfg. Co., 948 F. Supp. 40 (N.D. Ill. 1996).

Phillips v. AWH, 415 F.3d 1303 (Fed. Cir. 2005) (en banc).

PhoneDog v. Kravitz, 2011 U.S. Dist. LEXIS 129229, 2011 WL 5415612 (N.D. Cal. Nov. 8, 2011).

Playboy Enters., Inc. v. Welles, 279 F.3d 796 (9ᵗʰ Cir. 2002).

Polaroid Corp. v. Polarad Electronics Corp., 287 F.2d 492 (2ⁿᵈ Cir. 1961).

Procter & Gamble Mfg. Co. v. Hagler, 880 S.W.2d 123, 128–29 (Tex. App. 1994).

Qualitex Co. v. Jacobson Products Co., 514 U.S. 159 (1995).

Rambus Inc. v. Infineon Techs. AG, 318 F.3d 1081 (Fed. Cir. 2003).

Realnetworks, Inc. v. DVD Copy Control Ass'n, 641 F. Supp. 2d 913 (N.D. Cal. 2009).

Recording Industry Ass'n of America, Inc., v. Verizon Internet Services, Inc., 359 F.3d 1229 (D.C. Cir. 2003).

Rescuecom Corp. v. Google Inc., 562 F.3d 123 (2ⁿᵈ Cir. 2009).

Riley v. California, 134 S. Ct. 2473 (2014).

Roberson v. The Rochester Folding Box Company, 171 N.Y. 538 (1902).

Robert Thomas v. Bill Page et al., No. 04 LK 013, Circuit Court for the Sixteenth Judicial Circuit, Kane County, Ill. (2007).

Ron Paul 2012 Presidential Campaign Committee, Inc. v. Does, (N.D., Cal. January 13, 2012).

Rosetta Stone, Ltd. v. Google, Incorporated, 676 F.3d 144 (4ᵗʰ Cir. 2012).

Salinger v. Random House, Inc., 811 F.2d 90 (2ⁿᵈ Cir. 1987).

SCO Group v. Novell, Inc., No. 10-4122 (10th Cir. Aug. 30, 2011).

Shoars v. Epson America, Inc., No. SCWI 12749, Cal. Sup. Ct., Los Angeles Cty. (1989).

Smyth v. Pillsbury Corp., 914 F. Supp. 97 (E.D. Pa. 1996).

Sony Corp. of America v. Universal City Studios, Inc., 464 U.S. 417 (1984).

Staggers v. Real Authentic Sound, 77 F. Supp. 2d 57, 64 (D.D.C. 1999).

State Street Bank & Trust Co. v. Signature Financial Group, 149 F.3d 1368 (Fed. Cir. 1998).

Stern v. Delphi Internet Servs. Corp., 626 N.Y.S. 2d 694 (1995).

Steve Jackson Games v. U.S. Secret Service, 816 F.Supp. 432 (W.D. Tex. 1993).

Stratton Oakmont, Inc. v. Prodigy Services Co., 1995 WL 323710 (N.Y. Sup. Ct. 1995).

Sue Scheff, Parents Universal Resource Experts vs. Carey Bock and Ginger Warbis, Case Number: 03-022937 (18). Circuit Court, Broward County, Fla. (Sept. 2006).

The Chamberlain Group, Inc., v. Skylink Technologies, Inc., 02 C 6376 (2004).

321 Studios v. Metro Goldwyn Mayer Studios, Inc., 307 F. Supp. 2d 1085 (N.D. Cal. 2004).

Tiffany (NJ) Inc. v. eBay Inc., 600 F.3d 93 (2ⁿᵈ Cir. 2010).

TiVo Inc. v. Echostar Corp., 597 F.3d 1247 (Fed. Cir. 2010).

TiVo Inc. v. Echostar Corp., 646 F.3d 869 (Fed. Cir. 2011).

TiVo v. EchoStar, 516 F.3d 1290 (Fed. Cir. 2008).

Toney v. L'Oreal USA, 406 F.3d 905 (7th Cir. 2005).

Trade-Mark Cases, 100 U.S. 82 (1879).

TrafFix Devices, Inc. v. Marketing Displays, Inc., 532 U.S. 23 (2001).

Two Pesos, Inc. v. Taco Cabana, Inc., 505 U.S. 763 (1992).

U-Haul Int'l, Inc. v. WhenU.com, Inc., 279 F. Supp. 2d 723 (E.D. Va. 2003).

UMG Recordings, Inc. v. MP3.Com, Inc., 92 F. Supp. 2d 349 (S.D.N.Y. 2000).

UMG Recordings, Inc. v. Shelter Capital Partners LLC, 718 F.3d 1006 (9th Cir. 2013).

United States v. Aleynikov, 673 F.3d 71 (2nd Cir. 2012).

United States v. Elcomsoft Co., Ltd. and Dmitry Sklyarov, Case No. CR 01 20138 (N.D. Cal. 2002).

United States v. M.J. Trujillo-Cohen, CR-H-97-251 (S.D. Tex. 1997).

United States v. Smith, 978 F.2d 171 (5th Cir. 1992).

United States v. Smith, No. 91-5077 (5th Cir. 1992).

Universal City Studios, Inc. v. Corley, 273 F.3d 429 (2nd Cir. 2001).

Viacom International, Inc. v. YouTube, Inc., 676 F.3d 19 (2nd Cir. 2012).

Wal-Mart Stores, Inc. v. Franklin Loufrani, Oppositions Nos. 91150278, 91154632, and 91152145 (T.T. A. B., March 20, 2009).

Wal-Mart Stores, Inc. v. Samara Brothers, Inc., 529 U.S. 205 (2000).

Warner Bros. Entertainment, Inc. v. RDR Books, 575 F. Supp. 2d 513 (S.D. N.Y. 2008).

Whalen v. Roe, 429 U.S. 589 (1977).

Wheaton v. Peters, 33 U.S. 591 (1834).

White v. W. Pub. Corp., 12 CIV. 1340 JSR, 2014 WL 3057885 (S.D.N.Y. July 3, 2014).

Williams & Wilkins Co. v. United States, 420 U.S. 376 (1975).

XimpleWare v. Versata, et al., Case No. 5:13cv5161 (N.D. Cal. Nov. 5, 2013).

Zacchini v. Scripps-Howard Broadcasting Co., 433 U.S. 562 (1977).

Zazu Designs v. L'Oreal, 979 F.2d 499 (7th Cir. 1992).

Zeran v. America Online Inc., United States Court of Appeals, No. 97-1523, (4th Cir. 1997).

About the Authors

 Steven L. Baron is a partner in the Chicago-based law firm of Mandell Menkes LLC. He has significant experience in complex commercial litigation and dispute resolution, with particular emphasis on matters involving intellectual property, media, First Amendment, advertising, marketing, and class action defense. Mr. Baron represents media and entertainment companies, advertising and marketing agencies, graphic artists, authors, publishers, recording companies and recording artists, information technology businesses, Internet service providers, and other clients with intellectual property and media interests.

Outside of the courtroom, Mr. Baron guides clients in selecting and clearing trademarks and prosecuting trademark and copyright applications before the United States Patent and Trademark Office and Copyright Office. He also counsels clients on matters involving rights of publicity and privacy. To assist clients in their commercial relationships, Mr. Baron drafts, reviews, and negotiates a host of agreements, including intellectual property licenses and assignments, software escrow agreements, confidentiality and non-disclosure agreements, work-made-for-hire agreements, employment agreements, merchant agreements, and website terms of use and privacy policies.

Edward Lee Lamoureux is a Professor in the Department of Communication and the Department of Interactive Media at Bradley University in Peoria, IL. Ed received a BA from CSU, Long Beach (Speech, 1975), an MA from WSU, Pullman (Speech Communication, 1980), and a PhD from the U. of Oregon, Eugene (Rhetoric and Communication, 1985). Lamoureux earned Certification in Intellectual Property Management from the Center for Intellectual Property, University of Maryland University College. He has served as an expert witness in trademark litigation and testified as an expert before the Library of Congress's Copyright Office, Section 108 Study Group.

Professor Lamoureux came to Bradley as Director, Basic Speech Course (Department of Communication) in 1985. Ed teaches "Intellectual Property Law and New Media," "Introduction to New Media Theory," "Interactive Media Development at Cisco," "Rhetorical Perspectives in Organizational Communication," "Contemporary Problems in Sports Communication," "The Entrepreneurial Mindset in Communications and Fine Arts," and "Privacy in the Connected US."

In addition to intellectual property, new media, and privacy, his research interests include ethnography, rhetoric, religious communication, conversational analysis, and teaching and learning in virtual worlds. Ed's creative production has included audio production and web work as well as communication training via digital embellishments. Lamoureux was on the Founding Committee for the Multimedia Program at Bradley and served as Interim Director and Director of the Multimedia Program for 3 years. Lamoureux served as the editor of the *Journal of Communication and Religion* (sponsored by the Religious Communication Association) for two consecutive 3-year terms, 1998–2003. As a member of the President's Committee for Entrepreneurship and Innovation, a group that established the Turner School of Entrepreneurship and Innovation, Ed serves as the Slane College of Communications and Fine Arts liaison to the School. He taught the first online course at Bradley and taught the first Bradley course(s) in virtual worlds. Ed is Professor Beliveau in Second Life.

Ed is a singer/songwriter who appears at local venues, sometimes as "The Professor." Married (since 1981) to Cheryl; they have 4 adult offspring (Alexander, Samantha, Kate, and Nicole). Lamoureux will publish *Privacy, Surveillance, and the New Media You* for Peter Lang Publishers in early 2016.

Claire Stewart is the Associate University Librarian for Research and Learning at the University of Minnesota Libraries. Previously, she served for 20 years at the Northwestern University Libraries, managing a number of digital projects and initiatives and serving as a campus copyright expert. Claire holds an MLIS from Dominican University and a BA from Saint Mary's College, Notre Dame, IN.

Index

General Editor: Steve Jones

Digital Formations is the best source for critical, well-written books about digital technologies and modern life. Books in the series break new ground by emphasizing multiple methodological and theoretical approaches to deeply probe the formation and reformation of lived experience as it is refracted through digital interaction. Each volume in **Digital Formations** pushes forward our understanding of the intersections, and corresponding implications, between digital technologies and everyday life. The series examines broad issues in realms such as digital culture, electronic commerce, law, politics and governance, gender, the Internet, race, art, health and medicine, and education. The series emphasizes critical studies in the context of emergent and existing digital technologies.

Other recent titles include:

Felicia Wu Song
  Virtual Communities: Bowling Alone, Online Together

Edited by Sharon Kleinman
  The Culture of Efficiency: Technology in Everyday Life

Edward Lee Lamoureux, Steven L. Baron, & Claire Stewart
  Intellectual Property Law and Interactive Media: Free for a Fee

Edited by Adrienne Russell & Nabil Echchaibi
  International Blogging: Identity, Politics and Networked Publics

Edited by Don Heider
  Living Virtually: Researching New Worlds

Edited by Judith Burnett, Peter Senker & Kathy Walker
  The Myths of Technology: Innovation and Inequality

Edited by Knut Lundby
  Digital Storytelling, Mediatized Stories: Self-representations in New Media

Theresa M. Senft
  Camgirls: Celebrity and Community in the Age of Social Networks

Edited by Chris Paterson & David Domingo
  Making Online News: The Ethnography of New Media Production

To order other books in this series please contact our Customer Service Department:

(800) 770-LANG (within the US)
(212) 647-7706 (outside the US)
(212) 647-7707 FAX

To find out more about the series or browse a full list of titles, please visit our website:

WWW.PETERLANG.COM